RIATA AND SPURS

RIATA AND SPURS

The Story of a Lifetime spent in the Saddle as Cowboy and Detective

Facsimile of 1927 Edition

by

Charles Angelo Siringo

New Foreword

by

Marc Simmons

SOUTHWEST HERITAGE SERIES

SUNSTONE
PRESS

SANTA FE

Sunstone books may be purchased for educational, business, or sales promotional use. For information please write: Special Markets Department, Sunstone Press, P.O. Box 2321, Santa Fe, New Mexico 87504-2321.

Library of Congress Cataloging-in-Publication Data

Siringo, Charles A., 1855-1928.
    Riata and spurs : the story of a lifetime spent in the saddle as cowboy and detective / by Charles Angelo Siringo ; new foreword by Marc Simmons.
        p. cm. -- (Southwest heritage series)
"Facsimile of 1927 edition."
Originally published: Boston and New York : Houghton Mifflin, 1927.
    ISBN: 978-0-86534-573-7 (softcover : alk. paper)
    1. Siringo, Charles A., 1855-1928. 2. Cowboys--West (U.S.)--Biography.
3. Detectives--West (U.S.)--Biography. 4. Pinkerton's National Detective Agency--Biography.
5. Peace officers--West (U.S.)--Biography. 6. Frontier and pioneer life--West (U.S.)
7. Crime--West (U.S.)--History--19th century. 8. Crime--West (U.S.)--History--20th century.
I. Title.

F596.S54 2007
978'.02092--dc22
[B]
                                    2007061709

Published in

WWW.SUNSTONEPRESS.COM
SUNSTONE PRESS / POST OFFICE BOX 2321 / SANTA FE, NM 87504-2321 /USA
(505) 988-4418 / ORDERS ONLY (800) 243-5644 / FAX (505) 988-1025

CONTENTS

I

THE SOUTHWEST HERITAGE SERIES

The history of the United States is written in hundreds of regional histories and literary works. Those letters, essays, memoirs, biographies and even collections of fiction are often first-hand accounts by people who wanted to memorialize an event, a person or simply record for posterity the concerns and issues of the times. Many of these accounts have been lost, destroyed or overlooked. Some are in private or public collections but deemed to be in too fragile condition to permit handling by contemporary readers and researchers.

However, now with the application of twenty-first century technology, nineteenth and twentieth century material can be reprinted and made accessible to the general public. These early writings are the DNA of our history and culture and are essential to understanding the present in terms of the past.

The Southwest Heritage Series is a form of literary preservation. Heritage by definition implies legacy and these early works are our legacy from those who have gone before us. To properly present and preserve that legacy, no changes in style or contents have been made. The material reprinted stands on its own as it first appeared. The point of view is that of the author and the era in which he or she lived. We would not expect photographs of people from the past to be re-imaged with modern clothes, hair styles and backgrounds. We should not, therefore, expect their ideas and personal philosophies to reflect our modern concepts.

Remember, reading their words and sharing their thoughts is a passport back into understanding how the past was shaped and how it influenced today's world.

Our hope is that new access to these older books will provide readers with a challenging and exciting experience.

II

FOREWORD TO THIS EDITION
by
Marc Simmons

For a number of years prior to 1922, one of Santa Fe, New Mexico's most colorful and famous residents was Charles Angelo Siringo (1855-1928), popularly known as "the cowboy detective." A small, wiry man, he was friends with practically everyone in town, from the governor to the dog catcher.

In 1916 Governor William C. McDonald persuaded Siringo to accept a commission as a New Mexico Mounted Ranger for the state Cattle Sanitary Board. The only thing unusual about that was Charlie Siringo's age, a ripe 61. Undaunted, he saddled up and with a pack horse started for his headquarters at Carrizozo in Lincoln County.

His duty was to run down outlaws and stock thieves in southern New Mexico. Bill Owens, described as a fighting son-of-a-gun, became his partner. As Siringo reported later, "Poor Bill lasted only a short time."

The pair got into a gun fight with cattle thieves at Abo Pass east of Belen. Owens was shot through the lungs, but he emptied his pistol and killed two of the outlaws before he went down.

"During my two years as a ranger," Siringo said, "I made many arrests of cattle and horse thieves and had many close calls with death staring me in the face." Obviously, Governor McDonald had made a wise choice when he tapped this hard-riding, fast-shooting "senior citizen" for the dangerous ranger job.

Charlie Siringo's career in the West was as adventurous as it was long. Raised in Matagorda County, Texas, he took to life in the saddle before he was shaving.

As he put it, "When I was twelve years of age, in the spring of 1867, I became a full-fledged cowboy, wearing broad sombrero, high-heeled boots, Mexican spurs and the dignity of a full-grown man."

After trips up the Chisholm Trail, he landed a cowboy job in the Texas Panhandle, still a teenager. He fought prairie fires, had run-ins with rustlers and saw the last herds of buffalo roaming the Staked Plains.

The years drifted by and Charlie Siringo drifted with them. At age thirty he was tending store at Caldwell, Kansas and putting in nights writing up his previous experiences on the range.

When his book, *A Texas Cowboy*, appeared, its author achieved fame overnight. Eventually, it sold a million copies. *A Lone Star Cowboy*, published in 1919, contained many of the stories in his earlier book and the author says in his preface: "This volume is to take the place of *A Texas Cowboy*...." The latter portion of the book dealt with his life as a Kansas merchant, as a Pinkerton detective, and his term as a member of the New Mexico Mounted Rangers who concentrated on tracking down rustlers.

Meanwhile, soon after publishing his recollections, Siringo joined the renowned Pinkerton Detective Agency, whose branch offices covered the West. He remained with the firm for two decades, getting in and out of more scrapes than a modern TV sleuth.

The Pinkerton men first gained national attention just before the Civil War when they foiled a plot to assassinate Lincoln on the way to his inauguration. Later they made headlines in trying to break up Jesse James' gang, an effort that cost several detectives their lives.

Pinkertons were often hired as strike-breakers. They proved so successful that they earned the bitter hatred of organized unions. Siringo participated in one episode at Coeur d'Alene, Idaho.

There in 1892 occurred huge labor riots attended by the dynamiting of mines and the murder of managers. In trials that followed, Agent Siringo gave crucial testimony that led to the conviction of eighteen union leaders for these crimes. Soon afterward, the home office sent him in pursuit of Butch Cassidy's Wild Bunch.

After leaving the Pinkertons, Charlie Siringo returned to the Southwest and did a good bit of roaming before settling in Santa Fe.

Because of the name he'd made in publishing, he had access to many persons, on both sides of the law, who were on their way to winning a place in the history books. From them he got first hand information that he later incorporated in a new book called *Riata and Spurs*.

In that work, the writer had wanted to include some of his own daring adventures while serving with the Pinkertons. But the Agency threatened a lawsuit if he revealed any of their professional secrets. So the cowboy detective had to delete some of his best material.

Siringo in his later years lived in near poverty, making small amounts of money from his book writing and consulting on western films for Hollywood producers.

Charles Angelo Siringo fell victim to a heart attack on October 8, 1928 in Altadena, California. Humorist Will Rogers, who knew and respected him, sent a telegram upon learning of his passing. It read: "May flowers always grow over his grave."

III

FACSIMILE OF 1927 EDITION

RIATA AND SPURS

THE AUTHOR TRAILING TRAIN-ROBBERS IN THE MOUNTAINS AND DESERTS OF COLORADO, UTAH, ARIZONA, AND NEW MEXICO

These horses were the first to set foot in the ancient Moqui village of Oraibi (*see page 239*)

RIATA AND SPURS

*The Story of a Lifetime spent in the Saddle as
Cowboy and Detective*

BY

CHARLES A. SIRINGO

WITH AN INTRODUCTION BY
GIFFORD PINCHOT

AND WITH ILLUSTRATIONS

BOSTON AND NEW YORK
HOUGHTON MIFFLIN COMPANY
The Riverside Press Cambridge
1927

The Riverside Press
CAMBRIDGE · MASSACHUSETTS
PRINTED IN THE U.S.A.

TO MY FRIEND
ALOIS B. RENEHAN
OF SANTA FÉ, NEW MEXICO
IN APPRECIATION OF MANY KINDNESSES

PREFACE

To my native State, the original home of the cowboy and the longhorn steer, the author is indebted for furnishing wild cattle and horses on which to manipulate his RIATA and SPURS.

The little poem below, by Mrs. Lee C. Harby, expresses my feeling:

O prairie breeze, blow sweet and pure,
   And, southern sun, shine bright,
To bless our flag where'er may gleam
   Its single star of light!
But should thy sky grow dark with wrath,
   The tempest burst and rave, —
It still shall float undauntedly —
   The standard of the brave.

By deeds of arms our land was won,
   And priceless the reward;
Brave Milam died and Fannin fell
   Her sacred rights to guard.
Our patriots' force with mighty will
   Triumphant set her free,
And Travis, Bowie, Crockett, gave
   Their lives for liberty.

And when on San Jacinto's plain
   The Texans heard the cry,
'Remember, man, the Alamo!'
   They swore to win or die.
Resistless in their high resolve,
   They forced the foe to yield,
And freedom crowned the victory gained
   On that illustrious field.

PREFACE

O Texans, tell the story o'er,
  With pride recall each name,
And teach your sons to emulate
  Their virtues and their fame!
So shall your grandeur still increase,
  Your glory shine afar —
For deathless honor guards the flag
  Where gleams the proud Lone Star!

CONTENTS

Certain parts of the book are reprinted, in revised form, from the author's privately printed narratives called *The Lone Star Cowboy* and *A Cowboy Detective*.

ILLUSTRATIONS

xii ILLUSTRATIONS

From originals in the author's collection

INTRODUCTION

TWENTY years ago in Boise, Idaho, the murderers of Governor Steunenburg were on trial, and the fear of other assassinations was so strong that public officials had moved out of their own homes to the hotel for greater safety. It was a stirring time, and it was then I met McParland, a detective in the case, and nationally known as the man who had been mainly responsible for breaking up the Molly Maguires in Pennsylvania. McParland was old and nearly blind, and he had as his bodyguard a small, slight, friendly, and quiet man by the name of Charles A. Siringo. I was attracted to Siringo at once, as I think he was to me, and the proof of it is that we have been friends and have kept in close touch ever since.

Charlie Siringo's story of his life is one of the best, if not the very best, of all the books about the Old West, when cowpunchers actually punched cows, that ever passed under my eye. I am more than glad that some account of what he has done and seen and gone through is now to reach a wider audience.

No one book can contain the whole story of Siringo's most adventurous life, but what is contained between these covers is genuine. In these days, when so much is written about the West by authors who never saw a cow-pony outside of a circus, it is worth something to be able to lay your hand on a book written by a man who is the real thing, and who tells the truth.

Many a man has seen rough times, though few such as Siringo has lived through, but not many can tell of what they know in a way to make the reader happy. Very few fighting men who have lived lives of great and continuous danger and hardship have kept the milk of human kindness sweet and unclotted in their souls. There are not many like my friend Charlie Siringo.

GIFFORD PINCHOT

HARRISBURG, PENNSYLVANIA
November 11, 1926

RIATA AND SPURS

RIATA AND SPURS

. .

CHAPTER I

MY FIRST COWBOY EXPERIENCE — TWO YEARS IN YANKEE-LAND — LIFE IN NEW ORLEANS

I was born and brought up amidst wild, long-horn cattle and mustangs in the extreme southern part of the Lone Star State. I first saw the light of day, and had my first warm meal on the seventh day of February, 1855, in the county of Matagorda, Texas.

At the age of four I got my first 'book-larnin'' from a Yankee schoolmaster by the name of Hale. A year later war broke out between the North and South, and my beloved schoolmaster hiked north to join the Yankee army.

During the four years of bloody rebellion I saw much fighting on land and water, along the Gulf coast, between the Federals and Confederates. During that time our food consisted of fish, oysters, cornbread, and sweet potatoes. Coffee was made of parched corn and sweet potatoes.

When the cruel war was over, and I was twelve years of age, in the spring of 1867, I became a full-fledged cowboy, wearing broad sombrero, high-heeled boots, Mexican spurs, and the dignity of a full-grown man. I had hired out to run cattle for a man named Faldien, at a wage of ten dollars a month. During the season our work was mostly around Lake Austin, and on Bay Prairie, where now stands the thriving little city of Bay City.

The country was literally covered with wild mustangs and long-horn cattle. We did nothing but round up and brand mavericks from one to four years old, and I soon became handy with the lasso, as these wild mavericks had to be lassoed, thrown, and branded with Mr. Faldien's brand. The unbranded cattle were public property, and our object was to 'make hay while the sun shined' by putting Mr. Faldien's brand on as many cattle as possible. There were many other branding outfits in the field, doing the same for themselves.

In 1868 my widowed mother married again and sold our home and cattle. The land brought seventy-five cents an acre, and the cattle one dollar a head. Then we boarded a Morgan Steamship at Indianola, and started for Yankeedom by way of Galveston and New Orleans; thence up the Mississippi River on a steamboat to Saint Louis, Missouri, and by rail to Lebanon, Saint Clair County, Illinois.

Now the misery of a boy began. I had to work out in the cold fields during the late winter months, only half clothed, at a wage of eight dollars a month, which I never got the benefit of, as it went to buy whiskey for my drunken Yankee stepfather. But thank the stars, during spring he hit the road for parts unknown; then I drew the wages myself, as my mother and only sister went to Saint Louis, Missouri, to try their luck in a strange city. That same sister still lives in Saint Louis, having married a prosperous business man. Four girls and one boy spring from that union, and most of them have families of their own, and are prosperous. Mother and sister had promised to write to me, giving their city address, but for some reason they failed to do so — hence a Texas long-horn kid was left alone among strangers, and in a strange land.

During the summer I quit my heart-breaking job with Mr. Moore, and went to Lebanon to learn the carpenter trade. I had bound myself to an old skinflint who was building a new house in the edge of town. He made me sign a contract that I would work for him three years to learn the trade. I worked one whole day, from sunup to sundown, turning a grindstone to grind a lot of rusty tools. That night, by the light of the moon, I walked twelve miles east, and next morning hired to a farmer with a heart, by the name of Jacobs, for twelve dollars a month. During the harvest I made a half a hand binding and shocking wheat. Late in the fall, 1869, I quit my job and walked to Saint Louis, a distance of twenty-five miles, in hopes of finding mother and sister.

Little did I dream of the difficulty in finding two people in a city of nearly half a million souls. No need to recite the hungry spells, and the hard beds on platforms and dry-goods boxes for two long weeks until I secured a job as bell-boy in the swell Planters' Hotel. My wages were ten dollars a month, but I averaged several dollars a day from tips. Often a crowd of gamblers playing for high stakes in a room would give me a ten- or twenty-dollar bill to buy a tray-load of drinks, telling me to keep the change. The other dozen or more bell-boys did equally well in the way of easy tips, and when off duty we spent the money like drunken sailors.

One year later, in the fall of 1870, I had a rough-and-tumble fight with one of the bell-hops while on duty, and was slapped on the cheek by the chief clerk, Cunningham. This slapping stirred up the anger in my system, and I threw up the soft job of bell-boy.

With a few dollars in my pocket I started for the levee to board a steamboat headed toward Texas, but on the road to the levee I butted into a gambling game, and lost every cent of my money. Late in the evening I stole my way onto the Bart Able, which was ready to steam down the Mississippi River for New Orleans, and hid among the freight sacks and boxes.

While loading freight from an old abandoned steamboat, in a town in Arkansas, I fell over backward into an open hatchway about thirty feet deep and was fished out by the captain and crew more dead than alive.

On waking up, I found myself in a clean bed in the captain's private room. When we reached New Orleans I was able to walk, but couldn't bend my back, and the back of my head had a lump on it the size of a cocoanut.

After eating a nice dinner on the Bart Able, the boat steamed back up the river for Saint Louis, leaving me in a strange city with not a cent in my pocket. After two days of hunger, and sleeping on cotton bales, I was picked up by a kind-hearted man, William R. Myers, of the Couens Red River line of steamboats, and taken to his home.

When we rang the bell, Mrs. Mary P. Myers opened the door. She was evidently shocked at the sight of a dirty-faced urchin at her husband's side. Mr. Myers introduced me as a young Texan whom he had brought home to fill up, as I was half starved.

The five o'clock dinner was ready to be served by the two negro servants, but, bless you, I had to endure the agony of having the meal delayed until I could take a bath in the neat bathroom.

Don't wonder if my stomach was puffed out like that of a 'poisoned pup' when dinner was over. It was, and the world appeared like one round ball of glory and contentment.

That night in the parlor I was made tell my pedigree, and past life. The result was, this old couple, who had no children, offered to adopt me as their own son, and to give me a fine education, with a start in business when I should be twenty-one years of age.

Of course I consented, as the rosy picture of more juicy porterhouse steaks, broiled on a charcoal fire, loomed up in the future.

The next forenoon Mrs. Myers took me down to one of the

clothing establishments and fitted me out like a young prince. I objected to the peaked-toed gaiters and asked for a pair of star-top, high-heeled boots, but the good lady thought boots would make me look too much like a 'hoosier.'

Seeing that she was lavish with her money, I asked her to buy me a violin, so that I could learn to play 'The old blind mule came trotting through the wilderness,' and other favorite Texas songs. This she agreed to do, and later carried out her promise.

After the crick in my back and the lump on my head had 'vamoosed,' and the rare beefsteaks had painted my cheeks with a rosy tint, I was sent to Fisk's Public School to start my education.

One week in school and I had a rough-and-tumble fight with another boy in the schoolroom. In making my 'get-away' for the door, I ran over the good-looking young teacher, Miss Finley, who was trying to prevent my escape. The poor girl fell flat on her back, and I stepped on her pink silk waist as I went over her for the door. No doubt she thought it was a Texas stampede. A few days later, I was sent to a pay school. This old professor had only a few select scholars, all boys, to whom he taught the German, French, and English languages. In the course of a few months I had to shake the dust of New Orleans from my peaked-toed gaiters on account of stabbing one of the scholars with a pocket-knife. He was much larger than I and had my face bloody.

Night found me wrapped in slumber among the cotton bales on board the Mollie Able, en route to Saint Louis. My slumber was not a peaceful one, as I awoke often to worry over my future, should the boy Steamcamp die. I had seen the blood gushing from his wound as he ran screaming over the grassy lawn where we had been playing during the afternoon recess.

On reaching Saint Louis, after eight days and nights of hiding in the cotton bales and stealing food after the deck hands finished their meals, I spent a day trying to find mother and sister. Then I crossed the river on a ferryboat and walked to Lebanon, Illinois, thence to the Jacobs farm, where I was received with open arms, and put to work in the harvest field where I had worked the season previous.

When the harvest was over, I longed for the easy life under Mrs. Myers' wing. Therefore I drew my wages and struck out afoot for Saint Louis. I arrived there in time to board the Robert E. Lee, which was starting down the river on her great race with the Natchez. Thousands of dollars were bet on which one would reach New Orleans first. I slipped onto the steamer and kept hidden most of the time when the captain or the other officers were in sight. The cook kindly gave me food. We landed in New Orleans ahead of the Natchez, and there was great rejoicing aboard. The citizens of New Orleans presented the captain with a pair of gold antlers to place on the bow of his swift steamer.

On the same evening of our arrival I hunted up Babe Fisher, a yellow negro whom I knew could be trusted, and who afterward became a noted outlaw, to find out if the victim of my fight had recovered. I was informed that it required the skill of two doctors to save young Steamcamp's life, but he was now about as sound as ever. This encouraged me to ring the doorbell at the Myers mansion. My dirty face was showered with kisses by Mrs. Myers, who was happy over my return. When Mr. Myers returned at night from his office, he too, gave me a hearty welcome.

Mr. Myers made three visits to the German professor before he could induce him to take me back as one of his pupils. Now I took up my same old studies, German, French, and English. I was a hero among the scholars for winning the fight with young Steamcamp, who had been the bully of the school. He had never returned to take up his studies after recovering.

Everything went on lovely, and I continued to enjoy the juicy beefsteaks which were served every evening, fresh from the charcoal furnace on the brick-paved back yard.

In the latter part of November a big fire broke out near our school, and the street was lined with people going to the fire. I asked the professor if I could go and see the blaze. In a gruff voice he answered 'No!' I then yelled 'Good-bye,' and broke for the door.

It was night when the excitement of the fire died down. I then walked to the levee, and after a wait of an hour or more I slipped onto the Saint Mary, a Morgan steamship bound for Indianola, Texas. I kept hid out all night, and next morning was put to work scouring brass railings to pay for my food and passage.

After a stormy trip we arrived in Indianola, Texas, one morning about sunup. On viewing the old wharf, from which I had stepped onto the gangplank of the Crescent City about two years previous, I shouted deep down in my heart: 'Back home at last to the dear Lone Star State'; the natural home of the cowboy and long-horn steer.

The winter was spent working for H. Selickson, in his beef factory, where cattle were butchered for their hides and tallow; my wages being fifteen dollars a month. Early in the spring of 1871 I visited among my friends in the town of Matagorda, and on the peninsula, the place of my birth. About the first of April I hired out to Tom Nie, now known as the 'Onion King' of Laredo, Texas. He was making up a crew of cowboys to work on the Rancho Grande, on Tres Palacios Creek, about twenty-five miles northwest from the town of Matagorda.

We went by sailboat to Palacios Point, where the Rancho Grande Company had an outside camp. There we joined other cowboys, making a crew of twenty, and from there went overland to the Rancho Grande headquarters. We found the headquarter ranch a busy place, getting ready for the spring work. Here there were a company store, a church house, and the pleasant home of Jonathan Pierce.

The two Pierce brothers, Abel ('Shanghai') and Jonathan, were in partnership with Sam Allen, and a man named Pool, of eastern Texas. They owned this Rancho Grande, and the more than one hundred thousand long-horn cattle scattered over hundreds of miles of grassy range.

There were about fifty cowboys at the headquarter ranch; a few Mexicans and a few negroes among them. We had un- limited credit at the company store. My credit was stretched almost to the breaking point, in purchasing a cowboy outfit, including saddle, bridle, spurs, pistol, bowie-knife, bedding, sombrero, silk handkerchiefs, slicker, high-heel boots, etc.

'Shanghai' Pierce and his crew of cowboys had just arrived from the Rio Grande River with three hundred wild Mexican ponies for the spring work. He had paid two dollars and fifty cents a head for them. They were what was termed 'wet' ponies on the Rio Grande. In other words, were stolen stock; hence the low prices.

We always started the day's work at the first peep of day, and never thought of eating a noon meal. Often it would be pitch dark when we arrived in camp, where a warm camp-fire meal awaited us. These meals were made up of meat from a fat heifer calf, with corn bread, molasses, and black coffee. The negro cook, who drove the mess-wagon, generally had two kinds of meat, the calf ribs broiled before the camp-fire, and a large Dutch oven full of loin, sweet-breads, and heart, mixed with flour gravy.

For breakfast we often had pork and beans that had been simmering over hot coals all night. In those days knives and forks were seldom used in the cow-camps; each cowboy used his bowie-knife or pocket-knife to eat with. Nor were there tents to sleep in when it rained. The boys slept on the ground, covered with a canvas or wagon-sheet to turn the water.

The crew of which I was a member consisted of fifteen men and boys. We started work on the Navidad River, in Jackson County, gathering a herd of eleven hundred head of steers for Mr. Black, who had brought his crew of green Kansas boys, overland from Wichita, Kansas.

In gathering this herd of old 'mossy horn' steers, from four to twenty years old, I had a new experience. They were mostly wild timber cattle, which only graze out in the edges of the prairies at night, going back to the timber after day-light. We had to make raids on them before sunup, by which time they would be back in the brushy timber, where it was impossible to round them up, or rope and tie down the un-ruly ones.

It is hard to believe, but nevertheless true, that some of these old steers had a fine coating of moss on their long horns. The trees were all covered with moss; some of it more than a foot long.

By the time we got this herd 'put up,' and turned over to Mr. Black and his crew, we were a worn out bunch of cowboys. Every steer had to be roped and thrown to be road-branded, and we had to stand guard every night, half the crew the first part of the night, and the balance until daylight. During rain and thunderstorms every cowboy had to be in the saddle all night, singing and whistling to the restless cattle to avoid a stampede. At such times there was no sleep for any one but the cook. Stampedes were frequent on stormy nights, and we had to stay with the running herd until the steers became exhausted.

The rest of the season, up to Christmas, we put in our time branding mavericks and calves. The mavericks were not so plentiful, or so old, as when I took my first lessons as a cowboy in 1867. Among the timber cattle we found some unbranded bulls and cows, four and five years old, but on the prairies they ranged from one to two years of age, being calves that had escaped the branding-iron the previous seasons. During this year of 1871 the Rancho Grande Company branded twenty-five thousand calves and mavericks.

I finally wrote to Mr. and Mrs. Myers in New Orleans telling them that I had attained the desire of my life by becoming a full-fledged cowboy, in the Lone Star State. In a few weeks an answer was received to my letter. In it was a twenty-dollar bill, and a pass on the Morgan Steamship Line from Indianola to New Orleans, the money being for my expenses en route.

In the letter they begged me to return and finish my education. I wrote them that the life of a cowboy was good enough for me and offered to return the money and the pass. In a later letter Mr. Myers wrote me to tear up the pass, and to buy a suit of clothes with the twenty-dollar 'william.' Many years later this old couple died, and were buried in the town of Pocatello, Idaho. Mr. Myers had lost his wealth in a bad speculation with a thieving partner in Florida. Before old age put them under the sod, I had the pleasure of repaying them for all the money spent on me when I was a wild, reckless lad.

Such is life. I often think of what a narrow escape I had from becoming an educated business man, had I remained in New Orleans.

After the branding season was over I joined Bob Partain's crew, and we established winter quarters at the camp-house three miles from Palacios Point. Our work was shipping steers

A COW CAMP IN THE MOUNTAINS OF NEW MEXICO ABOUT 1890
Showing a calf stretched out to be branded and ear-marked

to New Orleans and Cuba. Twice a week a Morgan steamship would tie up at the wharf at Palacios Point, and it was our duty to put about five hundred cattle aboard. Gathering crews would deliver the steers to our outfit, and we had to night-herd them until ready to ship.

During cold northers and sleet storms we had a tough job night-herding. Often 'Shanghai' Pierce would be present to help us sing to the cattle during bad storms. 'Shanghai' felt at home on the back of a pony. He was quite different from his brother Jonathan, who was never so happy as when plough-ing with a yoke of oxen. In all the years that I knew Jonathan I never saw him in a saddle.

When spring came I was assigned with a new crew in charge of Mr. Wiley Kuykendall, who had married a sister of the Pierce brothers. 'Mr. Wiley,' as we cowboys affectionately called him, spent very little of his time in bed. He was fond of black coffee, steaming hot from the camp coffee pot, and only when asleep did the smoke from his black pipe cease. He was up with the cook every morning, so as to get his cup of hot coffee.

I shall always hold the name of 'Mr. Wiley' in kind remem-brance, as in the summer of 1872 he gave me my first start in the cattle business, by allowing me to put my own brand, which had not been recorded, as the law required, on a few mavericks. This made me bold, so that thereafter I al-ways carried a rod of iron tied to my saddle, as a branding-iron, to be made red-hot in a brush, or cow-chip fire, when riding over the prairie alone, and a fine-looking maverick showed up. The short piece of iron was bent at one end and used to run my brand on the animal's hip.

In the late summer our crew was sent to Lavaca and Cal-houn Counties to gather steers and ship them on board Mor-gan steamships, in Indianola, for the New Orleans market.

Later we were sent to Wharton and Colorado Counties to gather steers to be shipped by rail from Richmond and Houston.

It was while driving a herd of these fat steers to Richmond that I was bitten on the foot by a rattlesnake, which proves that even the bite of a snake can't kill a tough cowboy.

We had just swum the herd across a swollen stream, which caused me to get wet to the skin. While I was guarding the herd, part of the crew having gone to dinner, I disrobed to let my clothes dry in the hot sun. While I was standing bare-footed in the tall grass the snake put two gashes across one foot. This caused the death of his snakeship, as I was angry and beat him to a pulp. My foot and leg became badly swollen, so that I couldn't wear my left boot for a week; still I never missed doing my full share of the work, which included standing guard over the herd half of each night.

During the fall Mr. Wiley severed his connection with the outfit, and soon after I did likewise. I had been working for the Rancho Grande Company nearly two years, without a settlement or knowing how my account in the company store stood. My wages were twenty dollars a month, and whenever I needed cash, all I had to do was ask old Hunkey Dory Brown who was in charge of the store, for the amount, and he would charge it on my account. I was a surprised and disappointed boy when I found that I had only seventy-five cents to my credit. This I blew in for a bottle of peaches and brandy and some stick candy, before leaving the store to ride away on my own pony.

CHAPTER II

At the time Mr. Wiley Kuykendall quit the firm, the Pierce Brothers had sold their cattle interests to Allen and Pool for the snug sum of $110,000, which was a fortune in those days. This shows what men with Yankee blood in their veins could do with long-horn cattle.

As a young man, before the Rebellion, 'Shanghai' Pierce had drifted from the State where they make wooden nutmegs and went to work for W. B. Grimes, on Tres Palacios Creek, splitting live-oak rails at a wage of one dollar a day. In later years Mr. Pierce used to point out this old rail fence, which he put up, as the folly of his youth.

Late in the fall the Rancho Grande headquarters was established at John Moore's ranch home, at the mouth of Tres Palacios Creek — Mr. Moore being appointed general manager. John Moore had an only son, Bennie, who was put in charge of a crew to ride over the prairies to cut off the horns of old stray bulls — that is, animals which had no recorded owner, as they had drifted with the hordes of other cattle during northers and sleet storms from the north, during the four years of bloody rebellion, when the men and boys of middle and northern Texas were too busy fighting the Yankees to look after their cattle. During the late fall much of my time was spent with Bennie Moore's crew helping rope and throw these wild bulls. It was fun for me, and I asked no pay.

Previous to selling out to Allen and Pool, 'Shanghai' Pierce had made a contract with the Cuban Government to furnish them one hundred thousand head of bulls to feed their soldier boys. Before quitting the Rancho Grande Company I had helped put some of those bulls on board the Morgan steamships. For some reason only part of this great number of bulls were ever shipped. No doubt the soldiers rebelled, and swore off eating bull-beef. For many years afterward these old bulls with both horns chopped off could be seen leading a contented life on the grassy prairies of Colorado, Wharton, Jackson, and Matagorda Counties.

During the winter of 1873–74 some of these old bulls put easy money into my own pocket. Their hides were worth five dollars each, when dried. As they were strays I considered it no sin to kill and skin them. I would ride up close to the bull, and plant a bullet from my powder and ball Colt's pistol behind his ear.

During the winter of 1872–73 I made my home at the Horace Yeamans ranch on Cash's Creek. Old man Yeamans had a son, Horace, about my own age, and we went into partnership skinning dead cattle. They died that winter by the tens of thousands all over this coast country bordering the bay of Matagorda. The country had become overstocked through the natural increase and the hordes which drifted from the north during cold northers and sleet storms. Often a boggy slough would be completely bridged over with dead and dying cattle, so that the ones following could walk over dry-footed.

Horace and I did most of our skinning that winter at Hamilton's Point where the little city of Palacios now stands. Here the famished brutes could go no farther south on account of Tres Palacios Bay — hence they died by the thousands.

We made big money all winter. As a side issue I had put my brand on a lot of mavericks during spare times. In the spring my brand was sold to George Hamilton, he paying me two dollars a head for all cattle in my brand, gathered by the different branding outfits during the coming seasons. The last money he paid me was in 1879 — several years after making the trade!

Now I had a new brand recorded in Matagorda, the county seat, to put on other mavericks. I had the foresight to select a stray brand, which I knew was not on record — hence had no owner. I had seen grown cattle in this brand. The chances were that this brand belonged in one of the northern counties of the State.

The first money received from this new brand was for a twelve- or fifteen-year-old-steer which I found in W. B. Grimes's slaughter pen ready to be butchered for his hide and tallow. Never shall I forget the look on old man Grimes's face when I demanded ten dollars for this steer. He couldn't understand how a smooth-faced boy could have the gall to claim such an old animal, on the strength of a new brand only on record a few months. Showing him the recorder's certificate convinced this shrewd old Yankee that I was the rightful owner. He paid me for a few others later.

During the late fall Horace Yeamans and I made a camping trip along the Bay shore to lay in a supply of bacon for the winter. The marshes were full of wild hogs. We killed only fat sows.

In the late spring Mr. Grimes gave me charge of his range stock of horses. I had to attend the horse round-ups in Matagorda, Wharton, Colorado, and Jackson Counties to brand up the W. B. G. colts.

When the branding season was over, I took a contract to break wild ponies at two dollars and fifty cents a head. Some days I would ride as high as five head of these wild ponies which had never been saddled before. Most of them were vicious buckers. They had to be roped and thrown in order to get the hackamore — a rope halter — and the leather blind onto them. When the animal was allowed to get up on his feet, his eyes being blinded, he always stood quite still until the saddle was fastened on his back. Then the blind was raised in order to allow him to wear himself out bucking around the corral with the saddle.

Now he was put outside the corral, and the leather blind lowered back over his eyes. Then, when seated in the saddle the blind was raised, and the bucking and running began. It often required two hours' time to get him docile and back to the corral. Then he was turned loose among the others in the corral, and a fresh one saddled.

I had no help in this work. In those days a cowboy considered it a disgrace to have help in saddling and managing a wild bronco. Now, in these later years a bronco-buster nearly always has a helper to get the saddle on the bronco's back and to guide him over the prairie.

After I had ridden each of these ponies about a dozen times — the last few times with a bridle-bit in his mouth — they were turned over to the owner as 'broke.'

The winter was spent with Horace Yeamans in the skinning of dead cattle, and the branding of mavericks during spare times. By this time I was old enough to begin to feel my oats — as a horse-trainer would say about his racer. Therefore I attended many dances during the winter — some of them twenty-five miles distant from the Yeamans ranch. One day when ready to ride away to one of these distant dances, in company with Miss Sallie Yeamans, I thought seriously of heaven and hell while being dragged over the prairie by a wild bronco.

The proper way to mount a skittish horse is to pull his head around toward you with the left arm and grab the saddle-horn with the right hand, then put your foot in the stirrup. This I failed to do in mounting Satan — a large sorrel bronco.

My number five high-heel, star-top boot was shoved into the stirrup before grabbing the saddle-horn. The result was Satan went to bucking and I fell over backward with my left foot hung in the stirrup.

The long hackamore rope, fastened to Satan's nose, had been held coiled up in my left hand. It fell to the ground, and while being dragged on my back I could see a negro cowboy, who was present, running his best, afoot, trying to catch the end of the rope. At one time he was within a few feet of the dragging rope. Then I felt hopeful. But when I saw the end of the rope crawling farther away from the negro, I lost hope, and began to wonder what kind of a place hell was, and whether I should be treated with kindness.

After a few hundred yards of dragging, with Satan's hind hoofs flying over my upturned face, I began to kick frantically with my left leg. This brought the foot out of the stirrup. As the end of the hackamore rope went past me I grabbed it and hung on like grim death to a dead 'nigger.' Now I was dragging on my stomach, which wore the bosom of my white 'stake-and-rider, Sunday-go-to-meetin'' shirt into a frazzle. I finally had to turn the rope loose. Satan was found with a wild bunch of ponies a month or two later, still wearing the saddle on his back.

I finally sold him cheap to a drunken Irishman by the name of Martin. He and Dan — another gentleman from the 'ould sod' — were building dirt dams to hold stock water for the Rancho Grande Company. I had Satan pretty tame when sold to Martin. But next morning Martin was quite sober and concluded to give his pony a little training. Their camp was located in the timber near a narrow road. Martin mounted the pony and told Dan to go a short distance up the road and hide behind a pile of brush, then when he came galloping by, to spring suddenly out of the brush. He said he

wanted to get the pony trained not to scare at strange objects.

When Dan picked Martin up with a skinned face and body,
he swore at Dan for scaring the pony too hard. He said Dan
ought to have sprung out of the brush easy.

That spring I was put out of active business. I was seated
on the ground by the camp-fire smoking, late in the evening,
when Sam Grant, a 'nigger' killer, rode up and dismounted.
Picking up my pistol, which lay on the opposite side of the
fire from where I was sitting, he examined it, then threw it
away, at the same time pulling his pistol, with the remark,
'Why don't you have a good one like mine!' He then fired
at my heart.

My hands were clamped around my left leg — the knee
being on a level with my heart. The large dragoon bullet
struck the knee going through and lodging near the skin on
the opposite side. He was raising the pistol as though to fire
again when a negro cowboy, Lige, galloped into camp out of
the heavy timber and brush. This, no doubt, saved my life.
Grant swore to Lige, who had dismounted and was holding
me up with one hand, that his pistol went off accidentally.
Then Grant galloped away saying he would send a doctor
from Deming's Bridge Post-Office, the old Rancho Grande
headquarters.

The doctor came late at night and cut the bullet out. Lige
assisted me to the Yeamans ranch a few miles below on the
creek.

It was thirty-five years later when I learned from my friend
Nolan Keller, the true secret of this attempted assassination.
A certain wealthy cattleman, who is now dead, hired Sam
Grant to kill me, on account of my boldness in branding mav-
ericks and killing stray bulls for their hides. At that time
Nolan Keller was foreman for this cattleman and learned the
secret of his deal with Grant.

When able to ride, and walk with a crutch, I made my home with Mr. John Pierce at the old Rancho Grande headquarters. All I had to do was assist little Johnny Pierce — now a banker of Palacios, Texas — and 'Shanghai' Pierce's little daughter, Mamie, to and from the schoolhouse, two miles distant.

It was my duty to care for their ponies and to see that the youngsters were not hurt. At the same time I was getting some book learning, by attending school myself. I found it a pleasant home at the Pierce residence. Mrs. Nanny Pierce and her old mother, Mrs. Lacy, were like mothers to me.

A few weeks after starting to school the red-headed schoolmaster, Mr. Carson, concluded to whip me so as to convince the other scholars that he wore men's size pants, but when he started in I pulled a knife and threatened to carve him into mincemeat if he didn't go back and sit down, which he did.

I remained until school was dismissed, so as to take the Pierce children home. Next morning I saddled my pony, bade the Pierces good-bye, and headed east with my crutch tied to the saddle.

At the Sam Allen ranch on Simms Bayou I lay over a few days to rest. Mr. Sam Allen, for whom I had worked when he was in partnership with the Pierce brothers, treated me royally. He was a fine old man, but at meals he wouldn't allow his cowboys to cut bread from the loaf. He said it was bad luck. It had to be broken.

While visiting my Aunt Mary McClain, of Houston, and Uncle Nicholas White, of Galveston, I had the pleasure of shaking hands with the Confederate President, Jeff Davis. While attending the first State Fair ever held in Texas, at Houston, Uncle Nick, who was an old confederate soldier, introduced me to Mr. Davis.

On leaving Galveston, Uncle Nick slipped some greenback money into my pocket, and presented me with the old Spencer repeating rifle which he had carried through the Civil War. Of course I was proud of the gift, as cartridge repeating rifles were scarce and hard to obtain in those days.

Another stop at the Sam Allen ranch, and then I hired out to Joe Davis, who had a contract to furnish beef to the building crews on the Gulf, Colorado, & Santa Fé Railroad at Virginia Point, near Galveston.

It was September when I found Mother sick in bed at the Morris ranch. As Mr. Morris and his son Tom were going to Indianola in their schooner, Mother and I scraped together all the cash we had and sent after lumber, etc., to build a home. But this money went to feed the fishes in Matagorda Bay, as the great storm of 1875, which washed Indianola off the face of the earth, scattered the Morris schooner and everything on board to the four winds of heaven. Morris and his son saved themselves by swimming.

This same storm cured Mother of her sickness. About ten o'clock at night, when the seventy-five mile wind took the roof off the Morris house, letting in the flood of rain, I picked Mother up out of her sick bed and jumped into the foaming water, which was more than waist-deep. Through my advice Mrs. Morris and her two little girls and two sons followed suit. It required all my strength to hang onto Mother and to keep the Morris family from drowning. Once they became tangled up in a bunch and were on top of Jimmie, the oldest boy, who was under the water. The wind was from the west, blowing us out into Tres Palacios Bay — two miles wide. Knowing that there was an osage hedge of large trees a few hundred yards to the westward, I decided to face the wind and tide to reach that haven of safety. Hence my little crew were drilled to keep only their heads above water and their feet in the mud — leaning their bodies toward the wind. All except Mother, who was as limber as a dishrag, heeded my advice.

Inch by inch we crept toward the hedge. It required nearly an hour's struggle to reach it. Then we were saved.

When daylight came the only living creature, outside of ourselves, in sight, was a bay bronco which Jimmie and I had caught from a wild bunch the evening before. He was tied at the end of a long rope fastened to a strong stake driven into the ground. He had been floundering in water almost over his back during the night, but now it was only knee deep — as the tide was going down. By looking across the bay we could see the shore piled high with rubbish and dead stock.

When the sun peeped over the eastern horizon we began to think of breakfast. The nearest ranch was the Yeamans home, five miles to the northward. Jimmie, who was younger than I, and I, decided to draw straws to see who should ride the wild bronco bareback to the Yeamans ranch after a wagon and grub. Jimmie drew the unlucky straw.

We used a shirt to make a blind for the bronco. When Jimmie was seated on his bare back, with the hackamore reins in his hands, I raised the blind and said 'go.' We had made a hackamore out of the stake rope that the bronco was tied with. In spite of the hard bucking, Jimmie stuck on his back, and finally got him headed north in a run.

It was noon when the wagon and grub arrived.

Strange to relate, this ducking cured Mother and she forgot about being sick. She lived to be eighty-six years of age and died a peaceful death in the Sisters' Sanitarium in New Mexico's capital city, Santa Fé. With almost her last breath she begged me to make my peace with God, while the making was good. Ten years have passed since that dear old mother was laid away in Rosario Cemetery. I have been too busy to heed her last advice. Being a just God, I feel that He will overlook my neglect. If not, I shall have to take my medicine, with Satan holding the spoon.

CHAPTER III

MY FIRST TRIP UP THE CHISHOLM TRAIL — A LONELY
RIDE THROUGH THE INDIAN NATION

In the early spring of 1876 I hired out to W. B. Grimes to help drive a herd 'up the Chisholm Trail' to Kansas, at thirty dollars a month. We gathered the herd of twenty-five hundred old mossy-horn steers on the Navidad and Guadalupe Rivers, in Colorado, Jackson, and Victoria Counties. None but old steers, from five to twenty years old, were gathered. Most of them were wild timber cattle which only venture out on the edges of the prairies at night — grazing back to the timber before sunup.

At first, while the herd was small, we would corral at night in one of the many public corrals scattered over this coast country. When the herd became too large, we had to night-herd, each cowboy being up singing to the steers half the night. In corralling these steers for the night we had great sport. Often we wouldn't get to camp with the bunch gathered that day until after dark. In that case the job of getting the whole herd into the corral was a severe one.

These public corrals, built of live-oak logs, had wings extending out from the gate several hundred yards; the outer ends of the wings being far apart. We would handle the herd gently until inside the wing enclosure, then a man up a tree would think Hades had broken loose. It became a case of shove. The yelling and beating of quirts against leather 'chaps' could be heard miles away. We were lucky to get half the herd into the corral the first attempt. Then the ones which had broken through the string of yelling cowboys were rounded up, and another attempt made.

Toward the last there would be many old fighting steers which couldn't be got back to the wing enclosures. Some would run for the timber near by, fighting mad. Then there was nothing to do but tie the mad brute down till morning. This being a dangerous job for a lone cowboy if the night was dark.

For the purpose of tying down these unruly steers pieces of hobble rope were kept tied on the saddles. One dark night I ran out of rope hobbles — having previously tied down three steers — and had to tie a mad brute down with my silk sash — used wrapped around my waist to keep up my pants, in place of suspenders. I could have tied him down with his own tail, but that way of tying an animal generally lames one leg for a few days. In tying a cow-brute down with its own tail, the hair on the end of the tail is divided into equal parts, then knotted together at the ends, forming a loop. Now the tail is wound once or twice around the animal's upper hind leg while lying flat on the ground, and the loop put between the split hoof. This keeps that leg drawn up so that the animal cannot stand on its feet very long at a time.

It was against the rules to hog-tie a trail steer, as it caused stiffness in the legs. Only the two hind legs were tied together, which allowed the animal to stand up, though he couldn't travel very far in that condition.

Sometimes we had to sew up the eyelids of these old mossy-horn steers to prevent them running for the timber every chance they got. It required about two weeks' time to rot the thread, allowing the eyes to open. By this time the animal was 'broke in.'

After gathering the herd of twenty-five hundred steers the job of road-branding began. Small bunches were cut off from the main herd and put in a corral. Then each animal had to be roped and thrown by cowboys afoot, who worked in pairs.

Now the road-brand, 'G,' was burnt into the hair sufficiently deep to last 'up the trail.'

Often the corral was ankle-deep with mud, making it tough on the cowboys' fine calfskin boots. Being wet they were hard to get off and on, therefore the boys generally slept with their boots on. At one time I wore my boots night and day for two weeks at a stretch, as they were number fives when they should have been number sixes. Cowboys took great pride in small feet.

When we finally got strung out up the trail, the crew consisted of twenty-five cowboys, the cook, who drove the mess-wagon, and the boss, Asa Dowdy.

Stampedes at night during the spring rains and thunderstorms were frequent. Then the boys had to remain in the saddle all night, otherwise they could sleep half the night. The striking of a match to light a cigarette, or pipe, or a pony shaking the saddle, often caused stampedes.

On reaching the town of Gonzales our boss did a foolish thing. He concluded to give the boys a full night's rest by corralling the whole herd in the large House corral, a few miles west of town. By night we had the whole herd in the corral. It was jammed full.

After supper, as was the custom when a corral contained wild cattle, all the boys took their bedding and night-horse to the corral and spread out their beds around it, equal distances apart.

Then the boys retired for the night, sleeping with their clothes on, and holding the bridle-reins, or hackamore rope, of the pony in one hand.

These public corrals were built round, so that in case of a stampede, the boys could, by yelling and the shaking of slickers, etc., get the herd to milling in a circle until exhausted. About midnight while we were all asleep, a storm sprang up.

A loud crash of thunder and lightning started a stampede. The frightened herd went through the corral where I was sleeping. I barely had time to mount my pony, which saved me from being trampled to death. The corral was built of live-oak logs and rails, the largest logs being at the bottom, next to the ground. The herd went through it as though it was built of paper. While running in the lead of the herd, during flashes of lightning, I could see fence rails on top of the steers' backs. The herd being jammed into a solid mass the rails couldn't fall to the ground.

The boss had slept in camp with his clothes off. In this condition he sprang onto his night-horse, tied to a wagon wheel, and was soon in the lead of the herd; but before getting there his pony ran against a tree and almost tore off one of his little toes, he being barefooted.

On reaching the edge of the prairie, about a mile from camp, the herd split in two halves, the boss and I staying with one bunch. When daylight came, and the steers had exhausted themselves, we were ten miles from camp, on an open prairie. I doubt if there ever was such a large herd of wild steers put into one corral before, or since.

On reaching the city of Austin, on the Colorado River, two hundred miles from its mouth at the town of Matagorda, we struck the Chisholm Trail proper. From here north to the line of Kansas, a distance of about seven hundred miles, it was one continuous roadway, several hundred yards wide, tramped hard and solid by the millions of hoofs which had gone over it. It started in at a ford three miles below the city. All smaller trails from the different Gulf-coast districts merged into this great and only Chisholm Trail.

Now half of our crew returned home overland, leaving us with a crew of twelve cowboys, with six picked ponies for each rider.

In going through the Indian Nation we had several bad rivers to swim, the Washita, and the South and North Canadians being the worst. Large bands of mounted blanket Indians gave us much trouble. They were in the habit of riding into camp when the cook was alone and eating all the cooked grub in sight. They also demanded the bosses to give them 'whoa-haws' (steers) for beef, or they would stampede the herd at night. In this way these roaming bands from the Comanche, Kiowa, Kickapoo, and Wichita Agencies, to the westward, near the Wichita Mountains, kept themselves well supplied with fresh meat. They were the cause of many stampedes among the hundreds of herds passing up the trail at this season of the year.

On reaching Salt Fork River our misery began. After breakfast the boss had gone on ahead with the two wagons. We had lately rigged up a wagon to haul a supply of wood.

About 10 A.M. the boss came running back and told us to hurry as fast as possible, as the river was rising fast. He said he managed to get the wagons over just in time, as the driftwood and trees began flowing soon after.

When we arrived at the river she was about a half-mile wide and full of driftwood. The lead steers were pointed into the foaming water. The boss and Otto Draub were on the left point, while Negro Gabe and I were on the right, to keep the leaders from turning back. Henry Coats was out in the lead, and the steers following him nicely. When the water became deep enough to swim, Henry Coats's horse refused to swim. He fell over on his side, and in the excitement the lead steers turned back onto Gabe and me, and swam back to the shore.

We made a dozen efforts to get the herd back into the water, but failed. By this time it was raining, and the wind blowing a gale. There we were in a fix, separated from our grub and bedding. The wagons had gone on to the Pond Creek Stage Station, a couple of miles from the river.

No doubt our failure to get the herd into the river was a God-send, for some of us might have been drowned. It makes it very dangerous for man and beast when struck by swift-flowing log or tree. Many trail boys and horses and cattle have been drowned in this way.

Now we drove the herd down the river, a mile or two, where there was a belt of timber. Late in the evening the rain ceased for a while, then a large camp-fire was built of wet logs, and never allowed to go out during our stay here. Night and day the fire was kept burning. Being so large and hot the rain couldn't put it out. For supper a fat steer was butchered, and each cowboy not on duty with the cattle, roasted enough to satisfy his hunger. It had to be eaten without salt. Early at night a new rainstorm, with much lightning and thunder, broke out. Hence every man had to be in the saddle to stay with the drifting herd till daylight, by which time we were several miles from camp. Every now and then the whole herd would stampede.

Two days later Negro Gabe and I were hunting lost steers when we found an ear of yellow corn on the trail. That night we slipped off from the other boys and built a small fire to roast meat, and parch corn in the hot ashes. Gabe contended that God had dropped this ear of corn there for our special benefit.

Had it not been for the fact that the Cimarron and Wild Horse were roaring torrents, other trail outfits would have arrived to furnish us with grub and bedding. We had the whole country between Salt Fork and Wild Horse to ourselves.

On the seventh day, in the afternoon, the boss, Hastings, and I were hunting steers lost in a stampede the night before, when we saw the tents of a company of United States soldiers on the opposite side of Wild Horse, which was a roaring, swift-flowing stream, about two hundred yards wide.

On being told by the captain that we could have all the grub we wanted by coming over to get it, I jumped my pony into the foaming water and swam across. Then a washtub was borrowed from the captain's wife. This was filled full of flour, bacon, coffee, sugar, and salt and guided to the opposite shore. I swam by the side of the tub, landing several hundred yards below, being carried down by the swift current. The tub was carried upstream and launched back into the water.

Thanking the captain's wife for the use of her boat, I mounted my pony and swam back to my companions. That night the boys had a picnic filling up. The bread was baked by rolling it on sticks and holding it over hot coals.

The next morning the sun came out and there was not a cloud in the sky. The river had gone down so that we had only about one hundred yards to swim. The cook and driver of the wood-wagon were found well rested at the Pond Creek ranch.

On reaching the Ninnescah River, at the mouth of Smoot's Creek, in Kansas, a permanent camp was established. Mr. W. B. Grimes, who had come around by rail, was there to meet us.

When Mr. Grimes returned to Wichita, thirty miles east, the boss and some of the boys accompanied him, to receive their summer's wages and free railroad transportation back to southern Texas. In those days it was the custom for all cowboys, who wished to return home, to receive free railroad tickets.

The herd was split into three bunches to fatten for the fall market. I remained with one herd of eight hundred steers. Our outfit consisted of a boss, four cowboys, a cook and mess-

wagon, with five saddle ponies to the rider. Five miles east
of the mouth of Smoot's Creek lived a New York family who
had taken up a quarter section of land and put in a crop.
From them we bought eggs and vegetables. They had acres
of watermelons and cantaloupes, but these didn't cost us a
penny. All we had to do was load the mess-wagon with dry
cow-chips from an old bed-ground and dump them at the
kitchen door, then load the wagon with melons. These cow-
chips were used as fuel, as there was no timber or wood near
by.

Soon after pitching camp on the Ninnescah, one of our
trail boys, John Marcum, entered a Government homestead
in the forks of the Ninnescah and Smoot's Creek. He was
laughed at as a 'fool hoeman,' but he took the joking good-
naturedly. I have always had a desire to see this Marcum
farm, now that the country is thickly settled and highly im-
proved.

It was the first part of August before I had an opportunity
to see the cattle town of Wichita, Kansas. Another cowboy
and I rode the thirty-five miles from camp in quick time. The
first thing we did was to go to the New York store and fit out
with new clothes from head to feet. By the time the barbers
got through fixing us up, it was dark.

Now our ponies were mounted and we struck out in a gallop for Rowdy Joe's dance hall across the Arkansas River.
There were other dance halls across the river, but Rowdy
Joe had the name throughout southern Texas of running
the swiftest joint in Kansas — hence we steered for his place.

On nearing the toll bridge the one-legged man came out of
his shanty to collect the twenty-five cents toll. We both went
past him on the run, shooting our pistols off over his head.
The poison liquor we had drunk since our arrival in town
made us feel gay.

When halfway across the bridge the one-legged man turned both barrels of a shot-gun loose at us. We could hear the buckshot rolling along the bridge floor, under our ponies' feet. One shot hit me in the calf of my left leg, and the scar remains to this day, as a reminder of Wichita's hurrah days.

After celebrating a few days my cowboy pal and I returned to camp.

Late in the fall, after the first snowfall, a cowboy by the name of Collier and I concluded to quit the Grimes outfit and go to the Black Hills in Dakota to make our fortune gold mining. Drawing our pay we rode to Wichita on ponies owned by us.

In Wichita we 'whooped her up Liza-Jane' for a couple of days and nights and found ourselves broke. Then we gave up the Black Hills trip and started for the Medicine River, a hundred miles west, to hunt a winter's job. I finally secured a month's job to help move the Johnson herd of large long-horn steers down into the Indian Nation.

We established the winter camp on the Eagle Chief Creek, a tributary to the Cimarron River. Before reaching there a severe snowstorm and blizzard struck us, and I suffered greatly, standing night guard clad in summer clothes. The other boys had prepared themselves for winter. I didn't have even overshoes or an overcoat.

Up to that time cattle had never been wintered in that part of the Nation on account of the danger from Indians. Mr. Johnson was called foolish for taking the risk.

After drawing my month's pay from the boss, Mr. Hudson, I spent a few weeks trapping, etc. I had built a dugout about a mile from the Johnson camp. One snowy day part of the Johnson herd drifted over the roof of my castle. One steer fell through, missing me by a foot. I came very near roasting before the blazing fire in the fireplace. Finally I got a chance to crawl under the steer's flanks and make my escape. Then I swore off trapping, leaving my pelts behind. I started for Kiowa, Kansas, next morning, and about three o'clock in the evening the raging blizzard became so cold I concluded to head for a warmer climate.

I had been facing the north wind. Now my course was turned to the southeast, down the Eagle Chief Creek. After dark camp was pitched, but I went to sleep on my saddle blankets with an empty stomach, as I had brought no grub along, thinking I could reach the Drum ranch that night.

Now my route lay down the Cimarron River through sandhills and blackjack timber. During the all-day ride many deer and turkey were seen, but I was afraid to shoot off my pistol for fear of attracting Indians — there being fresh moccasin tracks everywhere.

That evening a jack-rabbit was killed with a club when he hid in a bunch of tall grass. He went into my stomach for filling that night.

Early next morning while absent from my camp-fire to get a cup of snow from a drift against a high sand-hill, to be melted for drinking-water, the tall grass around my camp caught fire. I had a swift job on my hands to save Whiskey Pete and my saddle. My leather leggins and slicker were burnt to a crisp. Only a small piece of saddle blanket was saved.

That night I had to sleep without even a saddle blanket to cover with, nor did I have fire to warm by, as my match-box had burnt up with my slicker. I hadn't gone far next morning when a fresh Indian camp, just vacated, was struck. After warming by the fire I continued down river, knowing that I would soon strike the Chisholm cattle trail. It was struck during the evening, and I turned south on it. About five miles ahead of me was the band of Indians whose signs had been seen all along my route.

That night I camped with a Government freighting outfit. They informed me that the fifty Kiowa Indians who had just passed were returning to their reservation from a hunting trip.

I rode into Erin Springs — the home of a wealthy squaw-man by the name of Frank Murray — late one evening. The woods were full of Chickasaw Indians and tough squaw-men, who had come to attend a big dance at Frank Murray's.

Whiskey was plentiful, being sold by Bill Anderson against the law. This Bill Anderson had served with Quantrell's band of Confederate soldiers, and had since become an outlaw.

I joined the gay mob and danced with half-breed Indian maidens until daylight.

This I consider the wind-up of a foolish cowboy's first trip up the Chisholm Trail.

CHAPTER IV

CAPTURING A BAND OF MEXICAN THIEVES —
ADVENTURES WITH BUFFALO

FROM Erin Springs I continued down the river to Paul's Valley — one of the richest spots on earth. Here it was no trick to raise from one hundred to one hundred and twenty-five bushels of corn to the acre. Corn sold for only ten cents a bushel. This brought many feeders to the valley to fatten steers for the market. Henry Childs and the Mitchells were the largest feeders in the valley.

Old Smith Paul, who was then ninety-two years of age, had been adopted by the Indians when a boy. When he grew to manhood he married an Indian girl and raised a brood of half-breeds. One of his sons was shot and killed years afterward in Ardmore, Oklahoma, by his own son.

Smith Paul owned most of this large valley, as he had it under fence. According to the law and custom, any Chickasaw Indian, or squaw-man, held title to all the land that he was able to keep under fence — so that he didn't get nearer than a quarter of a mile of any one else's fence. Most of this rich, black land he rented out to white farmers, who raised corn. In the early spring of 1877, while I was in the valley, this husky old man married a sixteen-year-old Texas girl. I was told that they had three children before he died.

Here I spent the winter breaking wild ponies at two dollars and fifty cents a head. My home was with one of the renters on Mr. Paul's land. While living with this renter and his hospitable family I paid fifty dollars for one crack shot out of my new Smith & Wesson pistol. One of the boys and I were back of the house, and I was bragging how I could knock a bird's eye out every shot with my pistol. The boy pointed out a redbird sitting on a limb, in a clump of bushes, saying: 'Let me see you knock his eye out.' The eye went with the bird's head when I fired. The shot killed one of the renter's fine work horses standing concealed farther on. I was let off by paying fifty dollars, half the animal's value.

During the winter a pretty little half-breed girl got me 'plumb locoed,' and I came within an ace of marrying her. All that prevented was the fear that being a squaw-man might ruin my chances of becoming President of these glorious United States. My schoolbooks had taught me that every boy has an equal chance of becoming President.

In the late spring I drifted to Tishamingo, the capital of the Choctaw Nation — thence west to Saint Joe on the Chisholm Trail. Here, in May, I secured a job with one of the north-bound herds of long-horns owned by Captain George Littlefield, of Austin. This herd consisted of thirty-five hundred head of mixed cattle. One of Mr. George Littlefield's nephews, Phelps White, now a millionaire stockman of Roswell, New Mexico, was one of the cowboys.

In passing through the Indian Nation we experienced many hardships in swimming swollen rivers. Dudley Pannell — later shot and killed in Tascosa, Texas — and I were the champion swimmers of the outfit, and did most of the dangerous work in the water. The herd being made up of mixed stock-cattle, it was a difficult matter to get them to take to the water. Small bunches had to be cut off from the main herd and shoved into the raging torrent. Then naked cowboys would swim on each side of the leaders to keep them headed toward the opposite shore. Often when out in midstream the leaders would turn and go to milling in a circle. Once I was caught in the center of the milling herd, and to save myself from being jammed to death, I crawled up onto the animals' backs, working my way from back to back until the edge of the herd was reached.

Often these milling bands would drift with the current a mile or two down the stream before we could get them strung out again. To make them string out, we would swim near the edge and splash water in the nearest animals' faces, at the same time yell and 'cuss.' In order to get the mess-wagon over these raging streams, a log raft had to be made to float it over.

On crossing the Cimarron River, at the mouth of Turkey Creek, we switched off from the Chisholm Trail and headed northwest for Dodge City, Kansas, via the United States Government Post of Camp Supply. The reason for leaving the Chisholm Trail was the fact that the 'fool hoe-men' were fast settling up the grazing country west of Wichita.

We arrived in Dodge City, Kansas, on the third day of July. The herd was to continue on up to Ogallala, Nebraska, and possibly farther north to Miles City, Montana — both great cattle towns. Therefore, I drew my pay and quit the job, to celebrate the glorious Fourth of July in the toughest cattle town on earth.

This celebration came near costing me my life in a free-for-all fight in the Lone Star dance hall, in charge of the noted Bat Masterson.

The hall was jammed full of free-and-easy girls, long-haired buffalo hunters, and wild and woolly cowboys. In the mix-up my cowboy chum, Wess Adams, was severely stabbed in the back by a buffalo hunter. Adams had started the fight to show the long-haired buffalo hunters that they were not in the cowboy class. We had previously taken our ponies out of the livery stable and tied them near the hall. I had promised Adams to stay with him till Hades froze up solid.

After mounting our ponies, Joe Mason, a town marshall,

tried to arrest us, but we ran him to cover in an alley, then went out of town yelling and shooting off our pistols. By daylight we had ridden eighteen miles to the D. T. Beals steer camp. Toward the last I had to hold Adams on his horse, he had become so weak from loss of blood. This wound laid him up for two weeks. This incident illustrates what fools some young cowboys were after long drives.

At this time the Atchison, Topeka & Santa Fé Railroad was building west from Dodge City, which filled the town full of cut-throats and bums, who follow up new railroads. The town was also the outfitting center for buffalo hunters within a radius of hundreds of miles, and that year of 1877 she became the great long-horn cattle center of the Universe. Wichita lost the trail drive through the 'fool hoe-man' settling up the cattle range to the westward.

The citizens of Dodge City seemed proud of their fat graveyard in the 'Boot Hill' Cemetery, where there were eighty-one graves, all the occupants except one having died with their boots on. Fort Dodge, a Government post, was located only five miles distant, and the soldier boys added merriment as well as devilment to the little yearling city.

During the seventies Miles City, Montana, Cheyenne, Wyoming, Ogallala and Sidney, Nebraska, were wild and woolly cattle centers. From these places large herds were driven to the open ranges, where new ranches were established. Most of these new ranches began improving the long-horn cattle by introducing short-horn bulls.

One of these new ranches afterward became noted as the Two-Bar 70 ranch. It was located on Snake River, near Soda Springs, Idaho. A wealthy citizen, by the name of Hawks, from Bennington, Vermont, established the ranch, and put his young son, William E. Hawks, Jr., in charge. Now, after the passing of over a quarter of a century, this man William

E. Hawks, Jr., has become the collector of the greatest store of cowboy literature and paraphernalia in the whole United States. At his fine home in Bennington, Vermont, he has what he proudly calls his 'Two-Bar 70 Tepee,' where these relics are displayed.

Soon after the Fourth of July I secured a job with the David T. Beals outfit to drive a herd of young steers to the Panhandle of Texas, where a new ranch was to be established. Bill Allen, of Corpus Christi, Texas, was the boss, and Owl-Head Johnson was the cook, and driver of the mess-wagon. 'Deacon' Bates, one of Mr. Beals's partners, a dyed-in-the-wool Yankee, accompanied us for the purpose of selecting the new range.

After crossing the Cimarron River into No-Man's-Land — now a part of the State of Oklahoma — we saw our first herd of buffaloes grazing a few miles to the southwest. Mr. Bates selected me to ride on ahead with him to get some fresh buffalo meat.

When within a mile of the herd, the ponies were tied in a gulch. Then we walked afoot out on the open flat, straight toward the woolly animals. When within about one hundred yards of them we raised our Sharp's 45 caliber rifles and fired. Two young animals, a bull and a heifer, dropped over dead. The whole herd then began bawling and milling around the fallen beasts.

I became frightened and wanted to run back to my pony, but Mr. Bates, who had ranched at Granada, Colorado, said buffaloes were harmless unless wounded, when they became vicious.

Still I felt timid and allowed the 'Deacon' to walk ahead. On reaching the edge of the milling herd, he pulled off his hat and began shooing them out of his way. At first they seemed to pay no attention to him, but finally they started away on the run. This trait of buffalo nature made it easy for hunters to slaughter them by the thousands. They will stampede at the sight of a horseman, but pay no attention to a man afoot.

A day or two later I roped my first buffalo. We had pitched camp for the night when a herd of the woolly animals ran past the camp, headed west. I had just ridden out a few hundred yards to turn back some steers which were going into the sand-hills. At a breakneck pace I rode after the fleeing buffaloes, not realizing that my pistol and bowie-knife lay on the ground in camp, until I had overtaken the rear end of the herd. Down came my lasso and an eight-months-old heifer was roped by the neck. The bawling of the calf brought the mother cow on the run. She made a dive for my pony. The thirty-foot rope was tied hard and fast to my saddle horn, so that the rope couldn't be turned loose. By 'socking' spurs to the pony I managed to drag the calf and keep out of the cow's reach. She soon scampered off after the fleeing herd. By this time I was many miles from camp, and it was getting dark.

I tried to throw the calf hard enough so that she would lie still until I could reach her on foot. But the instant she struck the ground on her side she would be on her feet again. Finally becoming angry, I dismounted and went at her with all the strength in my make-up. She was soon hog-tied with my silk sash. Then with a dull pocket-knife I cut the throat and peeled the hide off. Then I tied a chunk of meat to my saddle and rode toward camp. It was now pitch dark.

After going east about a mile I concluded to ride south in the hope of finding a stream of water, as the pony and I were thirsty. The streams in that country all run from the west to the eastward — hence my hopes of finding water. About three o'clock in the morning, while sound asleep on my saddle blankets, with the saddle for a pillow, a herd of stampeded buffaloes came running by, a few hundred yards to the west-

ward. The loud roar and the shaking of the ground frightened
my mount and I was dragged quite a distance, the end of the
hackamore rope having been wrapped around my body on
lying down.

There I was left afoot on the prairie, and dying for a drink
of water, but thanks to kind providence I soon heard a faint
snort off to the eastward. The pony had stopped, and I
mounted and headed him toward the southeast. I knew by
keeping this course we should strike the Bascom Trail, over
which the herd was being driven.

About 10 A.M. water was struck at the head of Sharp's
Creek, a tributary to the Beaver River, which was called the
North Canadian farther downstream. About noon the cattle
herd arrived on Sharp's Creek, and camp was pitched. The
outfit had traveled about fifteen miles from where I left them.
We had buffalo veal mixed with flour gravy for dinner. The
boys complimented me on my skill as a meat rustler, with only
a lasso as a weapon.

On arriving at the North Paladura Creek, we saw the first
house since leaving Crooked Creek, twenty-five miles south
of Dodge City, this being a buffalo hunters' trading store.
When within fifty miles of the Canadian River, camp
was established until 'Deacon' Bates and I could locate
a range large enough for fifty thousand cattle. We started
early one morning with a pack-horse loaded with grub and
bedding. On the north bank of the South Canadian River we
landed in Tascosa, which contained half a dozen Mexican
families, and a store owned by Howard and Rinehart. From
here we rode down the river. Finally Mr. Bates selected the
site for the home ranch on a little creek about a mile east of
Pitcher Creek. This was to be the center of the future LX
cattle range, which was to extend twenty miles up the river
and the same distance down the stream, and twenty miles

south to the foot of the Llano Estacado (Staked Plains), also twenty miles north to the foot of what was called the North Staked Plains. This constituted a free range forty miles square.

On our travels we had not seen a cow brute, and the grass was fine. Thousands of buffalo were roaming over this range, also deer and antelopes by the hundreds. We never ran short of wild meat to eat.

Finally we returned to the herd and moved it to the site of the home ranch, where the cattle were turned loose to fatten on the fine buffalo-grass.

Now Mr. Bates went to Granada, Colorado, to oversee the moving of their thousands of well-bred short-horn cattle to this new Panhandle ranch. Mr. David T. Beals and Erskine Clement — one of Mr. Beals's partners — were kept busy in Dodge City, Kansas, buying long-horn steers to put on this new range. By the time snow began to fall this grassy LX range contained thousands upon thousands of cattle.

Above Tascosa a Mr. Goodrich had a small cattle ranch, and down the river twenty-five to fifty miles Tom Bugby and Hank Creswell controlled the range. South of us there was not a cow brute this side of the Paladuro Canyon (head of Red River), a distance of about fifty miles, where Cattle King Charlie Goodnight had established a large cattle ranch the year previous.

Mr. Goodnight had the pick of the whole country when his ranch was selected. Nature had fenced his range down in the Paladuro Canyon. The valley down in the canyon was from one to five miles wide and about thirty miles in length, with walls on each side hundreds of feet high. There was only one place in the canyon where cattle could climb out, and a few rods of stone fencing fixed this. At the head of the canyon there was an abrupt wall. At its mouth Mr. Goodnight established his home ranch.

In the early winter Mr. Phelps White arrived with a herd of long-horns and established the L I T ranch above Tascosa. These cattle, and others which came later, were owned by Mr. White's uncle, Capt. George Littlefield. During the winter Lee & Reynolds established the L S ranch near Tascosa. Also Jim Kennedy — a son of the cattle king, of southern Texas — brought in a herd of steers and turned them loose above Tascosa. In the late fall Nick Chaffin established the Pollard ranch on lower Blue Creek, at the northeast edge of the LX range.

Early in the winter I started out alone down the Canadian River in search of some lost steers. I stopped at Adobe Walls to view the ruins of that noted place, where, in 1874, fourteen buffalo hunters — the notorious Bat Masterson being one of them — stood off a large band of Comanche Indians with their long-range buffalo guns for several days, until the United States soldiers arrived. Skulls and bones of dead Indians still lay on the ground near this old stockade.

On this trip I had the pleasure of meeting Mr. and Mrs. Thomas Bugby at their home ranch near Adobe Walls. I was told the history of their courtship, which sounds like a dime novel story.

In the fall of 1876 Mr. Bugby was driving through Kansas with a small herd of fine-blooded short-horn cattle, in search of a free range. In pitching camp one day, near a farmhouse, he discovered that they had lost their axe. He walked to the farmhouse to borrow one. The farmer's young daughter brought him the axe, and at the same time, from her bright eyes, shot his system full of Cupid's little arrows.

The next morning when Mr. Bugby returned the axe, he proposed marriage to this handsome young lady, and after papa and mamma were consulted, the deal was made. A Justice of the Peace tied the knot, and then the journey to the wild Panhandle of Texas was continued, with a new girl cook to dish up the grub.

Farther down the river I stopped at the Cresswell cattle ranch, and formed the acquaintance of Cattle King Hank Cresswell, and his foreman, Tom McGee, the afterward sheriff who was murdered by express robbers at Canadian, Texas.

From there I rode down Sweetwater Creek, to the 'wild-and-woolly' town of Sweetwater. Here there were two large outfitting stores, run by McCamy and a Mr. Weed, also several saloons and dance-halls. She was a lively place at night when the cowboys and buffalo hunters turned themselves loose.

During my two days' stay in Sweetwater, I became chummy with a saloon proprietor, who showed me the fine silver-plated ivory-handled Colt's 45 caliber pistol willed to him a short time previous by the noted horse-thief, 'Chubby' Jones. The story of Chubby Jones' death was also told to me by this saloon keeper and others in the town. I was already familiar with the history of Jones and his boss, 'Dutch Henry,' whose right name was Henry Born. All cowboys in the Indian Nation and the Texas Panhandle knew of these two noted characters.

It was claimed that Dutch Henry was at the head of three hundred horse-thieves who operated between Venita, Indian Territory, and Pueblo, Colorado. The bands who stole horses in the Nation would meet a band with stolen horses from Colorado, at some point in No Man's Land, and swap herds — the Colorado thieves returning to that state, and the others back to the Nation.

The undoing of Chubby Jones, as told to me, happened as follows:

A company of soldiers from Fort Elliot rounded up Chubby

and eight of his gang, on lower Sweetwater Creek. In the fight the army captain was shot through the stomach. This angered the soldiers who hung the nine thieves to a tree that night. When they started to string up Jones he asked, as a last request, that his pistol be given to the saloon keeper, which request was carried out.

A ride of eighty miles brought me back to the LX ranch with a small bunch of lost steers. I found a new boss in charge of the ranch. Mr. Allen had returned to his home in Corpus Christi, and an outlaw by the name of William C. Moore had taken his place.

This man Moore, up to a short time previous, had been the manager of the large Swan Cattle Company, of Cheyenne, Wyoming. He had just shot and killed his negro coachman, and made his get-away from the law officers in Wyoming, landing at the LX ranch on a broken-down pony. Previous to this he had shot and killed his brother-in-law in the State of California, which brought him to Cheyenne, Wyoming, to begin life anew.

Bill Moore was a natural leader of men, and one of the best cowmen in the west. He could get more work out of a gang of cowboys than any man I ever knew. But while working so hard for the LX outfit he was feathering his own nest by stealing from them. He soon started a brand of his own, and established a ranch at Coldwater Springs, in No Man's Land. He had two of the LX cowboys in with him on these steals, and they tried to induce me to join them, but I refused.

A few years later Moore sold his ranch and cattle for $70,000. Then he quit the LX outfit, and with this money established a cattle ranch in the American Valley, of western New Mexico. His stay in the American Valley was short, as he shot and killed two men, which placed a large reward on his head.

OUTLAW BILL MOORE
Manager of the LX ranch

After returning from Fort Elliot a young Texan by the name of John Roberson and I were put in a camp on the head of Amarillo Creek, at the foot of the Llano Estacado, about fifteen miles south of the home ranch. Our duty was to prevent cattle from drifting onto the Staked Plains. The cattle were in the habit of following bands of buffalo south onto the plains, and we experienced much hardship in cutting them off from the running buffalo herds. The cattle couldn't run fast enough to keep up with the woolly beasts, but they would stay on their trail until turned back. The company furnished us with free ammunition to shoot into these roving bands of buffaloes, in order to keep them off the range.

Soon after locating our camp on Amarillo Creek the main herd of buffaloes migrating from the north, passed a mile west of us. For three days and nights there was a solid string of them from a quarter to a half mile wide — sometimes in a walk and other times on the run. During daylight we could look to the northward, across the Canadian River breaks, a distance of about thirty miles, and see this black streak of living flesh coming down off the north plains. Their route was down Pitcher Creek, a mile west of our home ranch.

The next morning after this great string of woolly animals had crossed the Canadian River breaks, I trailed a bunch of cattle south onto the plains. It was an easy matter to distinguish the cattle tracks from those made by buffaloes. The former are sharp pointed while the latter are round pointed.

The cattle were found with the buffalo at Amarillo Lake — where the thriving little city of Amarillo, Texas, is now located.

I found the whole Llano Estacado one solid black mass of buffalo — just as far as the eye could reach, to the eastward, southward and westward. The great herd had scattered out to graze on the thickly matted buffalo-grass, nearly a foot high. There must have been a million of the woolly beasts.

Shortly after this Moore had me accompany him to the head of Paladura Canyon, so as to learn the country. Here I saw my first expert lancing of buffalo, by Apache Indians on swift buffalo horses. I accompanied a band of these reds out to a grazing herd, about fifty thousand in number.

When within a mile of the herd the Indian chief lined us all up abreast — that is side by side — close together. This was done to fool the buffalo — as they would have stampeded at the sight of horsemen.

They paid no attention to us until we were within a few hundred yards of them. Then they began to bunch up. Now we made a charge as fast as the horses could run. This started a stampede, and the lancing began at the rear end of the herd. Steel and stone lances were attached to long poles. The lance was driven into a buffalo's loin, and down he would go, helpless, but not killed. Some of the Indians on the swiftest horses were almost in the center of the herd, lancing one buffalo after another as they ran.

I did nothing but watch them at their expert work. Just ahead of me a buck on a yellow horse reached over to the right to bury the sharp lance in a buffalo's loin when his weight on the slender wooden handle, about fourteen feet long, snapped it in two, and down went Mr. Indian rolling in the grass. Buffaloes were dodging all around him. When he sprang to his feet a cow jumped over his head and knocked him down. Then he sat still until the rear end of the herd had passed. While sitting there some of the beasts jumped over him. At the wind-up of this free show I shot a buffalo and tied his hump-loins to my saddle for supper.

For a mile or two back, the plain was covered with hundreds of buffaloes trying to rise to their feet. Soon hundreds of the old bucks, squaws, and children arrived and butchered these struggling animals for their hides and meat.

About Christmas we had an exciting chase after thieves. Moore had sent a runner from the home ranch after Roberson and me to help round up eight Mexicans who had robbed Mr. Pitcher of everything he had. They had loaded all of his store goods into large freight wagons and headed across the plains in a southwesterly direction.

Nine of us rode night and day until they were overtaken, near the line of New Mexico. For a while they stood us off with their long-range buffalo guns. Finally Moore sent Jack Ryan to their barricaded wagons, under a flag of truce. They agreed to haul the stuff back and turn it over to Mr. Pitcher, who was one of the pursuing party, on our promise not to harm them.

This was agreed to, and we all started back toward Pitcher Creek. It had been promised that they could retain their fire-arms, but while camped for dinner we got the drop on them and took away their arms.

Now it was proposed to hang them all to a big cottonwood tree in the head of the gulch, where we were camped. But Dudley Pannell and I protested that this would be cowardly after giving our words of honor that they would not be harmed. As Pannell and I were well thought of, Moore decided in our favor, and several lives were saved.

Now Roberson and I returned to our camp at the foot of the South Plains. One morning I found cattle tracks among those of a large band of buffaloes. I went on their trail in a gallop on my blue pony. The trail continued up onto the plains past Amarillo Lake. A ride of about twenty miles brought me in sight of the buffalo herd, about fifty thousand in number. On reaching within a mile of them they stampeded toward the southwest. Now my misery began, trying to separate the dozen or more cattle from them.

It was almost night when my mount gave out completely and could hardly trot. Then I turned back toward camp, in a slow walk, for a night ride. Just as the sun was getting ready to go to roost I saw a band of Indians coming toward me from the west, on the run. Their steel lances were glistening in the sun. I thought of running, as they might be on the war-path, but despite the spurring, my mount couldn't be made to gallop.

Now my Winchester rifle and Colt's 45 caliber pistol were examined to see if they were in trim for war.

When the Indians galloped up to me I was standing facing them, with the rifle raised for action. The leader passed the time of day in the Mexican tongue, which I understood. Then he made inquiry as to whether I had seen any buffalo. Of course I told him about the herd which I had just left.

Seeing that my mount was played out this Apache chief invited me to go with them to their camp, a few miles west. The invitation was accepted, as I was hungrier than a wolf. After filling up in this Indian camp I went to sleep in a tepee filled with squaws and papooses.

By the latter part of January the buffalo had all gone south, with the exception of a few straggling bands. One of these bands, about one hundred head, made me think of the hereafter on the other side of the great divide, where Saint Peter lives.

Being out of meat, and seeing this band grazing at the head of a gulch, about a mile distant, I concluded to get some buffalo humps. In order to make sure of fresh meat I kept out of sight, by riding in the bed of the gulch.

When within a few hundred yards of the grazing band the pony was left with the bridle-reins hanging on the ground, to prevent his running away. Continuing the journey up the arroyo afoot, I came to the extreme head of it, a steep embankment. Now standing on my tiptoes a grassy valley spread out before my eyes, and over its surface grazed the contented animals, all but one old bull, lying down chewing the cud of contentment, within twenty or thirty feet of my nose.

This being the only animal within sure gun-shot I concluded to make a death shot on him. Then the rifle barrel was raised gently up onto the level ground. But I was not tall enough, even by standing on my tiptoes, to keep the rifle butt pressed to my shoulder, and at the same time bring the sight down on the sleeping bull. Hence the rifle was fired off-hand like a pistol. Aim was taken under the hump, where the bullet strikes the lights, and causes death.

At the crack of the gun the bull was on his feet and jumping toward me. Ducking my head down he leaped over me and fell dying in the bed of the gulch, at my feet. I sweated blood through fear that he might regain his feet and discover me.

Now peeping over the edge of the embankment I discovered the whole band almost upon me. I squatted down and they leaped over my head onto the dying and struggling bull. In looking upwards all I could see was flying buffaloes. The dirt bank caved in around me, through some of the animals getting too near the edge before making the leap for the bottom of the arroyo.

I felt relieved when the last ones went over me, and went running down the gulch. No doubt this old bull was their leader, and seeing him, at the crack of the gun, go over this embankment they followed.

After getting the loose dirt out of my clothes, the hump-loins were cut out of the dead bull, and a start made for camp. My pony had stampeded on seeing the narrow gulch filled with woolly beasts running toward him. He was found trembling with fright about a quarter of a mile from where I had left him.

Soon after this I had a different kind of buffalo experience. Seeing a lone bull grazing on a flat I rode to a round knoll, which hid me from his view. When within about one hundred yards of the small hill I left the pinto pony, with the bridle-reins hanging on the ground. Then crawling to the top of the knoll I fired a bullet from my Winchester rifle at the bull. He dropped to the ground, and I foolishly stood up.

In an instant the bull jumped to his feet with one front leg as limber as a rag. The bullet had hit him in the shoulder. He saw me while standing in plain view, a distance of about one hundred and fifty yards. Here he came for me with his front leg dangling at his side. The broken leg seemed to have no effect upon his speed.

Instead of pumping more lead into him, as the lamented 'Teddy' Roosevelt would have done, I started for my mount on the run. The rifle went up in the air when I started. It was a case of my legs running away with me. Once I looked back. That was enough, the bull was coming down the knoll not fifty yards behind me. My hair rising on end threw my sombrero off my head.

My greatest fear was that Pinto would become frightened and run before I could leap into the saddle. But he stood still until I could make the leap — then he wheeled around and was off like a bullet, just in time to save my bacon. The bull's horns raked some of the hide off his rump before he could get out of reach.

Now I rode around to my rifle and Mr. Bull was killed, and his hump-loins taken to camp. That night 'Pinto' received a double feed of corn for saving my life.

CHAPTER V

A TRIP TO CHICAGO — MY FIRST ACQUAINTANCE
WITH 'BILLY THE KID'

TOWARD spring Mr. Moore put a cowboy in my place, to camp with Roberson, and I was sent out with a scouting outfit to drift over the South Staked Plains in search of stray cattle. Our outfit consisted of a cook, Owl-head Johnson, and three riders, Jack Ryan, Van Duzen and myself. After starting on this trip we experienced a touch of hardship. Camp was pitched after dark one evening on the edge of a 'dry' lake, or basin. Enough buffalo-chips were gathered to cook supper. After retiring under our tarpaulins, spread over the beds on the ground, a severe snowstorm sprang up. By daylight our beds were covered with a foot of snow.

Crawling out of these warm beds into the deep snow was anything but pleasant. We had no buffalo-chips to build a fire — hence had to cut up the bed of the mess-wagon. There we were afoot on these snowy plains, as the pony staked out the evening before had pulled up the stake-pin and drifted south with the hobbled ponies. They were not found until late that evening, about ten miles from camp.

It was on this trip that I saw the piles of bones from thousands of ponies killed by orders from General McKinzie. They were at the head of Tule Canyon, which empties into Canyon Paliduro. It was here that General McKinzie and his United States soldiers rounded up the Comanche Indians, in 1874, when they broke away from Fort Sill, Indian Territory, on the war-path — killing hundreds of white men. The Indian ponies were shot and killed to prevent another break on horseback, the reds being made to walk back to Fort Sill.

One forenoon three thousand Comanche Indians gave us a 'scaring up,' as we didn't know whether they were on the war-path or not. On Mulberry Creek they came pouring down the hills from the eastward, on a gallop. We were completely surrounded. The chief made inquiry about buffaloes to the westward. They were from Fort Sill, Indian Territory, on a big buffalo hunt. The chief showed us a letter from the commanding officer at Fort Sill stating that they were peaceable, and friendly toward the white men.

After an absence of several weeks we arrived back at the LX ranch with a small bunch of steers. .

About the last of March all the cowboys were called in from the outside line-camps to prepare for the spring round-up. Moore hired every renegade outlaw and cowboy passing through the country for this big spring round-up.

One evening before bed-time the sky became red from a big prairie fire off to the south-eastward. The fire was being driven by a strong southeast wind, down into the Canadian River Breaks, from the Staked Plains.

Now the headquarter ranch became a busy place. Saddle ponies were rounded up and a start made for the big fire, by the dozens of cowboys. In a swift gallop Moore led the crowd in the pitchy darkness, over all kinds of rough places. A ride of about fifteen miles brought us to the fire. Then we became fire-fighters in dead earnest.

Large droves of cattle were running ahead of the fire. Some of these largest animals were shot and killed. Then the carcasses were split open. Now two cowboys would fasten their ropes to each hind leg of the dead animal, and by the saddle-horn drag it to the blaze.

If the fire was down in an arroyo, where the blue-stem grass grows tall, it was allowed to burn its way onto a level flat covered with short buffalo grass. Here the two cowboys dragging a carcass would straddle the blaze — the one on the burnt side close up, with his rope shortened, while the other, on the hot smoky side, would be at the extreme end of his rope.

Now the wet carcass was dragged slowly along the blaze. This would put out the fire, all but small spots, these being whipped out by cowboys following afoot with wet saddle blankets or pieces of fresh cow-hide. A few miles of dragging in a hot blaze would wear a carcass into a frazzle. Then another animal was killed to take its place.

Without a bit to eat, except broiled beef without salt, this strenuous work was kept up until about three o'clock the following evening, when the fire was under control, and our range saved. We arrived back at the ranch about sundown — a smoky, dirty, tired and hungry crowd.

Soon after this fire excitement Mr. Moore lost nearly half of his crew of cowboys. They 'hit the trail for tall timber,' in New Mexico and Arizona — some on stolen ponies. The cause of this cowboy outlaw stampede was the arrival of E.W. Parker — now a respected citizen of El Paso, Texas — and his large, well-armed crew of Government Star-route mail surveyors. But they kept their mission a secret, hence the boys had them spotted as Texas Rangers in disguise.

A few months later the first mail route in the Panhandle of Texas was established. It ran from Fort Elliot, Texas, to Las Vegas, New Mexico, a distance of about three hundred miles. Our home ranch was made Wheeler post-office. Previous to this all our mail came from Fort Bascom, New Mexico, two hundred and twenty-five miles west, on the upper Canadian River. It came by private conveyance, and each letter sent, or received, cost us twenty-five cents — newspapers the same.

By the middle of April our range was crowded with buffaloes again. They were migrating north. But there was no great herd like the one going south in the early winter. Not over half of the woolly beasts that went south ever returned. They had been slaughtered for their hides, worth one dollar each, at the south edge of the Llano Estacado. It was estimated that, during the winter, there were seven thousand buffalo hunters along the Texas Pacific Railway — then building west to El Paso.

Now these buffaloes were going north through Kansas and Nebraska to their summer feeding ground in Dakota, to be killed by the northern hunters. The following fall only a few scattering herds passed through the Canadian River Breaks, on their way south. Most of these met their doom that winter by the southern hunters. Thus were the millions of buffaloes wiped from the face of the earth in a few years.

About the middle of April Moore took all his cowboys, about twenty-five with two well-filled mess-wagons, and went to Tascosa, there to meet other outfits from different parts of the country. Many of these cattle outfits came from the Arkansas River in southeastern Colorado, and southwestern Kansas. When we pulled out of Tascosa for the upper Canadian River, there were dozens of mess-wagons, and hundreds of riders.

This general round-up, the first ever pulled off in the Texas Panhandle, started work near Fort Bascom, New Mexico, and continued down the river almost to the Indian Territory line. During the winter thousands of northern cattle had drifted south and lodged in the Canadian River Breaks. These were all driven north after the general round-up.

While these round-up crews were at Tascosa, that little burg saw the need of saloons and dance-halls to relieve the cowboy of his loose change. The supply of liquors, sardines, and crackers in Howard & Rinehart's store melted away like a snowball dropped into Hades.

In June, after the spring round-ups, our cattle were all shoved onto the summer range, on Blue Creek north of the river. I and another cowboy were placed at the extreme head of the Blue, to ride line. Our camp was pitched at a spring.

Every morning and evening I had to ride past a plum-thicket, which was a few miles west of our camp, at the edge of which lay the bodies of three murdered Mexican buffalo hunters. They were badly swollen, and the sight of them made me nervous. Strange to relate these corpses were never devoured by the many lobos and coyotes around them. This fact convinces me that there is truth in the theory that wolves won't eat a dead Mexican — possibly on account of his system being impregnated with chili (red peppers). A short time previous, these three men were murdered by Nelson and three companions, in order to get their ox-teams to haul buffalo hides to Dodge City, Kansas. These murderers were never arrested, as there was no law in the country — and not a law-officer nearer than Fort Elliot.

While camped at the head of the Blue, several herds of 'Jingle-bob' cattle passed near our camp. These thousands of cattle had belonged to Cattle King John Chisum, of the Pecos River, in New Mexico, until Colonel Hunter, of the firm of Hunter and Evans in southern Kansas, had played a dirty trick on him.

In the early seventies John Chisum had bought thousands of she cattle from the old battle-scarred Confederate soldiers in middle Texas, giving his notes as pay. These cattle were driven across the Staked Plains to the Horse-head crossing of the Pecos River — thence up the river over two hundred miles into New Mexico, where they were turned loose. Then Mr. Chisum introduced fine-blooded short-horn bulls to breed out the long horns on these Texas cattle. The notes given by Chisum for these cattle were finally outlawed, as they couldn't be collected in New Mexico.

In the winter of 1877 and '78 Colonel Hunter and his flowing gray beard hiked from Medicine Lodge, Kansas, to middle Texas and bought up these outlawed notes for five or ten cents on the dollar. These notes were tucked into a satchel, and in the early spring of '78 taken to Las Vegas, New Mexico, and placed in a bank. Now Colonel Hunter went overland down the Pecos to South Spring River, where Mr. Chisum had established his 'Jingle-bob' headquarter ranch. There a deal was made for about twenty thousand head of his picked cattle, at a fancy price.

Now Jesse Evans, Colonel Hunter's partner, went to Dodge City, Kansas, and hired fifty fighting cowboys to go to New Mexico after these cattle. As soon as the Chisum outfit got a herd 'put up' they were turned over to the Hunter and Evans cowboys.

When the last herd was gathered, and headed northeastward, for the line of Texas, Colonel Hunter and John Chisum went overland to Las Vegas to settle up. Among cattle-men Colonel Hunter's word was as good as his bond, hence Mr. Chisum had no fear about getting his pay.

The curtain of this play goes down when, in the bank, the old satchel was opened and Mr. Chisum was paid for the cattle in his own notes, with the years of accumulated interest.

As fast as a team could travel, John Chisum went back to his ranch. Then he tried to make up a fighting crowd to follow up these Hunter and Evans herds, and recover them. He offered 'Billy the Kid' and his warriors big inducements to do the job, but they knew the Hunter and Evans cowboys were armed to the teeth, and being already over the line in Texas, they declined.

In the middle of June Mr. Moore sent for me to take charge
of a herd of steers containing twenty-five hundred head. I
was told to take them out onto the South Staked Plains and
fatten them. My crew consisted of four riders, and a cook to
drive the mess-wagon, with five ponies to the man. Soon after
this three more herds of steers were sent to the South Plains
and I was put in charge of the four herds. This made me feel
of some importance. I had nothing to do but ride from one
camp to the other — sometimes twenty miles apart — to see
that the steers were kept on fresh range so as to put on fat by
the time cold weather set in.

The summer of 1878 was a wet one — hence the 'dry' lakes,
or basins, were full of rain water. During the summer Mr.
David T. Beals paid me a visit. He brought a young man,
Burkley Howe, from Massachusetts, and turned him over to
me to be taught the cow business. The first lesson I dished
out to Burkley Howe was on mustang meat.

I shot and killed a young mustang from a band of three
hundred head. Then a young buffalo was killed. Some of the
meat from each animal was taken to camp. I instructed the
cook to prepare each kind the same, but to have it in separate
vessels. When we squatted down on the grass to eat our supper, the cook pointed out the vessel containing the mustang
meat, which in reality was the buffalo meat. Of course the
other boys had been posted.

Burkley Howe could not be induced even to taste the horse
meat. Instead he filled up on the supposed buffalo beef, which
he declared was the finest he had ever eaten. When told of
the trick, after supper, he was mad all over, and tried to vomit.
This goes to show that the mind controls the taste.

About the first of October eight hundred fat steers were cut
out of my four herds and started for Dodge City, Kansas,
the balance of the steers being turned loose on the winter

range, along the Canadian River. Now I secured permission from Mr. Moore to overtake the fat steer herd and accompany them to Chicago.

Mounted on my own pony, Whiskey Pete, I started in company with a cowboy named John Ferris. We kept on the Bascom Trail. After crossing the Cimarron River we saw a band of about two hundred Indians, off to our left in a deep arroyo, traveling westward, single file. Being hungry we concluded to gallop over to them and get something to eat.

On seeing us coming they all bunched up and showed great excitement. This didn't look good to Ferris and me; so we galloped back to the Bascom Trail and continued north. About sundown we reached Mead City, a new town started a few months previous. Here there were a half dozen new frame buildings, their insides being turned 'topsy-turvy,' showing that the Indians had run the occupants off and ransacked the dwellings. There were Indian moccasin tracks everywhere.

Now we hurried on to the store, on Crooked Creek, arriving there after dark. Here we found the same conditions as at Mead City showing that the Indians had looted the store. Hearing some ox-bells down the creek we rode to them, about a mile distant. Here we found several yoke of oxen and a log cabin, the door of which was locked. Being hungry we broke the lock on the door and entered. A playful puppy inside gave us a hearty welcome. After the lamps were lighted we found sacks of grain for our tired ponies, and a cupboard full of nice food. Hanging over the still warm ashes in the fireplace was a pot of fresh beef stew. This proved a treat, and we filled up to the bursting point. About midnight we started on the last lap of our two hundred and twenty-five-mile journey.

A twenty-five-mile ride brought us to the toughest town on

COWBOYS AT DINNER IN INDIAN TERRITORY, 1883

This shows how a well-trained cow-horse will stand when the bridle-reins are thrown over his head

earth, Dodge City. It was now daylight, and the first man met on the main street was Cape Willingham, who at this writing is a prosperous cattle broker in El Paso, Texas. Cape gave us our first news of the great Indian outbreak. He told of the many murders committed by the reds south of Dodge City the day previous — one man being killed at Mead City, and two others near the Crooked Creek store.

Riding up the main street Ferris and I saw twenty-five mounted cowboys, holding rifles in their hands, and facing one of the half-dozen saloons, adjoining each other, on that side of the street. In passing this armed crowd one of them recognized me. Calling me by name he said: 'Fall in line quick, h—l is going to pop in a few minutes.'

We jerked our Winchester rifles from the scabbards and fell in line, like most any other fool cowboys would have done. In a moment Clay Allison, the man-killer, came out of one of the saloons holding a pistol in his hand. With him was Mr. Mc-Nulty, owner of the large Panhandle 'Turkey-track' cattle outfit. Clay was hunting for some of the town policemen, or the city marshal, so as to wipe them off the face of the earth. His twenty-five cowboy friends had promised to help him clean up Dodge City.

After all the saloons had been searched, Mr. McNulty succeeded in getting Clay to bed at the Bob Wright Hotel. Then we all dispersed. Soon after, the city law officers began to crawl out of their hiding-places, and appear on the streets.

I found Mr. Erskine Clement, a partner of Mr. Beals, at the Wright Hotel, greatly worried over the non-arrival of the steer herd, which Mr. Moore had written him had started two weeks before. He was surprised when told that I had seen no sign of them over the Bascom Trail.

Telegrams kept pouring in from the west, of the bloody deeds committed by the Indians, on their way to Dakota.

They were Northern Cheyennes, who had broken away from the Cheyenne Agency in the Indian Territory.

In passing through western Nebraska these Indians murdered many settlers. At one ranch-house they captured a widow woman and her two daughters. After a day's march they turned the mother loose on the prairie, stark naked, keeping her two daughters with them. After much hardship this woman found the cabin of a 'fool hoe-man,' who was living alone. He wrapped the robe of Charity and his overcoat around her, and took her to civilization.

About midnight my chum John Ferris was flat broke, and borrowed twenty-five dollars of my accumulated wages, amounting to over three hundred dollars. He had in this short time 'blown in' his one hundred and fourteen dollars. By morning he had borrowed fifty dollars from the livery man on his pony and saddle, and I had to get these out of 'soak' for him, before he could hit the road again. He went direct to Fort Sumner, New Mexico, where he was shot and killed by Barney Mason, one of 'Billy the Kid's' gang, and a brother-in-law of the fearless New Mexico sheriff, Pat Garrett.

The next morning after my arrival in Dodge City, Erskine Clement and I struck south to look up the lost herd of steers. We found the outfit traveling up Crooked Creek very slowly. They had quit the Bascom Trail to avoid long drives between watering places. This, no doubt, had saved them from running into the Indians.

In Dodge City the herd was split in two, four hundred head being put aboard of a train for Chicago. I went in charge of this first shipment, and Mr. Clement followed with the next. Two of the cowboys went with me, one of them being A. M. Melvin, who now, after forty years, lives with a happy family at Orient Heights, East Boston, Massachusetts.

Now for the first time in my life I became a cow-puncher,

carrying a lantern and a long pole with a spike in the end, to keep the steers punched up, when they got down in the crowded cars. In a few years the name, cow-puncher, became attached to all cowboys.

At Burlington, Iowa, we crossed the Mississippi River into Illinois, and there on the east bank of the great river unloaded to feed the steers.

During our two days' stay we three cow-punchers made a dozen or more trips on the ferry boat to Burlington, a swift city. Our trips were free, and everything in the way of liquor, cigars, meals, candy, etc., bought in Burlington was free. The fact that we wore our cowboy outfits, including pistols, may have had something to do with the people refusing to take money from us. But it was said that their object was to encourage cattle-men to ship by way of Burlington.

On the first night after leaving Burlington I came within an ace of being ground to death by the train. The thoughts of my narrow escape cause my flesh to creep, even to this day.

A sleet storm was raging. The train stopped to take on coal. We three cow-punchers left the caboose and ran up toward the engine, peeping through the cracks to see if any of the steers were down. About the time we reached the engine the train started. Then we climbed onto the first car and started back to the caboose, on the run. I was in the rear. In making a spring from the top of one car to the other — the space between being about two feet — my high-heeled boots slipped on the icy boards. There I lay flat on my back with my head and shoulders over the open space. I had grabbed the edge of the footplank with my right hand. This is all that saved me from sliding down between the cars.

Mr. Beals met us on our arrival in Chicago. After unloading at the stock yards he took me to dine with him at the Palmer House. He wanted me to take a room in his hotel, but I told him that the food and price, five to ten dollars a day, were too rich for my blood. Therefore I went to the Irvine House where the price was only two dollars a day.

That night I turned myself loose in the toughest part of the city, spending all the money I had, about two hundred dollars. Toward daylight I managed to find my way back to the Irvine House, where a nap was taken. About ten o'clock I struck out for the Palmer House to borrow some money from Mr. Beals. On the way there, while gazing up at the signs, I saw the name of Dr. Bruer, Dentist. This put me in mind of the teeth which needed filling, so up the stairs I went, not realizing that my pockets were empty of cash.

In the dentist office I found Mr. Bruer and his handsome young lady assistant. After seating myself in the dentist chair, the doctor asked me what kind of filling I wanted for the two teeth. I told him to fill them with gold.

In those days the filling had to be done by hand. The doctor used the punch and the young lady the mallet. They didn't stop for lunch. It was three o'clock when the job was finished.

Now I got down off the chair, and for the first time realized that I didn't have a cent to pay for the work. I asked the amount of my bill, and was told that it was forty-five dollars. I told the doctor that I would drop around in the morning and pay him. He turned pale, and so did his assistant. The large pistol and bowie-knife buckled around my waist may have caused them to turn pale. Finally the doctor asked the name of my hotel. I told him. Then he said: 'Now you won't forget to come up in the morning and pay me?' I answered him that he could depend upon it.

I found Mr. David T. Beals at the Palmer House and borrowed a hundred dollars. Then I started out to see more of the sights of a great city. But I took the precaution to tuck the dentist's forty-five dollars down in the watch-pocket of my pants, so that it wouldn't be spent. The next morning at nine o'clock I was in the dentist's office and paid over the forty-five dollars. The doctor and his assistant were happily surprised.

The doctor had me go to lunch with him. Then we spent the afternoon driving over the city in his buggy, drawn by a fine pair of black horses.

We visited the waterworks and climbed up to the top of the tall, rounded tower, from the inside. On reaching the top I looked over the edge, to the ground below, just once. That was enough. I was afraid the thing would topple over from my weight. The dentist laughed at me but he couldn't induce me to look over the edge again. After the drive was over, I hunted up Mr. Beals to get more money for the night's sight-seeing.

I can look back now and see that I was an 'easy mark' for the city people. Of course they knew at a glance by my bow-legs and high-heeled boots where I was from, and they charged accordingly for what was purchased.

After a few days' sight-seeing I boarded a train for Dodge City, Kansas. Mr. Beals and Erskine Clement accompanied me.

Arriving in Dodge City, Whiskey Pete was mounted early one morning for my two-hundred-and-twenty-five-mile lonely ride to the LX ranch. I arrived at the headquarters ranch late in the evening. A crowd of strangers were playing cards under a cottonwood tree near by. The cook informed me that they were Billy the Kid and his Lincoln County, New Mexico, warriors.

When the cook rang the supper bell, these strangers ran for the long table. After being introduced, I found myself seated by the side of good-natured Billy the Kid. Henry

Brown, Fred White and Tom O'Phalliard are the only names of this outlaw gang that I can recall.

When supper was over, I produced a box of fine Havana cigars, brought from Chicago as a treat for the boys on the ranch. They were passed around. Then one was stuck into my new ten-dollar meerschaum cigar-holder, and I began to puff smoke toward the ceiling.

Now Billy the Kid asked for a trial of my cigar-holder. This was granted. He liked it so well that he begged me to present it to him, which I did. In return he presented me with a finely bound novel which he had just finished reading. In it he wrote his autograph, giving the date that it was presented to me. During the next few weeks Billy the Kid and I became quite chummy. After selling out the band of ponies, which he and his gang had stolen from the Seven River warriors, in New Mexico, he left the Canadian River country, and I never saw him again. Two of his gang, Henry Brown and Fred Waite — a half-breed Chickasaw Indian — quit the outfit and headed for the Indian Territory.

During his long stay around the LX ranch and Tascosa, Billy the Kid made one portly old capitalist from Boston, Massachusetts, sweat blood for a few minutes. Mr. Torey owned a large cattle ranch above Tascosa. On arriving from the east he learned that Billy the Kid and gang had made themselves at home on his ranch for a few days — hence he gave the foreman orders not to feed them, if they should make another visit. This order reached the Kid's ears.

While in Tascosa Billy the Kid saw old man Torey ride up to the hitching-rack in front of Jack Ryan's saloon. He went out to meet him, and asked if he had ordered his foreman not to feed them.

Mr. Torey replied yes, that he didn't want to give his ranch a bad name by harboring outlaws.

Then the Kid jerked his Colt's pistol and jabbed the old man several times in his portly stomach, at the same time telling him to say his prayers, as he was going to pump him full of lead. With tears in his voice Mr. Torey promised to countermand the order. Then war was declared off.

Thus did Mr. Torey, a former sea captain, get his eye-teeth cut in the ways of the wild and woolly West.

This story was told to me by Billy the Kid and Steve Arnold, who was an eye-witness to the affair. But the Kid said he had no intention of shooting Mr. Torey — that he just wanted to teach him a lesson.

CHAPTER VI

DOWN THE CHISHOLM TRAIL AND BACK — I BOSS A HERD OF STEERS FROM TEXAS

AFTER lying around the home ranch a few weeks Mr. Moore put me in charge of a scouting outfit, to drift over the South Staked Plains, in search of any cattle which might have escaped from the line-riders.

While on this trip I went to church several times. A colony of Illinois Christians, under the leadership of the Reverend Mr. Cahart, had established the town of Clarendon, on the head of Salt Fork, a tributary of Red River, and there built a white church house among buffalo and wolves.

When spring came I was called in from the plains and put in charge of a round-up crew, consisting of a cook and twelve riders. Our first round-up was on the Goodnight range, at the mouth of Mulberry Creek. Here we had the pleasure of a genuine cattle-queen's presence. Mrs. Goodnight, a noble little woman, a dyed-in-the-wool Texan, attended these round-ups with her husband. Mrs. Goodnight touched a soft spot in my heart by filling me up on several occasions, with juicy berries which she had gathered with her own hands.

Mr. and Mrs. Charlie Goodnight are still alive, and living in the town of Goodnight, Texas, which has been made famous as the home of the largest herd of buffaloes in that State, and possibly the whole United States.

The foundation of this herd of buffaloes was started on this round-up in the spring of 1879. In the round-up at the head of Mulberry Creek was a lone buffalo bull. When ready to turn the round-up cattle loose Mr. Buffalo was roped and thrown, and a cow-bell fastened to his neck. When turned loose he stampeded, and so did the thousands of cattle.

In the round-up the following spring the bell-buffalo was with the cattle, and had with him several female buffaloes. During that summer Mr. Goodnight fenced his summer range on Mulberry Creek, and this small herd of buffalo found themselves enclosed with a strong barbed wire fence.

We wound up this spring round-up on the Rocking Chair range, at the mouth of McClellan Creek, where I saw about fifty thousand cattle in one bunch — more than I had ever seen before in one band.

Now we returned to the home ranch with about five hundred LX cattle, which had drifted away from the range during the winter. Shortly after our return Moore had us help him brand some large long-horn steers, late arrivals from South Texas. We did the branding on the open plains, at Amarillo Lake. While roping and tying down these wild steers we had real sport in seeing 'center-fire' saddles jerked over sideways from the pony's back, the riders with them.

Moore had got his cowboy training in California, where they use 'center-fire,' high horn saddles, and riatas (ropes) which they wrap around the saddle-horn when roping on horseback. The cinchas on these saddles being broad, and in the center of the saddle, it is difficult to keep the saddle tight on the pony's back. Moore had persuaded many of his cowboys to use these saddles and the long rawhide riatas, and a large order had been sent to California in the early spring. In the order were many silver-mounted spurs and Spanish bridle-bits. I sent for one of these ten-dollar bridle-bits, and am still using it to ride with.

I must confess that Moore never got a fall from his center-fire saddle, as he had learned his lesson early in life. He was also an expert roper with his seventy-five-foot riata. He could throw the large loop further and catch his animal oftener than any man in the crowd of about twenty-five riders.

Moore tried his best to persuade me, and such Texas-raised cowboys as Jim East, Steve Arnold and Lee Hall, not to tie our thirty-foot ropes hard and fast to the saddle horns when roping large steers. He argued that it was too danger-ous. No doubt he was right, but we had been trained that way.

Later poor Lee Hall was gored to death by a wild steer, roped down in the Indian Territory. The steer had jerked his mount over backward, and one of his spurs caught in the flank cinch, preventing him from freeing himself until too late to save his life. The spur which hung in the cinch and caused his death, was one of the fine silver-mounted pair which Moore sent to California for. After his death I fell heir to Lee Hall's spurs and they are used by me to this day, over fifty years later.

In the latter part of June Moore put me in charge of eight hundred fat steers for the Chicago market. My outfit con-sisted of a well filled mess-wagon, a cook and five riders. Late in the fall we arrived in Nickerson, Kansas, and turned the steers over to 'Deacon' Bates.

Leaving Whiskey Pete and a Missouri mare, which I had traded for, with a 'fool hoe-man,' five miles south of town, 'Jingle-bob' Joe Hargraves and I started west across country to meet another herd of fat steers. As the snow had begun to fly it was thought best to turn this herd toward Dodge City, Kansas — hence we were sent to pilot the outfit to Dodge City.

We finally found the steer outfit and turned them toward Dodge City. There the fat steers were put aboard two trains, and I took charge of one train, thus taking my second lesson in cow-punching with a spiked pole and lantern.

On arriving in Chicago, Mr. Beals met us. Then at the Palmer House Mr. Beals settled up my wage and expense account. With a few hundred dollars in my pocket I started out to see the sights again.

I had told Mr. Beals of my intention to quit his outfit and spend the winter in Southern Texas. He agreed that if I concluded to go back to work for the LX Company in the spring, he would arrange for me to boss a herd of steers up the trail. He had already contracted with Charlie Word of Goliad, Texas, for two herds to be delivered on the LX ranch.

A couple of days and nights of sight-seeing put me almost out financially. Then a train was boarded for Nickerson, Kansas. Whiskey Pete and the bay mare were found hog fat. The 'fool hoe-man' had shoved corn to them with a scoop shovel.

After purchasing a pack-saddle, and some grub, I had just six dollars in cash left to make my eleven-hundred-mile journey down the Chisholm trail to the gulf coast of Texas. Puck was not far off when he said: 'What fools these mortals be.' For here was a fool cowboy starting out to ride eleven hundred miles, just to be in the saddle, and to get a pony back home.

On the way down the trail I kept myself supplied with cash by swapping saddles, pack pony and watches, and running races with Whiskey Pete, who was hard to beat in a three-hundred-yard race.

At one place in middle Texas I lay over a couple of days to rest my ponies, and to make a few dollars picking cotton. One morning I was sent out by the farmer, with a bunch of barefooted girls, to pick cotton in a field which had already been picked over. These young damsels gave me the 'horse-laugh' for my awkwardness in picking the snowy balls of cotton. When night came I had earned just thirty cents, while the girls had made more than a dollar each. This was my last stunt as a cotton picker.

On Pecan Creek, near Denton, I put up one night at the home of old man Murphy — the father of Jim Murphy, who was a member of the Sam Bass gang of train robbers, and whose name is mentioned in the Sam Bass song, which was a favorite with trail cowboys.

The old Chisholm Trail was lined with negroes, headed for Topeka and Emporia, Kansas, to get a free farm and a span of mules from the State Government. Over my pack there was a large buffalo robe, and on my saddle hung a fine silver-mounted Winchester rifle. These attracted the attention of those green cotton-field negroes, who wore me out asking questions about them. Some of these negroes were afoot, while others drove donkeys and oxen. The shiny black children and half-starved dogs were plentiful. Many of the out-fits turned back when I told them of the cold blizzards and deep snow in Kansas.

My eleven-hundred-mile journey ended at the old Rancho Grande headquarters ranch, after being on the trail one month and twelve days.

The balance of the winter was spent on hunting trips after deer and wild hogs, and visiting friends throughout the county of Matagorda.

Early in the spring I mounted Gotch, a pony traded for, and bidding Whiskey Pete good-bye, he being left with my chum, Horace Yeamans, we headed for Goliad to meet Charlie Word. He was found near Beeville, thirty miles west of Go-liad, putting up a herd of long-horn steers for the LX Com-pany. He had received a letter from Mr. David T. Beals tell-ing him to put me in charge of one of the herds.

This first herd was to be bossed 'up the trail' by Liash Stevens.

The outfit was up to their ankles in sticky mud, in a large round corral, putting the road-brand on the steers, when I found them. I pitched in and helped and was soon covered with mud from head to feet. Each steer had to be roped and thrown afoot, which made it a disagreeable job in the cold drizzling rain. And to finish out the day's work, after my thirty-mile ride from Goliad, I stood guard over the steers until after midnight.

After the herd had been road-branded and turned over to Mr. Stevens and his crew of trail cowboys, Charlie Word asked me to help him get the herd started on the trail. Our first night out proved a strenuous one. Mr. Stevens had taken a fool notion to arm his cowboys with bull's-eye lanterns, so that they could see each other on dark nights. He had ordered a few extra ones and insisted on my trying one that night, which I did.

About ten o'clock a severe storm came up and we were all in the saddle ready for a stampede. While I was running at break-neck speed, to reach the lead of the herd, my pony went head over heels over a rail fence. The light from the lantern had blinded him, so that he failed to see it in time. The pony was caught and mounted, and the new-fangled bull's-eye lantern was left on the ground.

Strange to relate, this lantern is prized to-day as a souvenir of bygone days. It was picked up next day by a young rancher, who at this writing lives near Kingston, Sierra County, New Mexico.

I finally reached the lead of the herd, and from that time till daylight it was one stampede after another. Daylight found young Glass and me alone with about half the herd of thirty-seven hundred head. We were jammed into the foot of a lane, down which the cattle had drifted during the last hour of darkness. This lane was built with five strands of new barbed wire, and was cut off by a cross fence. Here the herd was jammed together so tightly that it was impossible to ride to the rear.

There we had to wait and pray that another stampede wouldn't start while we were hemmed in on three sides by a high wire fence. A stampede would, no doubt, have sent us to the happy hunting ground. It required two days' hard work to gather up steers lost during the night. They had become mixed up with range cattle. In that camp the price of bull's-eye lanterns took a tumble. It was almost impossible to give one away.

After the herd was strung out again on the trail I went on to Goliad to meet Charlie Word. Here he made up a crew of twelve riders, a cook and mess-wagon, with five ponies to the rider, and turned them over to me. With this crew I drifted northwesterly to the crooked-street, straggling town of San Antonio — now one of the leading cities of Texas. In San Antonio we had all of our ponies shod as we were going into a rocky country. Charlie Word had bought twenty-five hundred head of cattle from Joe Taylor, and it was our duty to gather them from this range.

We finally got the herd broke in, and started 'up the trail,' but not up the Chisholm Trail, which lay to the eastward about a hundred miles.

During that spring of 1880 the Chisholm Trail was impassable for large herds, as 'fool hoe-men' had squatted all over it, and were turning its hard packed surface into ribbons with ploughs. When about fifty miles west of Fort Worth, Charlie Word, who had come around by rail, drove out in a buggy to see how we were getting along, and to supply me with more expense money. At Doan's store, on Red River, we found Liash Stevens waiting for us. We swapped herds, as it had been decided to drive the herd I was with up into Wyoming.

I arrived at the LX ranch with thirty-seven hundred head of steers on the first day of July. Now part of my crew were paid off, and with the balance, six riders, I took the herd onto the South Staked Plains to fatten the steers.

One of the first things I did after riding into Tascosa was to step into Mr. Turner's restaurant to see his pretty daughter, Miss Victoria. I was not hungry, but to have the pleasure of this pretty miss waiting on me I was ordering all the good things in the restaurant. Just then a gang of cowboys came charging through the main street shooting off pistols.

As this was no uncommon thing for a live cow-town, I didn't even get up from the table. In a moment Sheriff Willingham came running into the café with a double-barrel shot-gun in his hand. He asked me to help him arrest some drunken cowboys who had just dismounted and gone into Jack Ryan's saloon, near by.

Just as we reached the Ryan saloon, these cowboys came out. One of them sprang onto his horse, when the sheriff told him to throw up his hands. Instead of throwing up his hands, he drew his pistol. Then Willingham planted a charge of buck shot in his heart, and he tumbled to the ground dead.

The dead cowboy was the one the sheriff was after, as he had seen him empty his pistol at a flock of ducks, which a lady was feeding out of her hand, as she sat in a doorway. In galloping down the street this cowboy remarked to his companions: 'Watch me kill some of those ducks.' He killed them all right, and the woman fainted. These nine cowboys had just arrived 'up the trail' with a herd of long-horn cattle, and were headed for the north. For fear they might make a raid on him in the night, which they threatened to do, the sheriff had me stay with him till morning.

Thus did Tascosa bury her first man with his boots on, which gave her the reputation of being a genuine cow-town.

Before the court-house and jail were finished Tascosa had a
bad murder case to try. The District Judge and attorney
came from Mobeta to try the case. Jack Ryan was foreman
of the jury, and the upstairs part of his saloon was selected as
the jury-room.

When the prisoner's case was finished, the jury were locked
up over the saloon. About midnight Jack Ryan and some of
the jurymen were holding out for murder in the first degree.
About that time Frank James, Ryan's gambling partner, got
a ladder and climbed up to the outside window of the jury-
room. He then called for Ryan, and told him that there was
a big poker game going on in the saloon, and that he needed
three hundred dollars. Jack gave him the money from the
bank-roll which he carried in his pocket, at the same time telling him to keep the game going until he could get down there
and take a hand.

Now Ryan called the jurymen together and told them
about the big poker game down in the saloon. He said it was
necessary for him to be there and help Frank James out;
hence he had come to the conclusion that the prisoner was innocent, and had no evil intentions of murdering his victim.

In a few moments Ryan had the few stubborn jurymen on
his side and the prisoner was declared innocent. At least this
is the story told to me by men who claimed to know the facts
of the case. This added another laurel to Tascosa's brow as a
wide-open cow-town.

CHAPTER VII

BILLY THE KID'S CAPTURE — I ESCAPE ASSASSINATION
BY A SCRATCH

About the first of September my steer herd was turned loose
on the winter range. Then we started out to brand calves.
When the branding season was over, Moore sent me onto the
South Plains in charge of a scouting crew.

A month later a runner hunted me up to deliver a letter
from Moore. In this letter I was instructed to turn the outfit
over to James McClaugherty, and to bring three of my picked
fighting cowboys with me to the headquarters ranch. I selected James H. East, Lee Hall, and Cal Polk as the fighting
men.

On arriving at the ranch Moore outfitted me for a trip to
New Mexico after Billy the Kid and LX cattle which he and
his gang had been stealing.

I finally started up the river with four large mules hitched
to a heavy mess-wagon, with Francisco as driver and cook.
My fighting crew consisted of five men: Big-Foot Wallace
(Frank Clifford), Jim East, Cal Polk, Lon Chambers, and
Lee Hall. In Tascosa we were joined by the Littlefield crew,
in charge of Bob Roberson. He had a mess-wagon, a cook,
and five riders.

We started out with only one horse apiece, with the exception of myself; I had two. As corn was scarce, it was
thought best to buy more horses if we should need them.

On reaching San Lorenzo, New Mexico, I boarded a buckboard to Las Vegas, to buy a supply of corn, grub and ammunition, giving the outfit instructions to lie over in Anton Chico,
on the Pecos River, until I got there.

I found Las Vegas to be a swift dance-hall town, and the first night of my arrival I went broke, playing monte — a Mexican game. I blew in all my expense money, about three hundred dollars, and about a hundred dollars which Bob Roberson had given me to buy ammunition and grub. A big-hearted merchant by the name of Houton gave me the goods I needed, he taking orders on the LX Company for pay.

On reaching Anton Chico with the wagon load of supplies, I learned that Billy the Kid and gang had slipped into town one night and stolen some fresh horses. They had come from the White Oaks country, to the southwestward. We finally pulled out for White Oaks, and the next morning early Pat Garrett, the sheriff of Lincoln County, New Mexico, rode into our camp. He said he was making up a crowd to go down the Pecos River in search of Billy the Kid and gang.

After consulting together, Bob Roberson and I decided to furnish Garrett part of our crew. Hence I turned over to him Lee Hall, Jim East, and Lon Chambers. Roberson loaned him Tom Emory and Louis Bozeman. Frank Stewart also joined Pat Garrett, he being his own boss and not subject to Roberson's orders. In Anton Chico, Pat Garrett picked up a few of his own men, his brother-in-law, Barney Mason, being one of them. They then started down the Pecos River.

In the Mexican village of Puerto de Luna, Garrett proved his bravery. A drunken Mexican enemy fired a shot at him from the open door of a saloon. Garrett remarked that he didn't want to kill the fellow, so he would just break his right arm. This he did with a well-aimed shot.

Roberson and I struck out for White Oaks in a raging snow-storm. When within a day's ride of White Oaks we came to the still smoking ruins of the Jim Greathouse road-ranch, a saloon and store. Here a posse from White Oaks, under the leadership of deputy-sheriff Jim Carlyle, had fought a battle, a few days previous, with Billy the Kid and his gang. While the posse had the gang surrounded in the Greathouse ranch, Jim Carlyle went in to have a talk with the Kid. For an hour or more the gang held Carlyle a prisoner, waiting for darkness to come so they could make their escape. They made him drink with them at the bar every time they took a drink.

Finally Jim Carlyle jumped through a window to make his escape. As he sprang through the window the Kid shot him. He fell on the outside and began crawling away. Then the Kid killed him with another shot from his pistol. In the darkest part of the night the gang made a break for liberty, and escaped.

The next day the posse set fire to the ranch, as it had become a rendezvous for outlaws. In following the gang's trail through the snow they came to the Spence ranch, where the gang had eaten breakfast. Now the posse burnt up Mr. Spence's buildings for feeding them.

By tramping all that day and part of the night the Kid gang reached Anton Chico, where they stole horses and saddles while my outfit was there waiting for me to return from Las Vegas.

We arrived in the new mining camp of White Oaks in a severe snowstorm. For a week we camped out in the open with the snow nearly two feet deep, then we rented a building to live in. Two of the leading merchants, Mr. Whiteman and Mr. Sweet, gave us unlimited credit for grub and horse feed. We concluded to make this our headquarters until Pat Garrett and crowd were heard from. He had felt sure that he would find Billy the Kid and gang down on the Pecos River.

White Oaks was only a year old, but she contained over a thousand population, mostly venturesome men from all parts of the land, who flocked there after the first find of rich gold ore.

An outlaw by the name of Wilson had put White Oaks on the map by stumbling onto a rich gold lead. He was making his get-away from Texas law officers, and cut across the county of Lincoln, New Mexico. At White Oaks Spring his pony played out, and seeing smoke from a cabin three miles down the gulch he headed for it.

This cabin proved to be the home of two old California placer miners, Jack Winters and John Wilson. They were washing gold out of the bed of Baxter Gulch, and hauling water on burros from White Oaks Spring. The ground was rich in gold, and they generally took the gold dust to Lincoln, the county seat of Lincoln County, every Saturday, returning to Baxter Gulch on Mondays. These two old prospectors gave the outlaw Wilson permission to make himself at home in their cabin until his pony rested.

On the day after his arrival, after eating dinner, Wilson started out to walk to the top of Baxter Mountain, to view the surrounding country. He took a pick on his shoulder, telling the old prospectors that he might find a gold mine. When half-way up the high mountain, Wilson sat down on a boulder to rest. While resting he began to chip pieces off this quartz boulder. When ready to proceed on his journey, he picked up a large chip from this boulder, and seeing specks of yellow in it, he stuck it in his pocket.

It was almost dark when he got back to the cabin. Jack Winters was cooking flap-jacks for supper, on the sheet-iron stove. As a joke he asked Wilson if he had found a gold mine. He replied that he had found a rock with specks of yellow in it. He then handed Winters the chip from his pocket. One glance at the rock sent Winters up in the air with a yell. This brought John Wilson out of his slumber; then he, too, became excited.

It required a lot of persuasion to get Wilson to go back up

the mountain, and show them the boulder from which this chip was broken, his argument being that he was worn out from his long tramp, and that the boulder would be there in the morning.

Finally the three started up the mountain-side with lantern and location stakes, the flap-jacks being left on the stove to burn up. On reaching the boulder, other similar quartz boulders were found farther up the mountain: finally, by the light of the lantern, the quartz lead about three feet wide was discovered. In picking into it wires of free gold were discovered.

Now the two old prospectors wrote out location notices on the stakes brought along. Wilson was asked his full name, so that he could be put in as a third owner. But he told them to locate it for themselves, as he had no use for a gold mine. Therefore two full claims, each fifteen hundred feet in length and six hundred feet in width, were located, running north and south, they being named the North Homestake, and the South Homestake, Winters claiming the former and John Wilson the latter.

It was midnight when the three tired and hungry men returned to the cabin, and finished the flap-jack operation. In a few days outlaw Wilson mounted his rested pony, and headed northwestward for the adobe village of Albuquerque, on the Rio Grande River, a distance of about one hundred and forty miles. He was presented with an old pistol and nine silver dollars, all the cash in camp, when he started. Shortly after his departure officers from Texas arrived on Wilson's trail, but whether they ever overtook him is a question, as he had several days the start. Shortly before our arrival in White Oaks, Jack Winters and John Wilson had sold the North and South Homestake to a Saint Louis Company — receiving $300,000 each for their rich claims. During one of his sober spells Jack Winters told me the story as outlined above.

At midnight our crowd ushered in the new year of 1881, in front of our picket shack. Each man emptied a Winchester rifle and a six-shooter in rapid succession. This was done to frighten the citizens of White Oaks, as we figured that they would think Billy the Kid had struck town. He had shot up the town a short time previous.

Our guess was correct, for it caused a regular stampede out of the saloons and billiard-hall. The town marshal, Pinto Tom, was playing billiards when the shooting began. He dropped his cue and broke for the back door, and took to the tall timber on the side of Carrizozo Mountain. It was noon next day when he returned. We had a man watching Pinto Tom to see what his actions would be.

Bob Roberson and I kept the neighbors around our shack supplied with fresh beef. A large steer would be dressed and hung up in a tree near by. The neighbors would help themselves to this beef, so that we had to butcher a fresh one quite often. One of these beef-eating neighbors, William C. McDonald, then a young surveyor, was the first governor of the State of New Mexico. He had become a wealthy cattle-man, and was opposed to people eating stolen beef, but I reminded him of the time when he seemed to relish it. He made a splendid governor, and when he died, and was buried in White Oaks, a short time ago, I lost one of my dearest friends.

Roberson and I didn't consider that we were stealing, as in Texas it was the custom to kill any one's animals for beef. Most of the fat steers butchered by our crowd belonged to Tom Catron, later United States Senator, and his nephew, Mr. Waltz. They owned a cattle ranch at Carrizozo Springs.

The first word we had of Billy the Kid was when three of our boys, Lee Hall, Lon Chambers, and Louis Bozeman arrived from Fort Sumner, with the news that Billy the Kid and gang had been captured, two of the gang being killed.

They explained the fight as follows:

On arriving in Fort Sumner, Garrett learned that the Kid and his gang had been there and had ridden east for Portales Lake. Hence the sheriff surmised that they would soon return. Therefore camp was pitched in an old vacated adobe house, fronting the Fort Sumner and Los Portales road. In front of this house there was an adobe fence, behind which one man was put on guard every night to give the alarm if men were seen coming toward Fort Sumner.

Several nights later, while Lon Chambers was on duty behind the adobe fence, a crowd of men was seen coming down the road. Chambers at once gave the alarm to Garrett and the boys who were playing poker. Then all lined themselves along the adobe fence.

When the man in the lead was opposite, Garrett stood up and called to him to throw up his hands. Instead he drew his pistol, and received two bullets through the body. These shots scattered the gang like a flock of quail. Many shots were fired at them as they took the back-track from whence they had come. The dead man proved to be Tom O'Phalliard. He breathed a few times after being carried into the house.

Then Garrett and the posse took up the trail in the deep snow. Twelve miles out they came to a dead horse which had been wounded in the stomach the night previous.

From now on two of the gang were mounted on one pony, which made their progress slow. Toward midnight that night a one-room rock house loomed up ahead, and the trail in the snow ended there, showing that the gang were inside the cabin.

Now the posse rode behind a high hill and built a fire. Just before daylight Pat Garrett and Lee Hall lay down along the west wall, near the corner, from whence the door could be covered with their rifles. Outside of this door stood four shivering ponies, the ropes around their necks being on the inside.

At the first peep of day one man walked out of the cabin, and the sheriff commanded him to throw up his hands. He jumped back toward the door, and received two bullets through the body. Then with his hands up, he walked to Garrett and Hall saying, 'I wish, I wish!' and fell over dead. This man proved to be Charlie Bowdre.

Now the gang inside began pulling one of the ponies inside through the doorway. When halfway in Garrett sent a bullet through the pony's heart. This blocked up the entrance.

Billy the Kid already had his little race mare inside, and it was their intention to pull the rest of the ponies inside, and then make a dash out of the doorway for liberty.

Now the sheriff and the Kid opened up a conversation, passing jokes back and forth. There were no windows in the cabin, and the gang tried to pick portholes through the thick stone walls, with their guns and knives, but this proved a failure.

All that day the gang held out without food, water, or fire.

They finally decided to surrender. Billy the Kid was the last to come out with hands up. There were only four of them left: Billy Wilson, Tom Picket, Rudabaugh, and the Kid.

On arrival in Fort Sumner the sheriff sent part of our boys to White Oaks, while he took Jim East, Tom Emory, and Frank Stewart with him to the railroad, at Las Vegas. There they boarded a train for Santa Fé, where the prisoners were put in the penitentiary for safe-keeping. In Las Vegas a mob was formed to hang Billy the Kid, but they were stood off until the train could pull out.

After the return of Tom Emory and Jim East, Bob Roberson decided, as the Kid was behind prison walls, to return home. I had concluded to stay until spring, and gather up any LX cattle that might be in the country.

As Jim East wished to return to Tascosa, and run for sheriff of Oldham County, Texas, I allowed him to go back with the Roberson crowd. I also let Lee Hall and Cal Polk go. As Tom Emory wished to stay with me, Roberson gave his consent.

I finally received several hundred dollars of expense money from Mr. Moore, with orders to stay in the country as long as I wished. We continued to feed our neighbors stolen beef — not exactly stolen, but butchered according to the Texas custom.

Well do I remember 'Shanghai' Pierce once riding into our camp, when one of his animals was being butchered; he said: 'Boys, the day is coming when every man will have to eat his own beef.' That day came before we old-time cowboys had time to realize it.

About the first of February I took Tom Emory with me and rode to Fort Stanton to examine the hides in Pat Coghlin's slaughter house there, he having the contract to furnish the soldiers with beef. Emory was mounted on his gray horse, while I rode one of the work mules, a dandy saddle animal.

We went first to the town of Lincoln and secured the services of Johnny Hurley — afterward killed by outlaws — as a witness in case we found any LX hides at Fort Stanton.

In searching the Coghlin slaughter house, in charge of 'Old Papen,' we found many LX hides — some freshly butchered. These were taken and stored.

Now I decided to see the 'King of Tularosa,' as Pat Coghlin was called, and warn him not to kill any more LX cattle. Arriving in Las Cruces I found Coghlin. He was a large, fine-looking old Irishman, with the 'ould sod' love for red 'licker.' On telling him of finding the LX hides in his slaughter house, and of my plan to search his range for LX cattle on my return, he promised not to butcher any more, if I would wait until April the first before rounding up his cattle, as he didn't want them disturbed until the grass became green in the spring. I promised, not realizing he was playing a dirty trick on me.

One night was spent in Tularosa. The next morning I started for the Pat Coghlin cattle ranch on Three Rivers — now the property of former Secretary of the Interior A. B. Fall — a distance of twenty miles.

On the way there I met a lone horseman. He introduced himself to me as Johnny Reily. Thirty-five years later I was reading a magazine on the front porch of the De Vargas Hotel, in Santa Fé, when an old gentleman passed me on his way into the hotel. I looked up, and our eyes met. He said: 'Didn't I meet you in 1881 on the road between Tularosa and Three Rivers?' And Johnny Reily, the wealthy cattle man residing in the El Paso Club at Colorado Springs, Colorado, sat down beside me to 'hark back' to the bloody Lincoln County War, in which he took a prominent part.

He told of one incident to show the cheap regard for human life in that noted war. He said he and Jimmie Dolan owned a store near Fort Stanton, and had been at war with Billy the Kid and his crowd. One night the Kid and some of his warriors pitched camp in the hills near their store. Early the next morning the Kid sent one of his men to the store with a peace treaty to be signed by Reily and Dolan.

After the paper was signed, they all went across the road to a saloon to take a drink. A drummer from the East, who had just sold them a bill of goods, accompanied them to the saloon. While filling the glasses to take a drink the traveling man criticized Billy the Kid and his lawless bunch. Here Billy the Kid's man told him to keep quiet, as he was not in the civilized East. He replied that as an American citizen he had a right to criticize lawlessness.

He hadn't more than finished the sentence when the Kid's man shot him dead. Reily said he and Dolan started to run to the door, but the fellow leveled his pistol at them saying: 'Finish your drink, boys, don't let a little thing like this excite you.' They finished the drink, and were glad to get back to the store alive.

At the Pat Coghlin ranch I put up for the night, and was royally treated by Mr. and Mrs. George Nesbeth, the couple who looked after the cooking and ranch work. A Mexican was in charge of the live stock. During the evening Mr. and Mrs. Nesbeth told me how they were present when Pat Coghlin made a deal with Billy the Kid to buy all the Panhandle, Texas, cattle that he could steal and deliver to him at Three Rivers.

The next morning when ready to start for White Oaks, by way of the wagon road, around the mountains, the Mexican foreman told me that I could save ten miles by taking a trail over the high mountain range. He agreed to send one of his Mexican cowboys to put me on the right trail.

Accepting his kind offer we started. When about five miles up the mountain-side a plain trail was struck, and the pilot returned toward home. About an hour later the trail made a bend to the left, and, to save time, I cut across to strike it farther up the mountain. This move, no doubt, saved my life, as assassins were 'laying' for me a short distance ahead on the trail.

Finally three shots were fired in quick succession, and my mule lunged forward, slipping on the ice-covered ground. She fell on her side throwing me over an eight-foot cliff. My pistol was hanging to the saddle horn, but I grabbed it and pulled it out of the scabbard as I went off the saddle. With the pistol ready for action, I lay quiet for a few moments, thinking the would-be assassins might show up. I then crawled up the cliff just in time to see two men running over a ridge, a few hundred yards distant. They were afoot and in sight only a minute. No doubt they thought I was killed, and were running back to where their mounts had been left.

The mule was found a couple of hundred yards up the mountain with her front leg fast in the bridle-rein. The ground was covered with blood, which had flowed from the wound in her breast. On investigation I found that one bullet had ploughed a furrow through the hind tree of my saddle, and another went through a blanket tied behind the saddle. The mule was not badly wounded, hence I reached White Oaks at dark, after an absence of about two weeks.

Over thirty years later my cowboy friend, John P. Meadows, of Tularosa, New Mexico, told me the secret of this attempted assassination. He had learned the facts in the case from Mexicans living at Three Rivers. Pat Coghlin had paid them to kill me, to prevent prosecution for the LX hides found in his slaughter house.

For the next month we took life easy in the lively town of White Oaks and continued to eat fresh beef. The only brand we looked for, in selecting an animal for slaughter, was fat. The town supported a weekly newspaper, the 'Golden Era,' hence we kept posted on local affairs. One of the boys then on the 'Golden Era' force, Emerson Hough, afterward attained a world-wide reputation as a writer.

Soon after my return to camp 'Big-Foot Wallace' (Frank Clifford) and I rode out in the hills to get a steer for slaughter. We butchered one on the edge of town, and the cook, Francisco, hauled the meat to our quarters in the mess-wagon.

On entering our picket shack, one of the boys told Wallace

that the town schoolmaster, Sheldon, was hunting him with a gun, to settle a difficulty they had got into that morning.

'Big-Foot' had just sat down to eat his supper. Jumping up he remarked: 'Well, I will go and hunt him!' So saying he pulled his Colt's pistol out of the scabbard lying on the floor, and stuck it in his right boot. Then he started downtown. I tried to persuade him to wait until after supper, when I would go with him, but he was too angry to wait.

Soon we heard six shots fired in quick succession, and a moment later, two louder shots. Jumping on my pony bareback I ran downtown. Finding 'Big-Foot' surrounded by a big crowd of men, I advised him to jump on behind me on the pony's back and return to camp, which he did.

He explained matters by saying that he met Sheldon and another man walking up the street toward him. On meeting, he asked Sheldon if he was hunting for him. Sheldon at once drew a pocket pistol and opened fire. 'Big-Foot' reached down to his boot-top to get his gun, but found that the leg of his pants had slipped down over the gun. By the time he got the pants leg up, and the pistol out, Sheldon had emptied his pistol and was running down the street. Just as he turned a corner 'Big-Foot' fired two shots at him, one of them knocking a button off his coat, and putting a hole in it. None of Sheldon's bullets had hit the target.

The next morning 'Big-Foot' received a summons from Justice of the Peace Frank Lea, to appear in his court at 10 A.M. on the charge of attempted murder. We all mounted and rode downtown. I employed lawyer John Y. Hewett — still a resident of White Oaks — to defend 'Big-Foot.' There were five of us in the crowd, and we wore our six-shooters and bowie-knives into the courtroom.

Pinto Tom, the town marshal, demanded that we take off

our firearms while court was in session. This request was
refused; then he called on Judge Lea to make us put up the
guns.

Now I called Pinto Tom to step outside with me, which he
did. There I told him that he was committing suicide, as the
boys were ready to fill him full of holes if he persisted any
further. This settled the matter, and the case proceeded.
'Big-Foot' was cleared of the charge.

Sheldon was never arrested for his part in the shooting
scrape — possibly because he did such poor shooting, which
convinced Judge Lea that he was harmless.

I received a confidential letter from Mr. George Nesbeth,
on the Pat Coghlin ranch, stating that Mr. Coghlin was not
keeping the promise made to me, not to butcher any more LX
cattle. The letter went on to state that he was trying to get
them all butchered before the first of April.

Now I got busy and sent Emory and Chambers to Three
Rivers with the mess-wagon, while 'Big-Foot' and I rode to
Fort Stanton to search the Coghlin slaughter house. We
found five freshly butchered LX hides. The ones previously
butchered had evidently been hauled off and hidden.

From Fort Stanton we made a hard ride over the White
Mountains for the Coghlin ranch, arriving there in the night.
Mr. and Mrs. Nesbeth got up out of bed and cooked us a
warm meal.

Early the next morning the rest of my outfit arrived; then
we cut out five LX steers from Bill Gentry's herd. Gentry,
the foreman, refused to give them up without orders from Pat
Coghlin. But we told him that if he wanted war we were
ready. He had seven Mexican cowboys with him.

Now we spent three days rounding up the Coghlin range,
only finding three more LX steers. Then we returned to White
Oaks, taking with us one of Coghlin's fattest steers, which

was butchered in White Oaks for the benefit of our meat-loving friends there.

We started toward home, rounding up cattle on small ranches through the Patos Mountains, then the Van Sickle range, now the large Block ranch, on the north side of Captian Mountains. On our way down the Pecos River we camped for dinner one day, on the west bank of the stream. The river was bank-full from melted snow at its head. We were sitting on the ground near the water's edge, with plates on our laps, eating dinner, when a man rode up on a black horse; he said, 'Boys, did you hear the news?'

When I replied 'No,' he continued:

'Billy the Kid has killed his two guards in Lincoln and escaped.'

At that moment Big-Foot Wallace gave a Comanche Indian yell, saying: 'Hurrah for Billy the Kid!' Then he dived headlong into the muddy water of the Pecos. He had on his boots, spurs, leather leggins, and six-shooter, with a belt of cartridges. When he came to the surface he yelled again: 'Hurrah for the Kid.' Then he swam ashore and wrung the water from his clothes.

This stranger didn't know the full particulars of the Kid's escape, but on our return to Roswell, two weeks later, we found out all about it.

We finally started up the river with our ten LX steers, having found two near the Chisum home ranch. Six miles above the abandoned post of Fort Sumner, at Sunnyside, I went ahead with the mess-wagon to buy horse-feed and grub.

On riding up to the platform, in front of the store, I dismounted, and, pulling my Winchester rifle out of the saddle scabbard, I walked into the open door. I had lost a screw out of the rifle, and wanted to buy another that would fit. As I entered the door several men went running out of the rear

entrance. There was no one left in the store but the proprietor, who seemed greatly excited. He said: 'Well, I'll be
d——d! We thought you was Billy the Kid. You look just
like him.' Then the store man went to the rear entrance and
called out: 'Come back, boys, it's a false alarm.'

Others had previously told me that I looked like Billy the
Kid. Now I felt convinced that it must be true. These men
had heard of Billy the Kid's escape, after killing his two
guards.

I then returned to Fort Sumner and lay over to attend a
Mexican dance that night.

Mrs. Charlie Bowdre — whose husband was killed by Pat
Garrett and Lee Hall — attended this dance. She was a good-
looking young Mexican woman and I danced with her often.
When the dance broke up before daylight, I accompanied
Mrs. Bowdre to her two-room adobe house. I tried to persuade her to allow me to go inside and talk awhile. Then I
bade her good-night. On meeting her the next fall she told
me the reason for her not letting me enter the house. Billy
the Kid was in hiding there at the time.

Now we struck out east for Portales Lake, on the west edge
of the Staked Plains. We camped one night at Stinking
Springs, and slept in the rock house where Billy the Kid and
his gang held out without fire, food, or water. Lon Chambers
and Tom Emory pointed out to 'Big-Foot' and me the spot
where Charlie Bowdre fell, when hit by bullets from Garrett's
and Hall's rifles. The stone walls inside showed the marks of
where the gang tried to pick portholes.

Arriving at Los Portales Lake — near where the thriving
county-seat town of Portales, New Mexico, is now located —
we pitched camp at Billy the Kid's 'cave.' It was here at a
large fresh-water spring — the lake being salty — that the
Kid and gang made their headquarters while stealing LX

steers. This 'cave' was not a cave — just an overhanging rock cliff, with a stone corral around it, on three sides.

From now on our misery began, gathering Canadian River cattle which in past winters had strayed away, drifting south with the buffaloes. They had become as wild as deer. Being short of horses we had to press the four work mules into service, to stand night-watch over the cattle. Farther east there was a chain of fresh-water lakes, on the head draws of the Yellow-House Canyon, a tributary of the Brazos River, and around them we found many cattle.

After leaving these lakes we were two days and nights without water. The first habitation we struck, after leaving Fort Sumner, was Walter Dyer's log house on the head of Paladuro Canyon, a distance of about two hundred miles.

Now over that same stretch of country dwell thousands of prosperous 'fool hoe-men,' and their happy families.

We arrived at the LX ranch on the twenty-second day of June, with twenty-five hundred head of cattle, after an absence of seven months.

CHAPTER VIII

A THREE-THOUSAND-MILE HORSEBACK RIDE —
A TRUE ACCOUNT OF BILLY THE KID'S
ESCAPE AND DEATH

ON returning to the ranch I found that we had no boss, as Mr. Moore had quit to look after his own cattle. Mr. David T. Beals, who was at the ranch, complimented me on my seven months' work. He said, on the strength of my letters, they had sent John W. Poe to Lincoln County, New Mexico, to prosecute Pat Coghlin.

Mr. Beals presented me with a fine-blooded colt, which I afterward sold for two hundred dollars. He also promised me that when his company met to select a new manager for the LX ranch, he would present my name and recommend me for the position.

John Hollicott, a slow, easy-going Scotch cowboy, was selected as general manager of the ranch, to take Moore's place, a few months later. Mr. Beals told me that other members of his company objected to me, as being too wild and reckless for such a responsible position.

As the 'fool hoe-men' were settling the country around Mobeta, Mr. Beals began buying up all land on the LX range, which bordered on streams, or took in watering places, such as lakes and springs. But he was only allowed to purchase every two sections of land out of three. Every third section was State school land, which could only be taken up by actual settlers. The State lands and the Gunter and Munson sections were for sale, and these constituted his purchases.

In the early seventies the State of Texas had made a deal with Gunter and Munson, of Sherman, Texas, to survey most of the Texas Panhandle, their pay being a deed to every third section (six hundred and forty acres) of land. There being about twenty-five counties in the Panhandle, you can imagine the number of sections these two Sherman lawyers owned after the survey was finished.

In the early eighties the State deeded three million acres of land, adjoining New Mexico, to the merchant J. V. Farwell, and his Chicago associates, as pay for the erection of a new capitol building in Austin. On this large tract of land the Capitol Syndicate established the XIT cattle ranch, which became one of the largest in the Panhandle. When the hoemen began to flock into the Panhandle, and land could be sold for twenty dollars and more per acre, the Capitol Syndicate cut up their large holdings into small farms, cutting down the number of cattle accordingly.

I spent the balance of the summer in charge of a branding crew. During the middle part of October a letter was received from John W. Poe, for Lon Chambers and me to be in Lincoln, New Mexico, to appear as witnesses against Pat Coghlin, on the 7th of November. We had to hurry, as it meant a horse-back ride of about six hundred miles.

I was instructed by Mr. Erskine Clement, who was in charge of outside matters, to put in the coming winter scouting along the Texas Pacific railroad, at the foot of the South Staked Plains, in search of stray LX cattle.

After a hard ride across country, part of the time without water, we reached Lincoln in the night, as per Mr. Poe's instructions, so that Pat Coghlin wouldn't know we were to appear as witnesses against him. Mr. Poe had arranged for us to board with a Mr. Cline, twelve miles down the Hondo River, and keep in hiding until we were called as witnesses.

On arriving at the Cline ranch, about daylight, we received a hearty welcome from Mr. Cline and his Mexican family.

After being in hiding twelve days Mr. Poe rode down to tell us that Pat Coghlin had been granted a change of venue to Doña Ana County. He instructed me to be in La Mesilla, on the Rio Grande, the first Monday in April, 1882, to attend court. He told Lon Chambers that he could return home, as he would not be needed, which he did.

Now, mounted on 'Croppy'—a milk-white horse with both ears frozen off close to his head — with 'Buckshot' for a pack animal, I started for Roswell. On arriving I rode out a short distance to Sheriff Pat Garrett's ranch, but found out that Garrett had gone to Dallas. Old man Ash Upson, who was living with the sheriff and his Mexican family, informed me that he had just received a letter from Garrett, with instructions to meet him at Pecos Station, on the Texas Pacific Railroad, with the covered hack on a certain day.

Mr. Upson and I decided to make this nearly two-hundred-miles trip together. He drove ahead with his covered rig and I followed with my pack outfit. But we pitched camp together at night. In riding along one day I passed a covered hack by the side of the road and heard my name called. Then I rode over to the camp, a few rods distant, and found my friend, Clay Allison, the man-killer. He introduced me to his new wife, a young corn-fed Missouri girl. Of course I had to lie over for the noonday lunch, so as to sample this Missouri girl's cooking.

Allison was in search of a new location to settle down. He selected a ranch near Seven Rivers, and started a small cattle ranch. Several years later, while intoxicated, he fell off a wagon and broke his neck. Thus did the killer of eighteen men die with his boots on.

On Christmas Eve, Ash and I put up for the night at the Jones ranch on Seven Rivers. Mr. and Mrs. Jones were warm friends of Mr. Upson's — hence they invited us to lie over

Christmas and eat turkey dinner with them, which we did. We certainly enjoyed the turkey, sweet potatoes, pumpkin pie, and egg-nog.

On this trip Ash Upson told me the history of Billy the Kid — whom he had known from childhood.

His true name was Billy Bonney; he was born on the 23d of November, 1859, in New York City. After his father's death, his mother married a Mr. Antrim, who soon after moved to Santa Fé, New Mexico, where Ash Upson was in the newspaper business. In Santa Fé Mr. and Mrs. Antrim opened a restaurant, and had Mr. Upson as a boarder. The Kid was then only five years old. A few years later, Ash Upson and Mr. Antrim moved to Silver City.

Soon after Billy the Kid went on a trip to Fort Union, and killed his first man, a negro soldier. On the LX ranch, in the fall of '78, the Kid told me that his first killing was a negro soldier, in Fort Union.

On returning to Silver City he killed a blacksmith in a personal encounter. He skipped out for Old Mexico to avoid arrest. In the city of Chihuahua, Mexico, he killed and robbed a Mexican monte dealer. He then 'hit the high places' for Texas, finally arriving in Lincoln County, New Mexico, where he went to work for an Englishman by the name of Tunstall.

In the winter of 1877 a mob, headed by Morton, from the Rio Pecos, shot and killed Tunstall. Now Billy swore that he would kill every man who had a hand in the murder of his friend Tunstall. He made up a crowd of warriors consisting of Tom O'Phalliard, Henry Brown, Fred Wyatt, Sam Smith, Jim French, John Middleton, R. M. Bruer, J. G. Shurlock, Charlie Bowdre, Frank McNab, and a fellow named McClosky, and started out to kill the murderers of Tunstall. This was the starting of the bloody Lincoln County War. Before the war ended, Morton and his crowd were killed.

Sheriff Brady undertook the job of breaking up the Kid's gang, and was killed by Billy, who shot him from behind an adobe wall, as he rode down the main street of Lincoln. As the sheriff lay in the road badly wounded, Billy ran out from behind the adobe wall and shot him through the head.

Now the whole country became a battle-ground, many good citizens joining the Kid's gang.

During this war Billy and a dozen of his men took refuge in lawyer McSween's residence in Lincoln. In the night they were surrounded by thirty-five 'Seven River Warriors,' and two companies of United States soldiers, under command of Colonel Dudley, of the Ninth Cavalry. The McSween residence was set afire. When the fire became too hot the Kid and his party dashed out of the kitchen door, shooting as they ran. Billy the Kid and Tom O'Phalliard were the only ones who escaped without a scratch. Lawyer McSween lay dead with nine bullets in his body. Ash Upson had previously moved from Silver City to Lincoln County, hence he knew all about this local war.

Ash and I arrived at Pecos Station at three o'clock on New Year's Eve. We had been traveling slowly, as Pat Garrett was not due to arrive at Pecos until after New Year's. There being no accommodations at Pecos Station Ash and I concluded to board the evening west-bound train for Toyah, twenty miles distant. Our horses were left in charge of a wolf-hunter. In Toyah we put up at the Alvarado Hotel, owned by a Mr. Newell.

After supper Ash took in the town, while I remained at the hotel to enjoy the company of Mr. Newell's daughter, Miss Beulah.

On New Year's morning a big shooting match for turkeys was to take place on the edge of the town. Miss Beulah expressed a wish that some one bring her a fat bird. Of course

BILLY THE KID

The Kid (from an old photograph); Lincoln Court-House, where he killed his two guards; Indian woman who fed him in hiding; house in which he was killed (the room marked with a cross).

BILL OF SALE GIVEN BY BILLY THE KID TO PROTECT THE PURCHASER OF A HORSE HE HAD SOLD

that meant me, so I promised that she should have a few turkeys. The Justice of the Peace, Mr. Miller, had sent to Dallas for the turkeys, which had cost him three dollars each.

When the shooting match started, a fat gobbler was put in an iron box, with only his head visible. The shooting was to be done with pistols, offhand, at a distance of thirty-five yards. Each shooter paid twenty-five cents a shot, with a free shot to follow if he killed the turkey. I paid my twenty-five cents and was put down as number eleven.

Ten men fired, but the gobbler was still alive. Now my Colt's forty-five pistol was raised and off went the bird's head. Then another was put into the iron box, and his head went off, or at least fell over on the box.

Here Judge Miller said he would have to bar me out from shooting any more. He explained that he had a large family to support, and that he ought, at least, to get his money back for his flock of turkeys.

With the two gobblers on my shoulder, I returned to the hotel and laid them at Miss Beulah's feet. Of course she thanked me.

From now on I was known as the 'turkey shooter.' Many times in riding along the railroad I was recognized by men on passing trains and hailed as the 'turkey shooter.' They knew my crop-eared horse.

That night we had a big turkey supper at the Alvarado Hotel, and a dance afterward. There were only two young ladies at the dance — Miss Beulah and a Miss Lee. The rest were married ladies.

During the whole night shots could be heard downtown, fired by hilarious cowboys and railroaders. Much of this shooting was over the heads of frightened Chinamen, there being about a dozen in town. They left for El Paso on the first train, and it was said that Pig-tails steered clear of Toyah ever afterward.

From Toyah I drifted east along the Texas Pacific Railway onto the southern edge of the Staked Plains, leaving the railroad at Sand Hill Station and circling around to the northeastward, to buffalo-hunters' camps. It had been reported that as buffaloes were getting scarce, stray cattle were being killed for their hides. But I satisfied myself that these reports were false.

I finally landed in Colorado City, at the head of the Colorado River, flat broke. Walking into the largest store in town, I introduced myself to the proprietor, Mr. Peter Snyder, for whom the now prosperous town of Snyder, Texas, was named. I asked for a loan of fifty dollars until money from the LX ranch could reach me. Without any 'hums or haws' he pulled out the amount and handed it to me. This shows the broadgauge spirit of these old-time Westerners. When my two-hundred-dollar post-office money-order, from Erskine Clement, arrived, I repaid Mr. Snyder.

Now my face was turned westward for a five-hundred-mile ride to La Mesilla, New Mexico, to attend court. In Big Springs I lay two days with a burning fever. Realizing the importance of my presence in court, I got up out of a sick-bed and continued my journey.

After dark, just as a cold norther and sleet storm had sprung up, I rode up to a section house, and called, 'Hello!' A man came out to the gate, and I told him that I was sick, and wanted to stay there for the night. He kindly told me to go into the house, that he would put up my horses and feed them.

On entering the door the blazing fire in the fireplace put new life into me. The lady sitting by the fire looked up, then gave a scream, which brought her husband on the run. She told him that I had smallpox. Looking at my face he discovered that it was really covered with fresh smallpox sores. Smallpox was raging in Colorado City, but I never dreamt that I had contracted the dreaded disease.

Now the section man told me that I would have to leave, although he hated to drive me out in the cold storm, then raging.

My journey was continued, but on riding about five miles I could stand it no longer. The ponies were tied to a telegraph pole and I lay down with my saddle for a pillow. At daylight my journey was continued to the next section house, they being ten miles apart, along the railroad.

Before riding up to the section house my face was tied up with silk handkerchiefs, so that the sores couldn't be seen. The section crew had just gone to work, and the man cook gave me a warm meal, which was carried upstairs to be eaten alone, for fear the cook would discover the sores on my face, and run me away. No doubt the cook thought I was an outlaw, trying to keep my face hidden from view. I continued the trick of keeping my face tied up at every section house stopped at *en route*. Hard rides were made to reach a doctor in Toyah.

On reaching that town I rode up to Dr. Roberson's office and entered. The doctor pronounced it a case of smallpox, but said the danger had passed, as my pulse was only slightly above normal. He gave me some salve to dry up the sores on my face and shoulders, the only places on my body where they had broken out. He also assured me that no one could contract the disease from me, as the fever had gone down.

With my face covered with handkerchiefs, I rode up to the Alvarado Hotel, and was greeted by Miss Beulah, who was out on the front porch. She wanted to know what was the matter with my face. I told her that my mouth was covered with fever blisters.

I hired a boy to care for my horses, and then went to bed. Miss Beulah brought my meals, but I put off eating them until after she left, so that she could not see the sores. The doctor had told me that I would be taken to the pest-house, where there were already several patients, if it was discovered that I had smallpox.

A few days in bed at the Alvarado Hotel and my journey to El Paso was continued, after bidding Miss Beulah a last farewell. I have never seen this pretty little tender-hearted girl since, although I have heard of her many times. She is now the wife of a well-to-do Texas cattle man. I still keep and cherish the leather pocketbook she presented to me on New Year's Day, 1882. Her name and address are written on the inside.

A ride of one hundred miles brought me to the Rio Grande River. That night I camped with a Mexican and his family, *en route* to El Paso from Laredo. Before retiring I moved my ponies to fresh grass, a few hundred yards from camp, Buckshot being staked out, and Croppy hobbled.

Early next morning I discovered both of my horses gone. I tracked them to the river. On the opposite shore, in Old Mexico, I found moccasin tracks in the sand where the thieves had dismounted to get a drink of water from the river.

Now I returned to camp and hired the Mexican's only saddle pony, his covered wagon being hauled by a yoke of oxen. I agreed to give him ten dollars a day for the use of the pony. The tracks of my two ponies were followed west to a range of mountains about thirty-five miles distant. In places I had to ride slowly in order to see the tracks.

It was nearly sundown when I came in sight of a spring, near which were my ponies. Buckshot was staked out to grass and Croppy hobbled, just as I had left them the night before. For a while I hid behind a hill, thinking the thieves would soon show themselves. Finally a shot was heard to the westward, about half a mile distant. I concluded the thieves had gone into the rough mountains to kill game for their supper. I took a drink from the cool spring and headed east, mounted on Croppy. It seemed plain to me that two prowling Indians, or Mexicans, afoot, had discovered my ponies and ridden them into Mexico.

It was daylight when I arrived in camp. After breakfast I gave the Mexican ten dollars for the use of his pony, then struck out up the Rio Grande River to El Paso.

Detective George Harold, whom I met in El Paso, is, no doubt, the slayer of the notorious Sam Bass, although a Mr. Ware got the credit for it. Ware has the reputation of killing this outlaw, as he was the leader of the posse who rounded up the gang in Round Rock, Texas. In this battle Sam Bass and his chum, Barnes, were killed. Dad Jackson and Underwood escaped. On the officers' side Grimes was killed and Morris wounded.

Sam Bass was the hero of more young Texas cowboys than any other 'bad' man, and the song about him was the most popular. It started out thus:

'Sam Bass was born in Indiana,
    It was called his native home.
And at the age of seventeen,
    Young Sam began to roam.
He first went out to Texas,
    A cowboy for to be;
And a kinder hearted fellow
    You'd scarcely ever see.'

This song seemed to have a quieting effect on a herd of long-horns during thunder-storms. Possibly the sweet, musical tune had something to do with it.

On the first Monday in April I appeared in Judge Bristol's court in La Mesilla, three miles from Las Cruces. John W. Poe and Pat Garrett were there, and so were Mr. and Mrs. George Nesbeth.

Pat Coghlin had employed Colonel Ryerson and Thornton to defend him in the court. Mr. Poe had secured Attorney A. J. Fountain to assist Prosecuting Attorney Newcomb. Several years later A. J. Fountain was murdered at the White Sands, between Tularosa and Las Cruces.

When the Pat Coghlin case came up for trial, that foxy gentleman pleaded guilty to butchering stolen cattle, after being warned by me not to. The Judge fined him two hundred and fifty dollars, along with the costs of the court. Thus did he dodge the penitentiary gates. Mr. Poe brought a ten-thousand-dollar damage suit against him. I have never learned how that damage case terminated.

Now I was free to ride back to the LX ranch in the Panhandle of Texas, a distance of about eight hundred miles. In bidding Mr. and Mrs. George Nesbeth good-bye they told me that they were afraid to travel over the White Sands road, for fear that Pat Coghlin would have them waylaid and murdered for appearing against him as witnesses. Hence they intended to stay in Las Cruces a month or two, and slip away when Coghlin got over his angry spell. They had taken up a homestead above Tularosa, near Blazier's sawmill, on Tularosa River, and intended to make their home there the rest of their lives.

At the point of the White Sands they were murdered. In a later chapter I will give the facts of this murder, and the trial of the two Mexicans, who confessed to committing the crime for one thousand dollars.

While in Las Cruces I contracted a severe case of heart trouble over a pretty little wealthy Mexican girl by the name of Magdalena Ochoa. Therefore I concluded to start a small cattle ranch in this, Doña Ana County, so as to be near the little miss.

Cowboy Charlie Wall told me of a place that would suit me for a ranch, this being Dog Canyon, the rendezvous of that murdering old renegade Indian Chief, Victoria. As Charlie Wall had to return to Fort Stanton, he agreed to go with me to Dog Canyon, to examine the water supply.

We started early one morning from the Montezuma Hotel. I threw a farewell kiss at Miss Magdalena, who sat in a window full of pretty flowers and roses, opposite the hotel. As I rode away, mounted on Croppy, she threw a kiss back at me which raised the temperature of my heart.

A telegram had been received in Las Cruces that morning, stating that old Victoria and his band of warriors had crossed the Rio Grande River at Colorow — above Las Cruces — during the night, and killed three white men. They were headed toward Dog Canyon, but this news didn't prevent Wall and me from making the trip. We decided, though, not to camp overnight at Dog Canyon.

After passing through San Augustine Pass, twenty-five miles out of Las Cruces, we left the wagon road and turned to the right, cutting across the desert for Dog Canyon, at the foot of the Sacramento Mountains. On the second day out of Las Cruces we ate dinner in Dog Canyon. It was a lovely spot, though the stream of sparkling water flowing out of the mountains through the canyon was small. I couldn't fully make up my mind to enter a Government homestead at this rendezvous of old Victoria.

After making a hurried examination of the land and water up next to the steep mountains, we rode north to La Luz, a Mexican village, where we put up for the night.

From La Luz Charlie Wall and I rode north to Tularosa,

then turned east, up Tularosa Creek. After crossing over the line of Doña Ana County into Lincoln County, we came to an alfalfa field to our left, where Charlie Wall had the year previous fought a battle with a crowd of Tularosa Mexicans who objected to his using water to irrigate this alfalfa field. When the smoke of battle cleared away four Mexicans lay dead upon the ground, and young Wall had two bullet holes in his body.

To prevent being mobbed by the angry Tularosa Mexicans, Wall and his companions made a run for Lincoln, to surrender to Sheriff Pat Garrett. The sheriff allowed them to wear their pistols and to sleep in the jail.

After continuing our journey up the river, young Wall, who was a modest, truthful fellow, gave me the full account of Billy the Kid's escape, the year before.

Charlie Wall, not being seriously wounded, did his loafing in the upstairs room of the Lincoln Court-House, where Billy was being guarded. In La Mesilla the Kid had been convicted for the murder of Sheriff Brady, and Judge Bristol had sentenced him to be hanged in Lincoln, on May 13, 1881.

On the morning of April 28th, while young Wall was present in the room, Pat Garrett, who was preparing to leave for White Oaks to have a scaffold made, remarked to the Kid's two guards: 'Watch him carefully, boys, for he has only a few days to live, and might make a break.'

Bob Ollinger, who had fought against Billy the Kid in the Lincoln County War, stepped to a closet, against the wall, and got his double-barrel shotgun. Looking over toward the Kid, sitting on a stool, shackled and handcuffed, Ollinger said: 'There are nine buckshot in each barrel and I reckon the man who gets them will feel it. You needn't worry, Pat, we will catch him like a goat.'

With one of his good-natured smiles the Kid remarked, 'You might be the one to get them yourself.'

Now Ollinger put the gun back in the closet and locked the door, putting the key in his pocket.

About five o'clock that evening Bob Ollinger took Charlie Wall and the other four armed prisoners across the wide street to the hotel for supper, leaving J. W. Bell alone to guard the Kid.

While eating supper, Wall says they heard a shot fired in the court-house. They all ran out on the sidewalk. Ollinger ran toward the court-house. In the middle of the street he met the frightened jailor, who said: 'Bell has killed the Kid.'

Ollinger quit running and walked to the court-house. He had to go around to a side stairs, as there was no upstairs entrance from the front. When passing underneath an up-stairs window, which was open, the Kid called out: 'Hello, Bob!' Ollinger looked up and saw the Kid, and the shotgun pointed toward him. Then he said, loud enough to be heard by Wall and the other prisoners across the street, 'Yes, he has killed me, too!'

These words were hardly out of the guard's mouth when a charge of buckshot went through his heart.

A moment later Billy the Kid hobbled out on the small front porch. Around his waist were two belts of cartridges and two pistols. In his hands was the shotgun. This he had secured by kicking open the door to the gun-closet. The Kid took aim at the dead body of Ollinger and fired. He then broke the gun in two and threw the pieces at the corpse.

By this time the sidewalk on the opposite side of the street was lined with people who had run out of their houses, on hearing the shots. Billy the Kid called to a Mexican, whom he knew, telling him to throw up a file. This was done, and the shackle chain was filed apart in the center, leaving a shackle and piece of chain on each leg.

Now the Kid told the Mexican to put a saddle and bridle

on the deputy county clerk's black pony — which had formerly been owned by the Kid — and bring him out on the street. This order was carried out.

The Kid now, after dancing a jig on the front porch, went to the side stairs, thence to the street, where the Mexican was holding the black pony. In trying to mount him, encumbered with the heavy load of guns and ammunition, the pony got loose and ran back to the stable in the court-house yard.

While waiting for the Mexican to bring the pony back, the Kid stood in the street. He would have been an easy target had it not been that most of the men watching him were sympathizers. Wall says he could have killed him, but he wanted to see him escape.

When the pony was brought back, the Kid gave the Mexican his rifle to hold, while he mounted.

Now the Kid galloped west, waving his hat and shouting: 'Three cheers for Billy the Kid.'

When the excitement was over, Charlie Wall says he helped the crowd care for the bodies of the two guards. Bell was found at the foot of the stairs with a bullet in his dead body.

The Kid told friends the secret of his escape. He said Bell was sitting in a chair reading. The Kid slipped his left hand out of the handcuffs and made a spring for the guard, striking him on the head with the iron cuff. Instead of pulling his pistol, which was buckled around his waist, Bell threw both hands up to protect his head from another blow.

Now the Kid grabbed the pistol from the holster. Then Bell ran toward the head of the stairs, and as he went to go down, the Kid fired. The body went tumbling down the stairs, falling onto the jailor, who was sitting at the foot of the stairs. This stampeded the jailor, who ran out on the street where he met Ollinger, telling him that Bell had killed the Kid.

After his escape Billy the Kid told his friends that he had starved himself, so that the handcuff could be slipped over his left hand. The guards supposed he had lost his appetite over the worry of his approaching doom. He said while in bed he used to slip the handcuff off to make sure it could be done easily.

In killing Bob Ollinger the Kid only gave him a dose of his own kind of medicine. While the Lincoln County War was raging, an acquaintance, who was in sympathy with Billy the Kid's crowd, stepped up to shake hands with Ollinger, who grabbed the extended right hand with his left. Then with his right hand he drew his pistol and shot the fellow to death.

On arriving in Fort Stanton, Charlie Wall and I separated. I continued on to Lincoln, where I lay over a few days. Pat Garrett and Mr. Poe had already arrived in Lincoln from Las Cruces.

The next day after my arrival the sheriff held an auction to sell Billy the Kid's saddle and pistol. The deputy county clerk and I were the only bidders for the Colt's forty-one caliber, double-action pistol, which the Kid held in his hand at the time of his death. My last bid was $13, what I thought it was actually worth. The deputy clerk bid $13.50 and got it. I heard that he afterward sold it for $250 on the strength of its past history.

While lying over in Lincoln I learned the true account of Billy the Kid's death from the three men who had a hand in the affair. These men were Pat Garrett, John W. Poe, and Kip McKinnie. Many stories have been circulated about the underhanded manner in which Garrett murdered the Kid. Therefore I will here give the true account of it.

About July 1, 1881 Pat Garrett received a letter from a Mr. Brazil stating that the Kid had been seen lately around Fort

Sumner. The sheriff answered the letter telling Mr. Brazil to meet him at the mouth of the Tayban Arroyo, on the Pecos River, after dark on July 13th.

Now Garrett took his two deputies, John Poe and Kip McKinnie, and started, horseback, for the meeting place. These three officers watched and waited during the whole night of July 13th, but Brazil failed to show up. On the morning of the 14th they rode up the Pecos River. When opposite Fort Sumner the sheriff sent Poe into that abandoned fort, where lived many Mexican families, to see if anything could be learned about the Kid. Then Garrett and McKinnie rode six miles up the river to Sunnyside, to keep in hiding until the arrival of Poe.

About night John Poe reached Sunnyside and reported to Garrett that he couldn't find out a thing of importance about the Kid. Then the sheriff said they would ride into Fort Sumner, after dark, and see Pete Maxwell, a wealthy sheep man, and the son of the famous Land Grant Maxwell. The Kid was in love with Pete Maxwell's sister, hence Garrett thought that Pete might have seen him hanging around their home.

It was dark when the three officers started on their six-mile journey. Arriving in Fort Sumner their horses were tied in an old orchard. Then they walked into Pete Maxwell's large, grassy yard. The residence was a long adobe building fronting south, with a covered porch the full length of the adobe house. Garrett knew the room in which Pete generally slept. The door of this room was open. The sheriff told his two deputies to lie down in the grass, while he went in to talk with Pete.

The sheriff lay over on Mr. Maxwell's bed and began questioning him about the Kid. No one besides Garrett was to know what Pete told him.

In the rear of the Maxwell dwelling lived an old Mexican

PAT GARRETT
Slayer of Billy the Kid

servant, who was a warm friend to the Kid. Previous to the arrival of the sheriff and his deputies, Billy the Kid had entered this old servant's adobe cabin. The old man had gone to bed. Billy lit the lamp; then he pulled off his boots and coat and began reading the newspapers, which had been brought there for his special benefit.

After glancing over the papers the Kid told the old man to get up and cook him some supper, as he was very hungry, having just walked in from the sheep camp. The old servant told him that he didn't have any meat in the house. Then the Kid replied: 'I'll go and see Pete and get some.' Now he picked up a butcher knife from the table and started, barefooted and bareheaded. As he walked along the porch to Pete's room, Kip McKinnie saw him coming, but supposed he was one of the servants.

When nearly opposite Pete's room, Kip raised up and his spur rattled, which attracted the Kid's attention. Pulling his pistol he asked in Spanish: 'Quien es? Quien es?' (Who's there? Who's there?) Not getting an answer he backed into Pete's room and asked: 'Pete, who's out there?'

Maxwell didn't reply. Now the Kid saw strange movements in the bed and asked: 'Who in the h—l is in here?'

With the pistol raised in his right hand and the butcher knife in his left, he began backing across the room. Pete whispered in the sheriff's ear: 'That's him, Pat.'

By this time the Kid had backed to the dim moonlight coming through the south window, which shone directly on him, making him an easy target for the sheriff. Bang! went Garrett's Colt's pistol, and down went a once mother's darling, shot through the heart.

After the first shot, the sheriff cocked the pistol and it went off accidentally, putting a hole in the ceiling.

The next day Billy Bonney, alias 'Billy the Kid,' was buried by the side of his chum, Tom O'Phalliard, in the old military cemetery.

A few months later Pat Garrett had the body dug up to see if the Kid's trigger finger had been cut off, but it had not. A man in the East was showing the first finger of a man, preserved in alcohol. He claimed it was Billy the Kid's trigger finger. The newspapers had sensational accounts of it.

Years later when the United States Government employed Will Griffin to remove all dead bodies of soldiers in the Fort Sumner Graveyard, to the National Cemetery in Santa Fé, the graves of Billy the Kid and Tom O'Phalliard were the only ones left.

Mr. Griffin, who is still a resident of Santa Fé, says at the time he moved the soldiers' bodies there was a board slab marking the Kid's grave. Now that old cemetery is an alfalfa field, and those two outlaw graves may have become obliterated.

Before leaving Lincoln, I bade Pat Garrett and John W. Poe good-bye, and never met them again for many years.

On my way home I stopped a few days to visit friends in White Oaks. I finally arrived at the LX ranch in the Texas Panhandle, after an absence of eight months, and after having ridden horseback about three thousand miles.

CHAPTER IX

I BECOME A MERCHANT IN CALDWELL, KANSAS —
HOW OKLAHOMA WAS OPENED TO SETTLEMENT

SHORTLY after my return from New Mexico, Mr. Hollicot put me in charge of eight hundred fat steers to be driven slowly to Caldwell, Kansas, on the southern boundary of that State. My outfit consisted of a cook and five riders, with six horses for each cowboy.

The fourth day of July we were on the North Staked Plains, and lay over to celebrate the glorious Fourth by resting. During the forenoon I killed my last buffalo. A small herd passed our camp and I roped a fat heifer calf, with the intention of taking it to Caldwell with us, but Lon Chambers and some of the boys begged that she be butchered for supper. Their wish was complied with, and we enjoyed buffalo calf-meat for several days.

The next morning while hunting lost horses I rode by a bleached buffalo carcass. On one horn initials had been cut. Through curiosity I dismounted to make an examination. Imagine my surprise on finding my own initials, C. A. S., and the year 1877 cut into the horn.

Now the killing of this buffalo bull came back to my memory. In the early winter of 1877 I was caught on these plains in a severe blizzard and snowstorm. Seeing a lone buffalo bull ahead of me, I made a dash for him, planting a bullet under his hump before he had time to escape. My pony being hungry and tired, I pulled the bridle off to let him graze, tying the end of the rope to the bull's hind leg.

Now to shield myself from the cold north wind I lay down

on the south side of the dead animal, with my head near his horns. While waiting for the pony to fill up, I cut my initials and the year on one horn. In order to get these horns to camp I had to drag the head at the end of a rope, as they couldn't be separated from the skull. Now, after the passing of forty-six years, this pair of buffalo horns are hanging on the wall of my bedroom to remind me of the days when millions of buffaloes roamed over the Staked Plains.

The bleached carcasses of these woolly beasts became a God-send to the wise 'hoe-men' who later settled on these plains. Buffalo bones almost became legal tender, after railroads were built. A wagon load of bones would purchase a good supply of food and clothing.

These new settlers who got the first grab at the pile of bones on the head of Tule Canyon, where General McKinzie, in 1874, killed the thousands of Comanche ponies, had a snap.

I once found a pile of human bones on the north Staked Plains. They were in a round pile, and bleached white. Many buffalo carcasses were near by. Whoever piled up these bones into a round mound must have known the gentleman who once carried them around with him. On top of the pile was the bleached shoulder blade of a buffalo, on which was carved:

'Here lies the bones of poor Kid Cones,
Whose greatest sin was the love of gin.'

We arrived in Caldwell, the 'Queen City of the border,' about the first of September. Soon after our arrival our herd of steers were turned loose on the new steer ranch on Turkey Creek, in the Indian Territory, which the LX Company had lately established.

Now with my outfit I attended the cattle round-ups in the western part of the Indian Territory, gathering lost LX steers. It was the last part of November when our work was finished.

Then we went to Caldwell, where Mr. David T. Beals was awaiting my return. He had purchased a farm on the Indian Territory line, two miles southeast of Caldwell, on which to winter the LX cow-ponies. I was given charge of this farm, and the more than one hundred head of cow-ponies.

Now I bought some town lots and contracted for the building of a new frame residence. Then I boarded a train for southern Texas to get Mother. I went by way of Saint Louis to visit my sister, Mrs. George W. Wines, and her family. While in that city I dropped into the Planter's Hotel to note the changes since I was bell-boy in that swell hostelry.

The red-headed bell-boy, Jimmy Byron, with whom I had the fight which caused me to throw up the job as 'bell-hop,' was now owner of the news-stand. We buried the hatchet of past hatred and shook hands. The former steward was now the proprietor, and 'Old Mike' was still the watchman. The chief clerk, Cunningham, who had slapped me for fighting while on duty, was still holding down his job, but I didn't shake hands with him.

My railroad journey was continued to the city of Galveston, in order to visit my Uncle Nick White and his family. Then a Morgan steamship was boarded for what was left of Indianola, since the great storm of 1875 had washed it away.

My boyhood playmates, Johnny and Jimmie Williams, were in Indianola with their sail-boat, and they took me to Matagorda.

In Matagorda I lay over a few days visiting my hundreds of friends. Then Jim Keller loaned me a horse and saddle and I rode to Mother on Cash's Creek.

Now I hired Fred Cornelius to take Mother and me over to the Sunset railroad, fifty miles north. Mother and I arrived in Caldwell, Kansas, a few days before Christmas. Furniture was bought and a 'Home, sweet home' established in my new house. I took charge of the horse ranch, southeast of town, and put in a pleasant winter.

About the first of March I received a letter from Mr. Beals, in Boston, Massachusetts, ordering me to take my crew of cowboys and cow-ponies back to the LX ranch in the Texas Panhandle. That night after receiving the orders, I attended church with Miss May Beals, a niece of David T. Beals. When church was over she introduced me to her pretty little fifteen-year-old, black-eyed chum, Mamie Lloyd.

Now I was a sure-enough locoed cowboy — up to my ears in love.

Six days later, in the Phillips Hotel, in Wellington, the county seat of Sumner County, Kansas, I was married to Mamie Lloyd — the only daughter of H. Clay Lloyd, of Shelbyville, Illinois. In nailing this pretty little miss to the matrimonial cross I 'shore' won a prize. But the poor girl lived only six years after our marriage, dying in my arms in Denver, Colorado. She left a five-year-old daughter, Viola, nearly to cry her eyes out over the loss of a fond mother.

Three days after marrying, I started for the Panhandle of Texas in charge of twenty-five cowboys, one hundred cow-ponies and six mess-wagons. A journey of eighteen days brought us to the LX ranch. After a few days' rest Mr. Hollicot sent me in charge of a crew to attend round-ups on Red River and Peas River, in the southeastern part of the Panhandle. We arrived at the LX ranch on July 1st with about three thousand head of cattle, which had strayed off during the winter. I started back to Caldwell with eight hundred fat steers, arriving there about September 1st.

Mr. Beals ordered me to take my outfit back to the Panhandle at once and get another herd of fat steers. This I started to do, but after Mr. Beals had taken the train for the East, I suddenly changed my mind. I then turned the outfit

MAMIE AND VIOLA, 1889

over to one of my cowboys, Charlie Sprague, who started for the Panhandle after the other herd. Then I swore off being a cowboy. I hated to quit the LX outfit, as Mr. David T. Beals was the best man I had ever worked for. He was an honest, broad-gauge cattle man.

Many years afterward I visited him in Kansas City, not knowing that he was almost at the point of death. On arrival in Kansas City, I dropped into the Union National Bank, of which Mr. Beals was president. The cashier, Mr. Neal, informed me that Mr. Beals was very sick, but would, no doubt, like to see me.

Arriving at the residence, 25 Independence Avenue, which, along with the grounds, covered half a city block, I rang the doorbell. The young lady servant informed me that the doctor had given orders that no one be allowed to see Mr. Beals. Writing a note to the sick man on a card, I departed. Before reaching the street, Mrs. Beals called me back. She said Mr. Beals would never forgive me if I left without seeing him.

When I reached the sick chamber Mr. Beals sat up, propped against pillows, and gave me a hearty welcome. He said my presence made him feel better. We 'harked back' to the good old cattle days until the five o'clock dinner was ready, then, strange to relate, the old gentleman accompanied me down to the dining-room and ate a hearty meal — the first for a long time.

Their son was David T. Beals, Jr. — almost grown to manhood. As a baby he had cost his father five thousand dollars in hard cash.

When about six weeks old he was kidnaped. Mr. Beals put advertisements in the city papers offering a reward of five thousand dollars for the return of the baby, and no questions would be asked. That money would be in the house ready to be handed over when the baby was returned. Two days later, after dark, a rap brought the cook to the kitchen door. There stood a man and woman, who told the cook to tell Mr. Beals to come and get this baby boy. Putting the infant in its mother's arms, Mr. Beals got the bag of money and gave it to the kidnapers, who departed.

After the death of Mr. Beals, young David T. Beals stepped into his father's shoes, and is now a successful banker, with a happy family of his own.

I rented a store room on Main Street and opened a tobacco and cigar store, with confectioneries as a side issue. I scraped together a few hundred dollars, in order to get started. After that the sailing was easy, as my credit was unlimited. Finally I rented an adjoining store room, and cut an archway between the two. In this I opened up an ice-cream and oyster parlor. Soon I had five clerks and attendants in my employ.

About this time there was great excitement over the opening of Oklahoma to settlement. Soldiers were kept on the border of the Indian Territory to keep the 'Oklahoma boomers' out of the 'promised land.' Still the 'boomers' would slip by the soldiers in the night. Many were arrested and jailed in Wichita.

While the soldiers were napping several hundred 'boomers' stole a march on them in the night. The next day the 'Oklahoma War Chief,' with Samuel Crocker as editor-in-chief, was issued in its new home, a frame shack hauled over the line from Kansas. This, the first newspaper ever published in Oklahoma, was issued several miles south of the line, on Chikaskia Creek, southeast of Hunnewell, Kansas.

Of course the United States soldiers, stationed at Caldwell, finally woke up and captured the 'Oklahoma War Chief' and its editor, burning the shack, and marching the big and little 'boomers' back over the line into Kansas.

Owing to the fact that their bitter enemies, the United

States soldiers and the Indian Territory cattle men, made Caldwell their headquarters, the 'boomers' left, and established headquarters in Arkansas City, Kansas, thirty-five miles east. This didn't suit the citizens and business men of Caldwell, so one night we held a mass meeting to remedy the matter. It was Saturday night. A collection of six hundred dollars in cash was taken up and a Mr. Miller and I were appointed a committee to visit Arkansas City, on the quiet, and induce the 'boomers' to reëstablish headquarters in Caldwell.

Bright and early Sunday morning Mr. Miller and I started east in a buggy, drawn by a spirited pair of sorrels. We arrived in the 'boomers'' camp, in the outskirts of Arkansas City, in time to eat dinner with Captain Bill Couch, his secretary, John A. Blackburn, and Samuel Crocker, who had brought the 'Oklahoma War Chief' back to life.

Mr. Miller and I explained our business, and showed the six hundred dollars collected the night before. And we promised that more money would be produced to feed the little hungry 'boomers' when needed.

There were many poverty-stricken 'boomers' with large families, who needed free grub and clothing. After dinner Captain Couch called the people together, and in a speech, told them of our mission. A vote was taken, and carried, to reëstablish headquarters in Caldwell.

Mr. Miller and I paid over the six hundred dollars, and returned home. Early the next morning the road along the Kansas border was lined with the six hundred big and little 'boomers,' some afoot and others in vehicles. Arkansas City was angry when she awoke to the fact that Caldwell had stolen a march on her while she slept.

Soon after this I became the 'Oklahoma Border' Cigar King. One hundred thousand cigars were ordered from an

Eastern factory, put up in my own special brand, called 'The Oklahoma Boomer.' They sold like hot cakes.

In order to catch the cowboy trade, coming to town from the Indian Territory, I had a large oil painting locked with iron chains to the overhead framework of the iron bridge across Bluff Creek. The painting showed a mounted cowboy with a long-horn steer at the end of his rope. Over this was my 'Oklahoma Boomer' cigar advertisement. Cowboys leaving town were in the habit of shooting this nice oil painting full of holes. The last time I saw it, about twenty years later, it was riddled with bullet holes.

On the first day of May, 1885, Caldwell put on her Sunday clothes and held a grand cowboy tournament at the fair grounds. Cowboys and cattle men from all over the Indian Territory were there to witness the sport.

One of the games was catching small rings with a long pole, while the pony was running his best, the prize being a fine ladies' gold ring. I had promised my sixteen-year-old wife that she should wear the ring, and the promise was fulfilled, as I won against the dozens of competitors.

In the steer-roping match I won a fine silver cup, hog-tying the steer in forty-four seconds. The first time I threw him, he jumped to his feet after I had dismounted. Then, springing back into the saddle, I had to throw him again. Even with all this lost time the silver cup was awarded to me, and it is kept as a relic of bygone days. My mount was a 'cracker-jack,' a black pony borrowed from Cattle King John Blair.

While running my store I wore high-heel cowboy boots and red silk sash around my waist. Finally my silk sash disappeared, and another couldn't be purchased in this northern country. There was nothing to do but wear suspenders to keep my pants up, and this almost broke my heart.

Several months later 'Shanghai' Pierce stopped off in

CHARLIE SIRINGO'S STORE AND ICE-CREAM AND OYSTER
PARLOR IN CALDWELL
Above: The Sign that Hung over the Bridge across Bluff Creek

Caldwell and took dinner with us. While at the dinner table Mr. Pierce expressed surprise at my wearing suspenders instead of a silk sash. Here Mamie, my girl wife, confessed that she had burnt my silk sash, so that I would have to wear suspenders. Of course I forgave her before she died.

The 'Oklahoma boomers' increased in numbers, and kept the soldiers busy running them out of the milk and honey land. Finally Congress passed a bill opening Oklahoma to settlement.

In the spring of 1889, when the grand rush was made for free homes in Oklahoma, it became the greatest human stampede ever pulled off. The rush was made from all sides, but the greatest crowd was on the Kansas border, where a large force of United States soldiers held the crowds back until the word was given to 'go.'

Two years and a half as a successful business man swelled my head, so that I thought I was a natural born financier. Caldwell became too small for a man of my caliber. Therefore, the store and other interests were sold, and in the early spring of 1886, I moved to the city of Chicago, a place more fitting for the expansion of my financial abilities.

A few months in that great city convinced me that the proper place for me to shine was in the saddle!

CHAPTER X

CHICAGO — THE HAYMARKET BOMB — I REMEMBER
THE BLIND PHRENOLOGIST AND BECOME A
DETECTIVE — THE TRIAL OF
THE ANARCHISTS

AFTER leaving Caldwell, Kansas, a train dumped us off in the great city of Chicago. We found a nice home in a private family on Harrison Avenue.

The city was all worked up over the killing of some laboring men in a riot at the McCormick Reaper Works, May 2d. The anarchists were up in arms over the matter. They called a meeting of protest to meet the night of May 4th, on Haymarket Square. For fear of a riot, Mayor Carter H. Harrison congregated three hundred police officers at the Desplaines police station, under the command of Bonfield.

While the meeting was in progress and the speakers were talking from the top of an empty wagon standing in the open square, the Mayor elbowed his way into the crowd, from whence he could hear all that was said. No one recognized him until he lighted a cigar near the wagon. Albert Parsons was closing the meeting with a speech advising the people to return home peaceably. On recognizing the Mayor by the flash of the lighted match, Parsons said, 'Haven't we behaved ourselves, Mr. Mayor?' Harrison answered 'Yes' — then walked to the Desplaines police station near by and told Bonfield to disperse his three hundred policemen, as the meeting was being closed and there was no danger of a riot.

After the Mayor had departed for his home, Bonfield marched the officers onto the Haymarket Square and ordered the crowd to disperse. Just then a bomb was lighted and thrown from the mouth of a dark alley into the midst of the closely packed police officers. The result was seven were killed outright and sixty others badly wounded. The crowd then scattered like a flock of quail.

It was close to midnight, and my wife and I had gone to bed, expecting to hear shooting, as the evening papers said a riot was sure to take place before morning. A few minutes after the explosion of the bomb, which shook the building we were in, as it was only a few blocks from the Haymarket Square, young Reynolds, a lawyer, whose room was next to ours, ran into our room and asked me to go to the riot with him. Pistol-shooting by the officers was then going on. My girl wife held on to me, so that I couldn't get up.

As I couldn't accompany him, Reynolds asked me to lend him my pistol. This I did, as it was under my pillow. He started off with the silver-plated, pearl-handled Colt's 45-gun in his hand. In less than half an hour he returned the pistol. He was as white as a sheet and trembling like a leaf. He said when he ran onto the square, pistol in hand, policemen opened fire on him, thinking, no doubt, that he was a crazy anarchist bent on revenge. He explained that several bullets whizzed past his head as he ran up a back stairs of a near-by building. He said he then went down a front stairs and flew for home.

For a month or more the city was in an uproar. A Citizens' League, with a million dollars at its disposal, had been organized to stamp out anarchy. I began to wish that I were a detective, so as to help down anarchy. I had been told by a blind phrenologist that I was cut out for a detective. It was in the year 1884, in the town of Caldwell, Kansas. Circulars were distributed announcing the coming of this noted phrenologist, who had studied under the famous Fowler. The meeting took place in the large Leland Hotel parlor. The room was packed with the invited guests. A chair was placed in the center of the parlor, and the large, fine-looking old man, with both eyes out, stood up holding its back. He called for a volunteer to come forward and sit in the chair. We all began calling for Henry Brown, our popular town marshal. It required a lot of pleading to induce the marshal to sit in the chair. Judging from his flushed face, he regretted having his head examined. There was not a favorable comment on his character.

I was the only one in the audience who knew the blind man was telling the truth. In 1878, on the LX ranch in the Panhandle of Texas, Billy the Kid had introduced me to the members of his gang, Henry Brown being one of them. It was in the fall of 1882 that I landed in Caldwell, Kansas, in charge of a herd of Texas steers. I was greatly surprised when I saw Henry Brown wearing a new blue uniform and a gold star. I shook hands with him, and he begged me to not give him away, as he said he had reformed and was going to lead an upright life in the future. I promised to keep his identity a secret. But I regretted doing so later, as, on April 30, 1884, he and his chief deputy marshal, Ben Wheeler, and two cowboys, John Wesley and Billie Smith, held up the First National Bank of Medicine Lodge, Kansas, a nearby town, killing the president and cashier. Enraged citizens of Medicine Lodge put an end to the four bad-men cowboys, Brown being shot dead and the others hanged.

After the blind phrenologist got through with Henry Brown, he called for another subject. The audience began calling for Theodore Baufman, the 'Oklahoma Scout.' 'Bauf' needed no coaxing. He strutted out, carrying his two hundred and fifty pounds of flesh and bones with the proud air of a king.

The blind man ran his hand over 'Bauf's' head just once, then said: 'Ladies and gentlemen, here is a man who, if the Indians were on the warpath and he should run across one lone Indian on the plains, would tell his friends that he had

HENRY BROWN, MARSHAL OF CALDWELL

BEN WHEELER, DEPUTY MARSHAL OF CALDWELL

seen a thousand warriors.' This brought yelling and laughter which caused Baufman to leave the chair in anger. I worked with 'Bauf' on the range in 1878, and knew that his worst failings were the fear of hard work and the stretching of the truth.

Next, the audience began calling for 'Mamie,' my sixteen-year-old wife. She took the seat and the blind man ran his hand over her head once. He then said: 'Here is a good-natured little somebody who cannot tell a lie or do a wrong.' The balance he told was what we all knew to be true. Next the crowd began calling for me. I went forward and sat down in the chair. The blind man laid his hand on the top of my head and then said: 'Ladies and gentlemen, here is a mule's head.' When the yelling and laughter had subsided, he explained that I had a large stubborn bump, hence was as stubborn as a mule. He then explained that I would succeed as a newspaper editor, a fine stock-raiser, or a detective.

So now, while I was worked up to a high pitch over the Haymarket riot, the blind phrenologist's words began to bear fruit. I finally concluded to start right by entering the greatest detective school on earth — Pinkerton's National Detective Agency. My steps were light and my hopes buoyant when I stepped into S. A. Kean & Company's bank and asked the cashier, Mr. Yure, for a letter of introduction to Mr. William A. Pinkerton, head of the Western Division of Pinkerton's National Detective Agency.

Mr. S. A. Kean wrote me a short letter which read as follows:

CHICAGO, ILL., *June* 29/86

Pinkerton Detective Agency,
City.

GENTLEMEN: The bearer, Mr. Charles A. Siringo, we know to be a person of good character, and having been a cowboy and brought up on the plains, his services and ability are commended to you.

S. A. KEAN & Co., *Bankers*

Armed with this letter of introduction, I went into the Pinkerton Agency. On the back of the Kean & Company letter, Mr. William A. Pinkerton wrote the following:

Captain Foley — The party referred to in this letter is undoubtedly a good man.

WM. A. PINKERTON

After presenting the letter to Captain Foley, I was allowed to meet the 'Big Eye,' as Mr. Pinkerton was called by his employees. He asked for references. I gave him the names of David T. Beals, president of the Union National Bank, in Kansas City; Sheriff James H. East of Tascosa, Texas, and Pat Garrett, slayer of Billy the Kid, of Lincoln, New Mexico. He said he would write to these parties, and if their answers were favorable, he would give me a position as cowboy detective, to work on Western criminals, in a new office they had just opened in Denver, Colorado.

Favorable answers came from the men whom I gave as references, and I was detailed to work in the anarchist Haymarket riot case, under the supervision of Superintendent David Robinson, and his assistant, John Flyn. My work was mostly at night, in the German saloons, where the anarchists congregated.

During the first part of August the anarchist trials started in the North-Side Court-House, with Judge Geary on the bench. I was detailed to be in the court-house every day during the trial and watch the jury, to see that no one tried to bribe them, by word of mouth, or by slipping them notes.

On the first morning, when the court opened, I took a front seat in the room, outside the railing, which enclosed the officials and lawyers. Directly in front of me sat the seven anarchist prisoners, Louis Ling, August Spies, George Engel, Michael Schwab, Oscar Neebe, Adolph Fischer, and Samuel

Fielden. There was one vacant chair reserved for the eighth prisoner, A. R. Parsons, who had been indicted, but never arrested, as he couldn't be found.

When it was announced that court was open for business there was a straining of necks among the defense lawyers and the prisoners, looking toward the rear of the courtroom. This caused the Judge and every one else among the great throng of curiosity-seekers in attendance to turn his face toward the rear hall, at the head of the stairs. Of course, I turned my face around to see what it all meant. What I saw was a medium-sized, dark-complexioned man coming forward through the aisle in a slow walk. When he reached the small gate in the partition railing, the leading counsel for the defense, General Black, a former officer in the Confederate Army, met him and shook his hand, calling him Mr. Parsons. The gate was then opened and he sat down in the vacant prisoner's seat. General Black told the court that Albert Parsons was present, ready for trial.

When the jury was finally empaneled, it was my duty to go to noonday lunches and evening dinners with them and the court bailiffs. I always ate meals in the same restaurant, keeping my eyes on the jury.

While the trial was going on, a beautiful young woman, Miss Nina Van Zant, said to be wealthy, sat on the Judge's platform. She was a friend to Judge Geary and his wife.

The month of August was very hot and the courtroom was like a furnace, so that I suffered greatly from the heat, as I was compelled to wear a coat, by order from the court. On one occasion I had pulled it off and was in my shirt-sleeves. The Judge ordered me to put on my coat. Of course, neither he nor any of the court officials knew who I was.

In the course of a month the jury of twelve men brought in a verdict of guilty against the eight prisoners. The Judge sentenced five of them, Albert Parsons, George Engel, August Spies, Louis Ling, and Adolph Fischer, to death by hanging. Michael Schwab and Samuel Fielden were sentenced to life imprisonment at hard labor. Oscar Neebe drew a sentence of fifteen years in prison.

While the trial was going on, Miss Nina Van Zant — the pretty and wealthy young friend of Judge Geary — fell in love with August Spies, and, after his conviction and sentence of death, married him in the jail.

Spies, Fischer, Engel, and Parsons were hanged, and Louis Ling blew his head off with a bomb, or dynamite cap, concealed in his steel cell the night before the execution was to take place. It was a mystery as to how Ling was able to conceal the explosive, as he and the cell were searched every day. He had said that he would never meet death by hanging.

After the anarchist operation ended, I did all kinds of small jobs, such as shadowing bank clerks and officials, down to looking up a lost child or jewel. I had one operation in 'Hell's Half Acre' which was a picnic — 'all same' getting money from your wife's relatives. I was detailed to shadow a long-legged, red-headed banker. He had to be in the bank most of the day, but at night he showed me a touch of high life. He would go into tough places and drink wine with the female inmates. I had to do likewise so as to see how much money his Royal Nibs was spending.

I was glad when October came. Then Mamie and little Viola were put into a Pullman sleeper and we turned our faces toward the setting sun, to make my headquarters in Denver, Colorado.

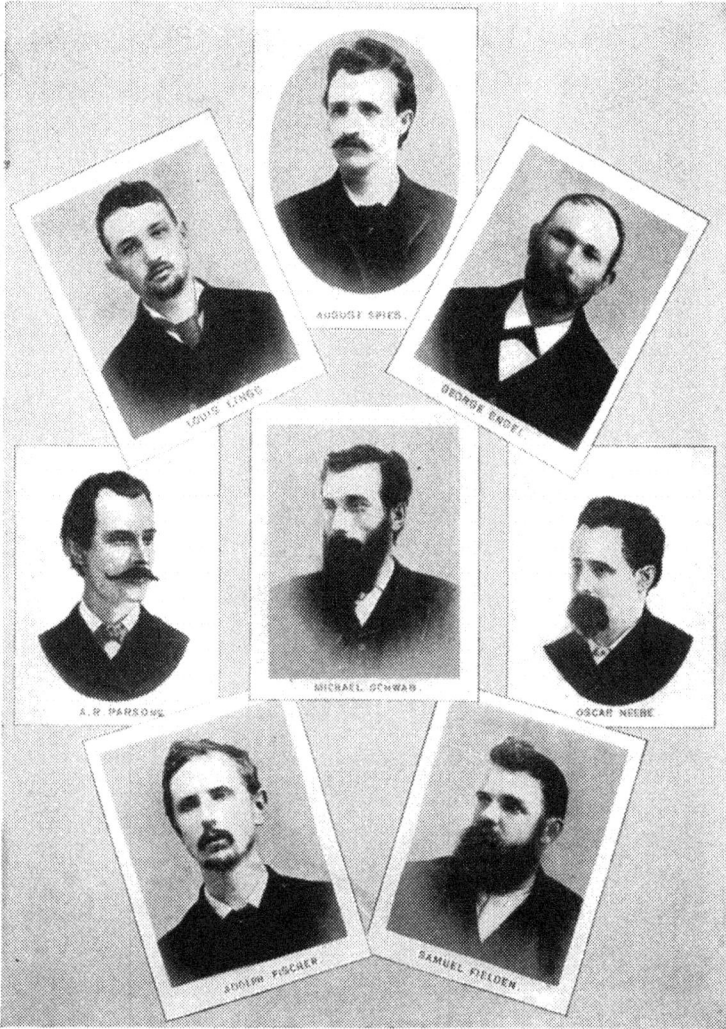

THE HAYMARKET ANARCHISTS

CHAPTER XI

A COWBOY DETECTIVE — I PLAY OUTLAW — IN JAIL
WITH TRAIN ROBBERS — BREAKING UP A
GANG OF ORE THIEVES

IN Denver, my work was of all kinds during the winter. Short trips were made out into the mountains to work on criminals. Early in the spring of 1887, Superintendent Eams sent me on my first cowboy operation.

What the daily press called anarchy had broken out in Archuleta County, in the southwest part of Colorado. There were only seventy-five voters, mostly whites, in this county, but they were ruled by the Archuletas, wealthy Mexican sheepmen of Amargo, New Mexico, who sent their sheepherders into the county to vote on election day. This caused the Americans to rebel. They marched the five county commissioners, 'Press,' J. M., and 'Don' Archuleta, and Bendito Martinez and a Mr. Scase, out of Pagosa Springs, the county seat, at the point of guns, over the line into New Mexico. They were warned never to return at the peril of their lives.

In order to hold their offices by law, the county commissioners had to hold a meeting in the court-house at Pagosa Springs within sixty days. Bendito Martinez came to Denver and hired me at eight dollars a day and all expenses, the fixed price charged by my agency, to go into Archuleta County as a cowboy outlaw and join the insurgents. It was understood that no one but himself was to know me. I was to make myself solid with Sheriff Dyke and the county clerk, E. M. Taylor, who had joined the insurgents.

In Durango, the extreme southwestern part of Colorado, I bought a horse and saddle and rode the sixty miles to Pagosa

Springs. There, as a supposed Texas outlaw, I joined the insurgents.

Finally, the deported county commissioners, along with the county attorney, James L. Russell, and the county judge, J. M. Archuleta, arrived from Armago, New Mexico, with sixty well-armed and mounted Mexican warriors. We insurgents, seventy-five strong, met them at the bridge spanning the swift-flowing San Juan River. Had they insisted on crossing the bridge into town, there would have been a great slaughter. But they finally withdrew and pitched camp in an abandoned Government post. Guards were kept on the bridge night and day for several days, when the insurgent leaders were promised an equal division of political pie in the future. Then the county officials held a meeting and departed for their homes in Armago, New Mexico.

During the excitement I saved the officials' lives twice when plots were laid to assassinate them. This came very near costing me my life, as a rope had been prepared to hang me as a spy. But I lied out of it and was made one of Sheriff Dyke's deputies at a wage of four dollars per day. This job was held down until I appeared before the grand jury in Durango, the county seat of La Platte County, Colorado. The result was sixteen of the insurgent leaders were indicted for running the county officials out of the county and burning their property.

On reaching Denver, I was hurried away to Mexico to try to locate a Wells-Fargo Express robber, who had stolen ten thousand dollars during a wreck at La Junta, Colorado. Armed with his description and photograph, I found him in the City of Mexico, going under an assumed name. He was safe from arrest while on Mexican soil, therefore all I had to do was to keep track of him until he returned to the United States. He invested some of his stolen money in diamonds to be smuggled into the United States and sold. I kept an account of every purchase he made.

While seeing the sights of Mexico City, I pulled off a stunt which shows what a great head I've got for avoiding danger. A railroad engineer, whose arm was in a sling from being in a wreck, and I went out to see the famous Church of Guadalupe, which is said to have been built by Montezuma in memory of the angel Guadalupe. After going through the church, and seeing the *serape* which this angel wore on her flying trip from heaven to Mexico City, and which is kept in a glass case surrounded with forty thousand dollars' worth of silver railings, we climbed the hill to the graveyard where all the noted warriors are buried. It covers several acres and an armed guard is kept on duty night and day. On coming to General Santa Ana's grave, I thought of Davy Crockett and his brave followers who met their fate in the Alamo, at San Antonio, Texas, through the inhuman blood-craving of this old general. The earth around where he sleeps was plastered over with all kinds of pretty relics. One particular piece took my eye and I told the engineer it should be in my cabinet of curios, even if it should cost me a leg. He said it would mean possible death or a long term in a Mexican dungeon if I were caught stealing from this 'heap big Chief's' grave. But when he found that I was determined to risk a fight to a finish with this copper-colored son of old Montezuma, he agreed to assist me by steering the watchman away to another part of the graveyard and keeping his back toward me by asking him questions about the city, which was in plain view.

The guard stood in sight with the seat of his white cotton pants toward me, when I and old Colt's 45 climbed over the tall sharp-pointed iron pickets and secured the prize. We wondered if Davy Crockett turned over in his grave to smile.

After two months of sightseeing, the Wells-Fargo thief and I were ready to board a steamship in Vera Cruz for New York City. But we learned that yellow fever had broken out in Havana, Cuba, where a stop was to be made. This changed our plans and we went by way of El Paso, Texas, to his home in Leavenworth, Kansas, where he was arrested and put behind steel bars. This ended my connection with the case.

Soon after reaching home, I was detailed on a double-geared operation into the White River country in western Colorado. One operation was to find out how a wealthy widow, Mrs. Tice, was being robbed by her partner in the cattle business and their cowboys. The other was to get for the United States Government the facts of a recent Ute Indian uprising.

Crossing the Continental Divide on a Denver & Rio Grande Railroad train, I bought a horse and saddle in the town of Rifle. A day's ride north brought me to the town of Meeker, made famous by the Meeker massacre in the early history of Colorado. A day's ride down the White River brought me to Mrs. Tice's cattle ranch. With the foreman and his cowboys I played myself off as a Texas outlaw dodging law officers. By being handy with the lasso and proving my skill in riding wild broncos, I soon secured convincing evidence that Mrs. Tice was being robbed.

After two weeks' rough riding, I departed for the extreme head of White River to investigate the great Indian uprising.

A week's work among trappers and ranchmen near the battle-ground convinced me that the blood-thirsty whites had murdered the Indians in cold blood. They were led by the long-legged sheriff of Garfield County, who soon absconded with the county's funds.

When Mrs. Tice brought her case before a local court to annul her partnership, I was the star witness. The foreman and some of his cowboys from White River were present to testify. But when they found out that they had been tricked and that I was a detective instead of an outlaw, they refused to go on the witness stand. Hence the partnership was annulled by the judge on the bench.

Now I was hurried away to Cheyenne, Wyoming, to consult with District Attorney Walter Stoll over the escape of Bill McCoy, who had been sentenced to hang for killing Deputy Sheriff Gunn of Lusk. Mr. Stoll felt sure that Bill McCoy was in hiding somewhere on the Keeline cattle range on the Platt River, above old Fort Laramie, where he had been one of the cowboys before being sentenced to be hanged. It was explained that the Keeline ranch was run by Tom Hall, who was supposed to be an outlaw from Texas. His crew was made up of Texans who were supposed to be going under assumed names. Two detectives from Dave Cook's Rocky Mountain Agency had been sent to the Keeline ranch to win the friendship of Tom Hall and his cowboys. But they were suspected and run out of the country.

At the terminus of the Cheyenne Northern Railroad, I bought a horse and saddle and rode to Howard's No. 5 Roundup road ranch, which was on the Douglas road. The snow lay deep on the ground, and the cowboys had all gone into winter quarters; therefore Howard and his wife had no business for their saloon, which was a money-maker during the summer seasons.

It would require too much space to explain how I got drunk with Howard and his wife, and of how I got in with Tom Hall and his fourteen Texan cowboys. I had to fall over a cliff of rock and sprain my leg. Tom Hall and Jim McChesney made a pair of crutches for me to walk on while recovering from the supposed injury.

Two months' work solved the McCoy case. He had been

liberated from jail by Tom Hall, whose true name was Tom Nichols. Hall had hired a criminal to commit a petty offense in Cheyenne, so as to be put in jail. There he sawed the steel bars with saws concealed in the soles of his shoes, liberating McCoy. He was paid five hundred dollars for the job.

Two days previous to my arrival, McCoy was mounted on Hall's pet roan race-horse and started over the mountains toward Utah. For a pack-animal, he used a big-footed bay horse, stolen from the sheriff's posse searching for McCoy.

Before closing the operation, I was allowed to read a letter written in New Orleans, just before McCoy left for South America on a sailing vessel. I had found out that Bill McCoy was a former cowboy friend of mine, named Bill Gatlin. I appeared before the grand jury in Cheyenne, with the result that Tom Hall and fourteen of his cowboys were indicted. When the sheriff and a large posse surrounded the Keeline ranch house, before daylight one morning, to arrest the gang, Hall remarked: 'That ——— Henderson is at the bottom of this.' I had been going by the name of Charlie Henderson, and they became suspicious of me when I failed to return from a trip to the railroad.

After the McCoy case ended in the spring of 1888, I was detailed to accompany 'Doc' (C. W.) Shores, the Sheriff of Gunnison County, Colorado, to Cawker City, Kansas, to dig up information as to the whereabouts of the Smith brothers, who were supposed to have held up the Denver & Rio Grande passenger train on Green River near the line of Utah. They had dropped out of sight and no trace of them could be found. It had been learned that their father and mother and a sixteen-year-old sister lived on their farm thirty miles west of Cawker City, where Shores remained until I could dig up the secret. In order to do so I had to fall in love with pretty black-eyed Miss Smith. When the secret was secured and I had read a letter from the brothers, written and mailed in Price, Utah, my heart grew cold for the pretty little miss. I then slipped away to Cawker City to rejoin Sheriff Shores. He at once wired his under-sheriff, Roe Allison, to search around Price, Utah, for the supposed train robbers.

Mr. Shores and I then departed for Denver, where we boarded a train for Price. While asleep in our berths on the Pullman car, the sheriff got a telegram from Roe Allison stating that he was on the way to Gunnison with the three train robbers. The sheriff and I remained on the sleeper the next day, arriving at Montrose about dark, just ahead of the eastbound train. We discussed the best plan for us to adopt. It was decided to put leg-irons and handcuffs on me, and pretend that I was a desperate criminal captured that day up the Gunnison River.

Shackled and handcuffed I was placed with the three sullen prisoners. Then the sheriff and I took the back track for the county-seat town of Gunnison, arriving there the next morning at ten o'clock. Half the population of the town was at the depot to see the four desperate criminals. We were marched to the court-house and jail with our leg-irons on. It was slow traveling, as the snow lay two feet deep on the ground. I brought up the rear and gave the people crowded on the board sidewalk some hard, contemptuous glances. Mr. Shores told me later that some of his friends said I was the toughest-looking man in the bunch.

All four of us were shoved into a steel cage just large enough for us to lie down in. We were given a few greasy quilts and blankets, and our meals were put into the cell. One of the Smith brothers had been shot through the head and the festered wound gave out a disgusting odor. To make matters worse, the two Smith boys and Rhodes were alive with vermin after their weeks of hiding on an island in the swamps of Green River.

After being in jail two weeks, I was taken out by a supposed officer from Wyoming, who was taking me there to be executed for murder. I had confided in my companions, telling them of breaking out of the Cheyenne, Wyoming, jail, after being sentenced to hang. The prisoners really shed tears when I shook hands with them before being handcuffed to the supposed officer.

I didn't have to appear as a witness against these men, as they confessed to the train hold-up after they were convinced that Shores had a 'cinch' case against them.

On returning to Denver from this operation, I found a new superintendent in charge of the agency. Eams had left and James McParland had taken his place. Mr. McParland had gained a world-wide reputation as a detective, when, in the early seventies, he was sent into the coal fields of Pennsylvania by Allen Pinkerton, of Chicago, to work in with the Molly Maguires. He joined the order and spent three years there under the assumed name of McKenna. His evidence caused twenty-three Molly Maguires to be hanged and thirty-four others to be sent to prison for long terms.

Shortly after McParland took charge of the branch agency in Denver, I was sent to Aspen, Colorado, to work on an ore-stealing operation for the Aspen Mining and Smelting Company. I was put to work in this rich silver mine with a husky miner, who, a few days later, had both eyes blown out and both arms blown off when he opened a new box of dynamite caps with his pocket knife. I happened to be far enough away to escape injury.

After working a month as a miner, I quit and joined Paddy McNamara and his gang of ore thieves. Finally we were all arrested and thrown into jail, with the result that one of the worst gangs of ore thieves in Colorado was put out of business.

The owners of two sampling works where we sold the stolen ore were let go free, after agreeing to sell out to the Aspen Mining and Smelting Company and to leave the State. One of them went to Washington and started a smelter which is operated to this day.

My next operation was for the Union Pacific Railroad Company in the States of Kansas and Nebraska, to find out if there was any crooked work going on. While on this operation I made the acquaintance of General Colby, in Beatrice, Nebraska. He let me ride his noted stallion Lindentree, which was presented by the Sultan of Turkey to General U. S. Grant when on his tour of the world. After General Grant's death, his son presented this beautiful gray stallion to General Colby.

I found Lindentree to be the best little big horse that I had ever straddled. He had a chest and nostrils twice as large as those of a common horse, and he galloped so lightly that he didn't seem to be touching the earth. He was the pick of three hundred Arabian horses in the royal stables. The Sultan had explained to General Grant that it was against the Turkish laws to sell, or give away, horses of royal blood, but in this case he would break the law. I still retain a fine photograph of this noble stallion, which is kept as a priceless relic of bygone days.

CHAPTER XII

SALTING OF THE MUDSILL MINE — A BRONCO BUSTER
— RUNNING DOWN DYNAMITERS IN NEVADA — THE
ANCHETA SHOOTING SCRAPE — I JOIN
THE WHITE CAPS

THE next big operation started soon after the railroad work
in Nebraska was finished. I was sent to Fairplay, Colorado,
to work on a mine-salting case. The Lord Mayor of London,
England, had paid $190,000 for the Mudsill silver mine in
Horseshoe Gulch, eight miles from Fairplay, in Park County,
Colorado. In addition to the cash payment, after two noted
mining experts had reported 30,000 tons of ore in sight, worth
thirty dollars a ton, the Lord Mayor gave the seller $40,000
worth of stock in the new company under the name of 'The
Mudsill Mining and Milling Company.'

After a contract had been let to Frazier and Chalmers to
build a $40,000 mill on the property, the New York expert
accidentally found silver in the samples, which was foreign to
that class of ore. He at once cabled the result to the Lord
Mayor in London. Then I was ordered to Fairplay to make a
secret investigation. After a week spent in Fairplay, I ordered
that the work on the mill be stopped, as the mine had been
salted.

By riding a bucking bronco for a man, whom I will call
Jacky, I won his friendship. He had been thrown from the
horse and was afraid to ride him again. The animal was a
vicious bucker, and the first time I rode him caused Jacky to
shout with joy. I agreed to ride him every day until he was
gentle.

There were two dance-halls in the town, and that night

Jacky and I got on a glorious drunk together, and danced with the free-and-easy girls until morning. In one of the dance-halls Jacky got into a fight with a tough crowd and I knocked one of them down with my heavy Colt's pistol, and made them leave the hall. Then I was the hero of the ball.

At daylight Jacky and I staggered to his room and went to bed together. He showed me an old shotgun wound in his hip, made by officers in Nebraska when he was captured for horse-stealing, under the name of Jack Allen. Under that name he was sent to the State Penitentiary for a term of years. When he was liberated, he went to the booming mining camp of Leadville, Colorado, and joined the notorious salter of mines, 'Chicken Bill.' I had got enough out of Jacky to convince me that he had helped salt the Mudsill mine.

Soon after this, Mr. McDermott, the New York mining expert, met me in Denver, and gave orders that I get at the bottom of the salting of the Mudsill mine, regardless of expenses, so that the Lord Mayor of London could get back his money through the courts.

I then returned to Fairplay, and spent money freely. I had explained to Jacky, confidentially, that my father in Texas was well-to-do and furnished me all the money that I needed; so Jacky and I made Rome howl every night at the dance-halls. Jacky had considerable money of his own, and he spent it. Shortly, I secured a partial confession from Jacky as to how he and his partner Andy had spent three years salting the Mudsill mine; that they had kept the tunnel locked during this time, and not even their best friends were allowed to enter. Later I got all the details of how they fooled the two renowned experts sent to Fairplay by the Lord Mayor. If it was all put in print, it would read like a dime novel.

After being in Fairplay quite a while, I sent for Mamie and Viola, so they could enjoy the cool mountain summer weather.

My friend 'Doc' Lockridge, who owned a pay-mine near Alma,
lived in the leading hotel of that town; hence it was arranged
that Mamie should go there as his niece from Kansas. I had
been to Alma to arrange matters. It was agreed that Mamie
was to call him uncle, and she was to be introduced as a widow
whose husband had died a couple of years previous.

It was Sunday morning when I rode the seven miles on
horseback to Alma from Fairplay. My excuse for going to
Alma was to visit my old cowboy friend Pete Stewart, who
conducted a saloon there. I met 'Doc' Lockridge in Stewart's
saloon and he invited me up to the hotel to take dinner with
him. In the ladies' parlor in the presence of other guests,
'Doc' introduced me to his pretty young niece from Kansas.
Little Viola had been left in the room for fear that she might
call me 'papa.' At the dinner table Viola did call me 'papa'
once, but it was after most of the guests had left the table.
We finally got her trained to call me Mr. Leon.

That night I retired with 'Doc' to his room, but I couldn't
sleep, so got up to get some fresh air and to do a little skir-
mishing like a thief in the night. It is certainly a funny business which makes it necessary for a man to tiptoe through a
dark hall to his own wife's bedroom. But, gee-whiz! what a
scandal would have been raised had I been caught going into
this 'young widow's' room.

My trips to Alma became frequent, and it was soon noised
about that I was in love with 'Doc's' niece. Then the land-
lady of the hotel and other lady guests, who had become attached to Mamie, aired my reputation as one of the worst
toughs and dance-hall loafers of Fairplay and advised her not
to associate with me. Some of the men who were 'stuck' on
the 'young widow' had told of my doings in Fairplay.

For the next few weeks I led a double life — about four
nights of each week I was carousing with Jacky and the dance-

hall 'girls,' and the balance of the time I was doing the tiptoe act and playing myself off as a respectable gentleman.

During the eight months that I was in Fairplay Jacky and I spent two weeks out in the mountains. This gave me an opportunity to get every detail of the salting. In the wind-up Jacky was arrested in Denver and confronted with his own photograph taken in stripes when in the Lincoln, Nebraska, penitentiary, under the name of Jack Allen. The result was he made a confession implicating his backers. The case was tried in the courts, and the Lord Mayor of London got back $150,000 of his money.

The Mudsill mine-salting case was passed on by the Circuit Judges of the United States, and is recorded in the Federal Reporter, volume 61, page 163, and is now used as a precedent in all mine-salting cases.

After a month spent in Denver doing all kinds of work, I was sent to Longmont, Colorado, on an important operation.

In Helena, Montana, a young man whom I will call Wraxhall had got into a scrape with a wealthy man of that section. In the fight which followed, the wealthy man was badly wounded and now lay at the point of death. In case he recovered, nothing was to be done with Wraxhall, so as to prevent a scandal. But in case of death, then he was to be prosecuted. The officers of Montana had lost trail of young Wraxhall and had turned the case over to us to find him, so that he would not become suspicious. He was not to be arrested unless his victim died. It was thought that he might be in hiding at his brother Frank's ranch, a couple of miles out of Longmont. I was detailed on the case and left Denver dressed as a tramp cowboy. I carried a description and photograph of young Wraxhall in my pocket.

I walked out from Longmont to the Frank Wraxhall ranch,

arriving there just at noon. Hoping to get a peep into the home, I rang the bell at the front door of the nice white house. A lady came to the door and I told her I wished to see Mr. Frank Wraxhall. She said he was eating his dinner, but that she would call him. Instead of seating me in the parlor, Frank Wraxhall conducted me out to the yard to hear my tale of woe. I told him my name was Charlie Le Roy and that I was stranded in Longmont with not a cent to buy my dinner; that I heard he had some wild horses to break and I had come out to get a job to break a few for my board until money could reach me from my home in Texas. He said I could have a free dinner, so he conducted me to a dining-room built off from the kitchen, where the hired men ate their meals. He agreed to talk to me about the horse-breaking after dinner.

About the time my dinner was finished, three men came out of the house. I asked one of the cowboys who these men were. He replied that they were all brothers. One, he said, was the Reverend Mr. Wraxhall, a minister of a church on Capitol Hill in Denver, and another was Oliver, just home from college, and the third was Frank, the proprietor of this ranch. I asked if there were any more brothers in the family. He replied yes, that there was a brother in Montana, who was a little older than Oliver.

Finally Frank called me to him in the yard and asked me if I could ride a wild bronco and stay with him if he bucked. I told him that I was brought up in southern Texas in the early days of the cattle business, and that ought to be recommendation enough. He replied that it wasn't, for he said he had been fooled in hiring riders from Texas, just on their word. So, for that reason, he kept an outlaw horse with which to test new riders. He said if I could stick on that horse until he quit bucking and whip him every jump, that I could have a job with him as long as he raised horses on the ranch. I told him

to trot out his outlaw horse, and he then sent a cowboy out
to the big pasture to drive up the wild bunch.

When corralled, the outlaw was caught. He was a vicious
iron-gray four-year-old, and very strong. We put the saddle
on him. Then Frank told me I had to ride him in the calf-
pasture, a small tract of an acre in front of the house. This
tract was enclosed with a high barbed-wire fence, and I protested that it was dangerous to ride a wild horse in such a
small lot enclosed with barbed wire. He said the horse had
never failed to throw every man who ever mounted him, and
he was sure he would throw me too, and for that reason he
didn't want to take chances on the horse getting away with
the saddle on.

In front of the picket fence surrounding the house I held
the blindfolded bronco. On the porch were three ladies, with
Oliver and the Reverend Mr. Wraxhall from Denver. Frank
stood near me at the front gate. Several cowboys and the
man cook were witnesses from another place.

After mounting, and just as I reached forward to raise the
blind from the horse's eyes, I glanced toward the front door
and saw the head of a black-haired man peeping around the
door casing. So here was my man, thought I, and I determined to get a better look at him while the horse was bucking.

As soon as the blind was raised, I struck the bronco with
my quirt and he went straight up in the air and changed ends
before he hit the ground. For the next twenty minutes I had
to ride, and on one occasion I had to throw one leg above the
saddle to keep from being cut by the wire fence. Several
times as the horse bucked by the front gate, I got a good look
at my man and he looked just exactly like the photograph
and answered the description. In the excitement he stood
among the ladies on the porch. All were clapping their hands
and cheering.

After the outlaw had worn himself out bucking, my man had disappeared again, but my work was done. The instructions had been to discontinue and return to Denver as soon as I was positive that our man had been found.

When the horse was subdued, Frank Wraxhall asked me to ride out in the big pasture and help drive up a bunch of cattle, as he wanted all the meanness taken out of the bronco while he was under control.

The cowboy and I returned with the cattle about night. After eating supper, I told Wraxhall that I was going to town to see if my money had arrived from Texas, as it should have been there several days previous. He complimented me on my good riding and assured me work at top wages, so long as I wished to stay. He offered me a horse to ride to town, but I insisted on walking. Next morning I boarded a train for Denver. On the same train were the Reverend Mr. Wraxhall and his wife returning home, but I kept them from seeing me.

Other men were then put on the case to shadow the depot in Longmont and also the Reverend Mr. Wraxhall's residence, so that we should know if our man came to Denver to visit his preacher brother, or left the country. In the course of time the wounded man in Helena, Montana, was out of danger, and then the operation was discontinued.

In the early fall of 1889 I was detailed to work on a dynamite case. Two wealthy mine owners of Tuscarora, Nevada, George Peltier, now a banker in Sacramento, California, and W. C. Price, who, at this writing is a resident of Pasadena, California, were blown up into the air with dynamite bombs. Mr. Peltier went up through the roof of his cabin and landed out in the street, on his mattress, still wrapped in the quilts and blankets, unhurt. Mr. Price was not so lucky; he went through the roof of his cabin and landed on the hard ground. He was laid up for repairs for quite a while.

A detective was sent from San Francisco to ferret out the dynamiters. After working a month or two, he had to leave in the night to save his life, as he had made false reports implicating innocent men. Then George Peltier came to Denver to consult with Mr. McParland, with the result that I was detailed on the case. Mr. Peltier instructed me to go to San Francisco and put up at the Palace Hotel, and remain there until he came from a pleasure trip to Southern California. This gave me a few weeks of high living, while seeing the sights of 'Frisco.

When Mr. Peltier arrived, he gave me the names of suspects, and two hundred and fifty dollars expense money. Then he left for Tuscarora. I followed a few days later, dressed as a tramp cowboy. In Elko, Nevada, I boarded a four-horse stagecoach for a fifty-mile ride to Tuscarora. The stage was loaded with passengers and Phil Snyder and I sat on the front seat with the driver.

Phil Snyder was one of the suspects; therefore I was anxious to win his friendship. The chance came when a coyote ran across the road ahead of us at a distance of about a hundred yards. Pulling my Colt's 45 pistol, I fired offhand while the horses were traveling in a swift trot. The coyote fell over dead, and I received the applause of Snyder and the other passengers. They all had to examine my pretty silver-plated pearl-handled pistol. In answer to questions from Phil Snyder, I claimed Texas as my native State.

Arriving at the post-office in the live mining camp of Tuscarora late in the evening, Phil Snyder introduced me to his chum, Tim Wright, also a suspect, as Charles T. Leon, a crack pistol shot from Texas. Tim informed me that he was rooming with a widow lady, whom I will call Mrs. Balcom, and he thought she had a spare room. Together we went there, and I secured a room fronting on the street, paying a week's rent in advance. I explained that the room would not be wanted for over a week, as I intended to buy a horse and saddle and go out in the mountains to live, as town life didn't suit me.

The next day Tim Wright and I walked out to the edge of town to look at a horse he said was for sale. I bought the animal and a saddle from the ranchman. Tim brought up the subject of my killing the coyote from the stagecoach. He pointed out a knot on a fence board, fifty yards away, and asked me to shoot at it. I pulled the pistol quickly and fired offhand. The bullet took the knot, the size of a silver dollar, out of the board. He tried to persuade me to shoot at another mark, but I had sense enough to let well enough alone, as my reputation was made.

A few days later I rode out with a Mr. Morrison to his slaughter house, and helped him butcher a steer for his butcher shop in town. He had a Chinaman working for him at this slaughter house, and I secured permission to move out and live with the Chinaman, who could not talk English. The next day I bought bedding and a camp outfit and moved. My object was to keep away from town so as to avoid suspicion.

Two weeks later Phil Snyder got me to go with him on a hunting and fishing trip into the high range of mountains. We were gone a week and killed two large buck deer, one apiece, and had all the fish we could eat; also quail and grouse.

Soon after our return to Tuscarora, Tim Wright introduced me to one of his friends, Wild Bill, who claimed to have no other name. He lived alone in a cabin on Lone Mountain, twenty-five miles from town. Tim gave me a hint that he was an outlaw. We three spent much of our time in the saloons, drinking. When Wild Bill returned to his cabin I went with him. Before starting, on horseback, I made a confidant of

Tim Wright and told him that I had got into a killing scrape in Texas, and had gone to Oklahoma to hide out; that my father, who owned a cattle ranch in Texas, sent money every month to an old school chum, Mr. Long, in Reno City, to be given to me. I asked Tim if he would object to Mr. Long sending the money to him, so that he could hand it to me on the sly. He consented and promised to keep everything a secret. I then wrote to Mr. McParland, in Denver, to send one hundred and fifty dollars to my friend, Charlie Long, in Reno City, Oklahoma, with instructions to send it to Tim W. Wright, in Tuscarora, Nevada.

I spent two weeks with Wild Bill on Lone Mountain, and found out that he was a counterfeiter. He showed me a steel plate for making twenty-dollar bills, which he had made himself. It was a fine piece of work. He showed his skill in working with steel by making me a combination miners' candlestick out of an old rasp. It contained a knife blade and half a dozen other tools, and can be closed up and carried like a pocket knife. It is kept to this day as a relic. From Wild Bill I got the names of Price's and Peltier's most bitter enemies. He said Tim Wright and 'Black Jack' Griffin were the leaders, and had a hand in dynamiting those two mine owners. On returning to Tuscarora, Tim gave me the hundred and fifty dollars sent to him by Mr. Long, in Oklahoma. Every month thereafter he received a hundred and fifty dollars for me. He felt highly honored at being trusted with my liberty.

From now on Tim Wright and I became bosom chums. We both roomed with Mrs. Balcom, but we were not in the same class when it came to burning the midnight oil and basking in the sunshine of her sweet smiles. She was in love with Tim.

On Christmas day I took my first sleigh ride, and for a few minutes I was 'going some.' The liveryman had just received a brand-new sleigh. I hired it and a spirited team of horses and took Miss Aggie Dougherty for a ride. We drove ten miles out on the stage road and then turned back. The stage and freight road was a mass of packed snow. On each side of the road about every hundred feet the stage company had a willow stuck into the snow so that on a stormy night the driver could keep on the road. One of these slender poles was bending over and the team ran into it. The end flew up and caught one of the horses in the flank. Then there was 'something doing' and we began to go some. If I had had the use of both hands the team might have been stopped before they got under full headway. My left arm was around the girl's waist, to keep her from falling out, as the sleigh had no sideboards. Before my arm could be disentangled and put back in its proper place, the team of flying broncos made a sharp turn off the road and went out of sight into the deep snow. The sleigh naturally went over them, high up in the air, upside down.

While standing on my head in the air, I could see my old Colt's 45 pistol, which had been carried loose in my hip pocket flying through space. At this place the snow was about ten feet deep. I found poor little Agnes standing on her head in a hole that she had made in the snow. I had made a hole of my own, so it took me quite a while to reach Aggie. By the time I got her on her feet into the hard road, the team was a couple of miles away, going like lightning. They had floundered back into the road. In order to find my pistol I had to swim out to the small hole where it had disappeared in the snow and then do some fancy diving.

A three-mile walk brought us to where the team lay tangled up in the harness. Both were on their sides. We had passed pieces of the sleigh scattered all along the road. Therefore there wasn't much of it attached to the team. After the pretty sorrels were on their feet, we started for town afoot, leading them. They had never been ridden, so we had to walk the five or six miles. On reaching town a large crowd greeted us and made me treat.

The liveryman let me off lightly by charging me only fifty dollars for the half-day's sleigh ride. He said the experience was worth something to a beginner. I thought so, too, for in future I vowed that side-boards would have to be put on the sleigh to hold the girl in place before it could be hired to Yours Truly.

The fact that I was riding with an eighteen-year-old girl, while my wife was recovering from an operation for pleurisy in Springfield, Missouri, where she had gone to be operated on by her father's family physician, may seem queer to you, dear reader. But the truth is I was working on old man Dougherty, who was a suspect, and Miss Aggie was only a side-issue to win points in the game.

In the spring Tim Wright and I made preparations to leave for the Wichita Mountains in the western part of the Indian Territory, on a prospecting trip for gold. I had told Tim wonderful stories of gold being found in these mountains by soldiers and hunters. I had concluded that the best way to get a confession out of Tim would be to get him in a strange country where he could talk with no one but myself.

When the gang found out that he was going to the Indian Territory with me, they became frightened for fear I might be a detective. That night they held another secret meeting in Mason's drug store and Tim got very little sleep. As a last resort they told Tim that they had positive evidence that all the money which I had spent in Tuscarora came from Price and Peltier's agents in San Francisco, and that if he would wait over another week they would produce my signature to the receipts for the money received at different times. Here's where the gang fell down. Tim told them that they were d——d liars, but he wouldn't tell them how he knew. He told me about their meetings later when we were on the road.

Next morning we boarded the stage for Elko, and most of the gang were at the post-office to see us off and to make one last effort to change Tim's mind. The faces of some of the gang appeared pale and careworn, and Black Jack looked daggers at me.

The whip was cracked and away we went. In Elko Tim and I boarded a Union Pacific train for Denver, Colorado. Tim's wealth consisted of six hundred dollars in cash and several hundred dollars' worth of rich ore which he had stolen from the Smith Brothers' mine, which he was taking along to sell in Denver.

In Denver we boarded a Fort Worth train for Wichita Falls, Texas. There we purchased two swift saddle horses and a couple of cowboy saddles; also a couple of pairs of heavy wool blankets. We crossed Red River into the Indian Territory, at the Burk Burnett cattle ranch.

From now on it became a game of hide and seek with us. The Indian police had found our trail and tried to capture us, but our horses were too swift. We camped on the highest peaks, changing locations often. Finally a squad of deputy United States marshals were sent from Fort Sill to round us up. This I learned when I left Tim in camp and slipped into Fort Sill after supplies, to be tied to the back of my saddle. Our camp was on the top of a round timbered mountain, twenty miles west of Fort Sill. From here we had a good view of the surrounding country.

Soon after my return with the supplies, we had to change camps in a hurry, to get away from the officers. In the night we moved to the top of a mountain on Otter Creek, twenty miles west.

We never ran short of wild game to eat, as deer and turkeys

were plentiful. Our next supplies were bought in Navajo, a village across the north fork of Red River, in Greer County, Texas. Here Tim and I put in one night; then returned to the Wichita Mountains.

In prospecting we found traces of gold, but not in paying quantities. When we ran out of supplies again, I rode the twenty-five miles to Fort Sill, leaving Tim to hold down our new camp on the top of a high mountain. We had both ordered our mail sent to Fort Sill. Tim gave me an order to get his, as he expected letters from his sweetheart, Mrs. Balcom.

On reaching Fort Sill late in the evening, I rode up to the post-office to get the mail before going to the store to buy supplies. What I got was a bunch of letters for Tim Wright. These I took to a secluded place on Medicine Bluff and read them. They were all from Mrs. Balcom. In all these letters she begged Tim to shake that dirty detective Charlie Leon, as it was known positively that he was a Pinkerton officer. One of these letters had been written that morning, giving the number of her room at the hotel. All of Tim's mail was shoved into a pigeonhole, under a rock at Medicine Bluff, there to rot. I never found out how long Mrs. Balcom remained in Fort Sill nursing her bleeding heart.

Soon afterward we hit the road for El Reno, Oklahoma. There we helped celebrate the first anniversary of the opening of Oklahoma to white settlement.

I had secured a complete confession from Tim Wright as to how he and his gang had blown up Price and Peltier with dynamite bombs. He said he lighted the fuse attached to the one under Mr. Price's cabin. They had cut the fuses of both bombs the same length, and set them off at the same time, so that the mine owners would sprout angel wings together.

In El Reno I owned a business lot which had been bought from an army officer for one hundred and fifty dollars, when

the town first started. This lot had gone up in price, as it was
near the center of town. I traded it, giving forty dollars to
boot, for a two-year-old race filly named Lula Edson, a sister
to the famous Lula Mack of Texas. Lula Edson had just won
five hundred dollars in a race against a speedy Texas horse.
Her time for the quarter of a mile race was twenty-two-and-
a-half seconds, almost a world record. The El Reno lot, so I
was told, sold for five thousand dollars a couple of years later.
This made Lula a costly piece of horseflesh for a fool ex-cow-
puncher to own.

In order to save a fight in the courts to get Tim Wright
back to Nevada, I concluded to ride the six hundred miles, on
horseback, to Denver, Colorado, before making the arrest.

Early one morning Tim and I headed north, using Lula
Edson for a pack-animal to carry our grub and bedding. The
second day out of El Reno we stopped at a large cattle ranch
in the Cherokee Strip, just over the line of Oklahoma. Here
we put up for the night, with the twenty cowboys congregated
there. The next morning, while we were seated at the breakfast table with the gang of cowboys, a stranger armed to the
teeth walked into the dining-room. His face looked familiar
to me, and I saw that he kept his eyes on me while eating.

As it was raining hard, Tim and I concluded to lie over until
next morning. As Lula had become a little tender-footed, I
decided to take her back over the line into Oklahoma and
have her shod at a cross-roads shop. I started immediately
after breakfast. As soon as I had left, the tough-looking
stranger, with two Colt's pistols buckled around his waist,
called Tim to one side and asked him if he had ever committed a serious crime. Of course Tim told him no. 'All right,
then go ahead,' said the fellow, 'but if you have ever committed a serious crime I would advise you to shake that detective you are traveling with. That is Charlie Siringo, and

he is after some one down here.' Tim told him that he must be mistaken, as my name was Charlie Leon. 'All right,' replied the fellow, 'I know what I am talking about.' When I returned in the evening, one of the cowboys told me that the stranger who had eaten breakfast there was the much-wanted outlaw 'Six-Shooter Bill.'

For several days Tim was sullen and seemed to be brooding over something. I pretended not to notice it. Not until after his arrest in Denver did I know that Six-Shooter Bill had warned him to shake me. He said he thought seriously of killing me, but that he couldn't believe that I was a detective.

Our six hundred miles' horseback ride to Denver, Colorado, ended one evening in May. Tim was arrested and taken to our office to face Mr. W. C. Price, who had come to be at the wind-up. At first Tim Wright denied everything, but he finally broke down and made a full confession before a notary public, agreeing to testify in court against his pals, after a promise from Mr. Price that he would be let off easy and would not be put in jail.

This ended my connection with the case after having worked on it nine months.

Poor Tim Wright went back to Tuscarora, Nevada, to his grass-widow, Mrs. Balcom, to repent in sackcloth and ashes for the letters that never came, after he had promised to write often. I had pigeonholed under rocks after I had read them all the letters Tim had sent by me to be mailed to his sweetheart.

During the fall my stubborn bump and quick temper came very near landing me in the penitentiary. It shows how a man's whole life can be changed by a mere hair's breadth. Gamblers call it luck, but I call it chance.

Mamie, my wife, was at death's door and I had been sitting up with her night and day. It was Saturday and I went down to the office to draw my week's salary and to ask Mr. McParland if I couldn't remain at Mamie's bedside until she got better.

With the salary in my pocket, I started home by way of Laramie Street, so as to get my old Colt's 45 out of 'soak.' Being short of cash, I had pawned the pistol for twenty dollars at the Rocky Mountain pawnshop, and in its place I was carrying a small pistol belonging to another operative.

Next door to the Rocky Mountain pawnshop a chemical factory had blown up and it was reported that a dead man was being brought out by the police and firemen. The police had rope stretched to keep the crowds back, and a special policeman named Rease was guarding the front door of the pawnshop and wouldn't let any one inside for fear a raid would be made on the valuable diamonds in the window and showcases. Being refused admittance, I stepped up on an iron railing to get a better view of the dead man who was being brought out. Just then young Solomon told me to get down and move away from the front of their shop. I told him to go to Hades or some other seaport. Then the big double-jointed special policeman pulled me down and tore my coat almost off. My gold-headed silk umbrella was broken all to pieces over his head, and, when he reached for his gun, mine was pulled out of my hip pocket and pointed at his heart and the trigger was pulled. While I was using the umbrella on the fellow's head, other policemen rushed at me. Just as the trigger was pulled, a policeman by the name of Ball threw both arms around me from the rear. His right hand grabbed the pistol, and the hammer came down on his thumb instead of the cartridge, thus saving me the expense of a trip to the penitentiary, for had the special officer been killed, it would have meant a trip 'over the road.' The sharp hammer had buried itself in Mr. Policeman's thumb, so I was told. I saw him many times afterward, but never made myself known to him.

By main strength and awkwardness six policemen put me in the 'hurry-up wagon,' and I was taken to jail, coatless, hatless, and umbrellaless. That evening I was liberated by Chief of Police John Farley, after Mr. McParland had come to see me. This ended the matter after my old Colt's 45 was taken out of 'soak,' and I had tried in vain to round up my hat and the gold head of my umbrella. They had vanished.

Poor Mamie died in my arms early in the winter, as I was holding her at the window to get fresh air. Her suffering had been something awful, and our physician, Dr. Herman H. Martin, shed tears when the end came. This was a surprise to me, for I didn't think a doctor could shed tears, as they become so accustomed to great suffering.

Mamie's aunt, Mrs. Will F. Read, formerly Miss Emma Lloyd, of Shelbyville, Illinois, came out from her home in Anna, Illinois, to comfort my wife in her last days on earth. When Mrs. Read returned to Illinois, I let her take Viola along, as she had no children of her own and begged me hard for the child to raise, as I had no way of caring for her.

It was in the early summer of 1890 that I closed the Nevada dynamite case. That leaves sixteen years of strenuous detective work to record my schooling in the study of human nature and the ways of the world. Soon after New Year's Day, 1891, I was sent to Santa Fé, New Mexico, to work for the Territory on the Ancheta shooting scrape. Ancheta was an educated Mexican who had been elected to the Territorial Senate, then in session. He and former Governor Stover fathered a public school law for the Territory, and this brought on a bitter fight by the natives, as it was argued that the Catholic schools already established were able to educate the youth of the Territory.

One night, when the executive committee of the Senate were holding a meeting, armed assassins rode up to the glass-front Griffin Block and fired into the office, putting nine buckshot into Mr. Ancheta's neck. A charge of buckshot entered a pile of law books in front of Thomas B. Catron, afterward a United States Senator, the shotgun being aimed at his breast as he sat behind the desk fronting the street. A rifle bullet barely missed Governor Stover and buried itself in the adobe wall near his head.

The next day the legislature appropriated twenty thousand dollars as a fund to run down the would-be assassin. It was thought that the lawless White Cap organization of San Miguel County were the instigators of the plot, as one of their members, Pablo Herrera, who had been elected to the legislature after serving a term in the penitentiary, fought the public school bill tooth and nail.

Governor Prince, T. B. Catron, and Edward L. Bartlett, the attorney general, were appointed a committee to handle the fund and run down the villains. The result was I was sent by McParland to Santa Fé to work on the case.

Arriving in the oldest town in the United States and the cradle of 'Ben-Hur,' I met the committee and was told to make friends with Pablo Herrera, and if possible join the White Caps who were strong in the county of San Miguel, of which Las Vegas was the county seat. The White Caps murdered stock men and cut fences. They marched in bands, placing white caps on themselves and their mounts.

By spending money in the tough dance-halls I soon won the friendship of Pablo Herrera, and when the legislature adjourned I was an invited guest on the train to his home in Las Vegas. There I was introduced to his two brothers, Juan and Nicanor, who were leaders in the White Cap organization. For a while I lived with Nicanor on his ranch, ten miles out of

Las Vegas. I had bought a horse and saddle and made frequent trips to town.

I learned that an important meeting of the White Caps was to take place in Tecolote on a certain night. I laid plans to be at that meeting. Pablo Herrera and I had been drinking all day, and when the time came for Pablo to start to the White Cap meeting I suggested that to pass off the time I would ride with him to Tecolote.

We started at 8 P.M., each carrying a quart bottle of whiskey in our saddle pockets. The ten miles was covered in an hour. We rode up to a large adobe hall built on a hill outside the Mexican village. The lights inside could hardly be seen, owing to the heavy curtains over the glass windows.

I suggested to Pablo that I wait outside for him, but he said that I was his friend and wherever he went I should go. He gave the secret knock at the door and it was opened. Seeing a Gringo at Pablo's heels, the guard tried to prevent my entrance, but Pablo being a powerful man brushed the half-breed Indian to one side. This caused a rush toward the front door which almost caused a riot. There were about two hundred Mexicans and half-breed Indians in the hall, among them being one negro who had married a Mexican woman.

Pablo put his hand on his big Colt's pistol buckled around his waist, and in the Mexican language, which I understood, he told the crowd to stand back. Then he made a fiery speech such as he had recently made in the Senate Chamber at Santa Fé. He soared to the sky in his Spanish eloquence, and said he had fought and bled for their noble order and would never bring any one into their hall who couldn't be trusted. This brought hand-claps and yells from the rough-looking crowd.

In the rear of the hall some new members were waiting to be initiated into the order. The proceeding was started over again for my benefit, and I became a full-fledged White Cap.

I had to swear that I would give up my life for the good of the order, or for a brother in need. This last clause was hard on my Territorial pocketbook, as I later found many brothers in need of a drink.

For the next few months I attended many secret meetings in the counties of San Miguel and Moro. I satisfied myself beyond the shadow of a doubt that the White Caps had had no hand in the shooting of Ancheta. Then I bade the Herrera brothers good-bye and started overland for Santa Fé, a distance of eighty miles.

Soon after this, Nicanor was sent to the penitentiary for a murder; and Pablo, who had in cold blood killed a couple of men, defied District Judge Smith and his court to arrest him.

When the court was in session, Judge Smith ordered his chief deputy, Billy Green, to bring Pablo Herrera's body before his court. The order was carried out when Pablo was killed and his body dragged into the courtroom by Billy Green and another deputy. But this caused the death of both officers, as they were both murdered and their bodies burned.

My next few months' work solved the mystery of the Ancheta shooting. At Oje La Vaca (Cow Springs) in the mountains of eastern Santa Fé County, I secured confessions from two of the Mexicans, who were with the crowd that shot Ancheta, on account of the public school bill.

While living with Francisco and his family in Oje La Vaca, I contracted smallpox in helping to bury a Mexican woman who had died from the disease. I thought I was safe, as I had had the smallpox in 1882. But from doctors I learn there is one case on record where a man had smallpox eight times. I am positive now of one poor devil who had it twice.

It is said that no good has ever come from whiskey. This I deny, as I should not be alive to-day had not my Mexican nurse got drunk and left me to die alone. The doctor had given me poison, so he confessed to me later — to put me out of my misery, as he didn't think I could live till morning. The medicine was to be given to me every ten minutes. After I had taken one dose, the nurse slipped away and got drunk. God bless him.

CHAPTER XIII

THE TROUBLE IN THE CŒUR D'ALENE — A CHANGE
OF SYMPATHIES — RECORDING SECRETARY OF THE
GEM UNION — THE SPECIAL MEETING — MAKING A
SPEECH FOR MY LIFE — THE PAGE CUT FROM THE
RECORDS — A HOLE IN THE FLOOR

IN the autumn of 1891 I was asked to go to the Cœur d'Alene
mining district of northern Idaho, where serious trouble was
brewing between the men and the Mine Owners' Association.
I was to work on behalf of the latter, and as my sympathies
were at first with the men I accepted the job only on condition
that I was at liberty to throw it up if I decided that the miners were in the right.

At a meeting with Mr. Finch, the secretary of the Mine
Owners' Association, and a Mr. Frank Jenkins, representing
Mr. John Hays Hammond, principal proprietor of the Bunker
Hill and Sullivan Mine, it was arranged that I should go to
Gem, the 'toughest' mining-camp in the district, and from
time to time send out reports as to the miners' probable move-
ments. I was to adopt the name of Allison, and no one except
John Monihan, the superintendent of the Gem Mine, was to
know my real identity.

I went to Gem. It was a little town of about a thousand inhabitants, including some five hundred miners employed in
the Helen-Frisco, Black Bear, and Gem Mines. It contained
half-a-dozen saloons and gambling halls, and was a lively place
at night. The town was situated in a deep canyon, with
wooded mountains on either side, and the Union Pacific
Railway from Wallace to Burk ran through the center of its
one and only street.

The first thing I did was to apply for a job in the Gem Mine where I was put to work on the night shift. Two weeks later I became a member of the Gem Miners' Union, whose secretary was a man called George A. Pettibone, Oliver Hughes being the president. Pettibone was also financial secretary of the Central Union, with headquarters at Wallace.

I was now in a position to learn what the men thought and what they intended doing, and the things I found out entirely changed my sympathies. The unions, I discovered, were being 'run' by a number of dangerous anarchists, who had completely duped the hard-working miners and were formulating demands to which the owners could not possibly agree.

A little later on I managed to get elected as 'recording secretary' of my branch of the union. This was a useful position from my point of view, since it would give me access to all the books and records. Seeing the character of the leaders, I had now no qualms of conscience as to revealing their schemes to my employers.

In due course things came to a head; the miners struck, and feeling at once became very bitter. The first action taken by the strikers was against 'scabs' — men who remained loyal or favoured the owners' cause. These were dragged from their beds at midnight and, after being marched up the canyon by a howling mob, were compelled to tramp through deep snow to Thompson's Falls, near the summit of the Bitter Root Mountains.

Soon after this the men of the Burk Union came to Gem to hold a joint meeting with our lodge, and plans were laid for the flooding of certain of the mines. These plans, in accordance with my duty as recording secretary, I put down in the minutes, but later on Hughes, the president, told me to cut this leaf out of the book, in case it should fall into the hands of the Mine Owners' Association.

Nothing suited me better! I cut it out — and straightway mailed it to Mr. Finch, the owners' secretary. I had to take it to Wallace after dark and post it myself, for the postmaster at Gem and all his assistants were union men.

The next excitement followed the owners' decision to import labor from other districts to work the mines. The unions decided to oppose this tooth and nail, and arms were collected and guards put out to capture the first train-load of 'scabs,' and send them back whence they had come.

One night a message was received that a trainload of 'scabs,' in charge of Joe Warren, a gunman, would arrive in Wallace early next morning. The town immediately began to buzz like a wasps' nest, and was soon full of armed union men from outside camps.

When the train came whistling down the canyon, Sheriff Cunningham, mounted on a sorrel charger, led his fighting deputies to the station to read a warrant of arrest for Joe Warren.

But alas! for his plans, the train didn't stop. Knowing, from my reports, what the blacklegs might expect, the owners had arranged for the line to be cleared, and with another whistle of derision the train proceeded under full steam up the canyon toward Gem and Burk.

With loud curses Sheriff Cunningham galloped after it, waving his warrant in the air. An ugly spirit was now abroad, and a mob of several hundred men promptly started on foot toward Burk, led by the sheriff and his deputies on horseback.

On reaching Gem, it was learned that the train had not stopped there either, and it transpired that Warren had unloaded his hundred armed non-union men some distance below Burk and marched them half a mile up the timbered mountain-side to the Union Mine, owned by John A. Finch and

Mace Campbell, where supplies had been stored in advance for them.

The sheriff and his deputies proceeded to the mine, and there arrested Warren for breaking the State laws by bringing in armed men. When they returned with their prisoner, who stood six feet four in his stockinged feet, and was as brave as a lion, the mob surged round, wildly excited, and clamored for his blood. They were only pacified when the sheriff told them that if Warren were killed the union would inevitably lose its fight, as United States soldiers would be brought into the district.

Several more trainloads of non-union miners, heavily armed, were afterward imported, and as all union members had by this time been served with injunctions by the Federal Court they dare not openly attack these 'blacklegs.' The hundreds of pickets who met the trains, however, used every possible means to intimidate them.

A 'wild and woolly' cowboy named Fred Carter brought in several bunches of volunteers. He was quite fearless, and often called the miners hard names when they reviled him. More than once I expected to see him killed, but up to this time the injunctions had kept the strikers from committing any open act of aggression. Many non-union men, however, caught alone at night, were set upon and beaten almost to death.

The strike dragged on through the winter, with myself still acting as recording secretary of my union. Toward spring I bought a building with twelve furnished rooms, giving Mrs. Shipley half the income for running the place.

We opened a store downstairs, and contemplated letting the rooms when the strike was over. It was nowhere near its end, however, and as I knew from secret action taken by the central union that serious riots were likely to occur before long I had a board fence, sixteen feet high, built round the rear of my building to keep out prowlers — a wise precaution, as future events were to show.

Pettibone, the Gem Union financial secretary, appeared to have taken a fancy to me, and told me many secrets which I should not otherwise have learnt, for to avoid any leakage all strike affairs were now arranged through the central union in Wallace. One of these secrets concerned a plot of a great rising in July, intended to run the 'scabs' and the mine owners out of the country and take possession of the mines on behalf of the workers. As on previous occasions, I passed on the information to my employers.

It was now, however, that suspicion began to fall upon me. The Mine Owners' Association was interested in a weekly paper called the *Barbarian*, published in the town of Wardner and conducted by a fearless individual named Brown. One issue of this sheet contained certain details about the Gem Miners' Union which could only have been given out by a member of that union. As I was the secretary and had charge of the books, the finger of accusation was pointed in my direction.

The upshot of the matter was that the secretary of the Butte City (Montana) Union, under whose charter all the Cœur d'Alene unions had been organized, came to Gem under the assumed name of Tim O'Leary to find out for himself just how the leakage occurred. Within a week he decided that I was the culprit.

I was warned of this by Johnny Murphy, a warm friend of mine, who had learned of O'Leary's decision. He told me that I had better leave the district at once, as I was in danger of being killed as a traitor. My job, however, was to stay, so I brazened the matter out to Murphy, saying that I was quite prepared to face the music.

The next day a special meeting was called to take place in the Union Hall at 8 P.M. Boys were sent all over the town, ringing bells and notifying union members of the importance of the occasion. Naturally I did not feel any too comfortable, for I knew the object of the meeting.

Putting on as bold a face as possible, I entered the hall with my record book under my arm. I found the place crowded with miners. On the raised platform sat the president, Oliver Hughes, Pettibone, the secretary, and Tim O'Leary, whose real name, by the way, was Dallas.

The meeting started by my reading the minutes in the ordinary fashion. Then O'Leary got to his feet.

'Brothers of the Gem Miners' Union,' he began, dramatically, 'you have allowed a traitor to enter your ranks. He now sits within reach of my hand. If you do your duty he will never leave this hall alive!'

The speech caused yelling, hissing, and much hand-clapping, and, of course, I had to clap my hands also, though it went sorely against the grain to do so.

When the applause died down, O'Leary continued his speech. The secrets of the Union published in the Wardner paper, he said, could have reached the Owners' Association only with the connivance of the man in charge of the record book. With that he glared at me.

The renewed burst of savage applause that broke out showed me the danger I was in, but just at that moment the president announced a ten minutes' interval while the record book was being examined. I was ordered to step down off the platform, and did so, though I kept my eyes fixed on the three men who were going through the book.

There is little doubt that they thought I would betray my guilt by trying to slip past the guard at the outer door, but I realized that the only thing to do was to see the matter through to the bitter end.

Under my left arm hung my Colt's 45, and at my waist, concealed by my clothing, I carried a sharp bowie-knife. If the decision went against me and the men attacked me, I determined to fight to the last, though the end would not be long in coming — one man against more than three hundred.

Presently O'Leary looked up with a scowl.

'Why is this page torn out?' he demanded.

'Ask the president,' I retorted. 'He ordered me to cut it out.'

'That's a lie!' Hughes declared. 'I never ordered you to cut a page out of this book.'

Taking a surreptitious grip of my pistol, I reminded him of the joint meeting of the Gem and Burk Unions, when he had ordered me not to put on record the resolution to flood the mines. To my immeasurable relief he was man enough to acknowledge this fact, which he had forgotten. This told heavily in my favor, and, in the end, the meeting was adjourned, the president informing the members that though there was obviously a traitor somewhere the evidence was not sufficient yet to point him out.

As I passed through the crowd, however, I knew that henceforth I should be a marked man. That night I slept with my loaded Winchester rifle and a sack of a hundred cartridges by my side.

From now on I was shunned by many of the union members; Pettibone especially had lost his former friendliness for me. I got no more secrets from him, though I learnt enough from other sources to be able to inform the owners that the rising was planned for early in July, and that Gem was to be its center. They accordingly barricaded the Gem Mine, and kept armed guards on duty night and day.

On July 9th I received a friendly warning not to attend the union meeting fixed for that evening, and this time prudence warned me that I had better heed it, the more so because a member of the Mullen Union, one 'Black Jack' Griffin, was in the town. This man, unfortunately, knew me to be a detective, for two years previously I had broken up his gang of desperadoes, who had blown up two mine owners with giant powder, though Griffin himself had escaped arrest. I felt pretty certain he had already discovered my identity and given me away.

Therefore, instead of entering the meeting with my minute-book as usual, I handed the latter to the guard at the door, together with a letter containing my resignation from the union, and went back to my own rooms to await events.

About two hours later, nothing having happened in the meantime, I slipped outside in the dark, and joined a group of Mullen miners, who did not recognize me as the 'traitor' to the union cause. They told me that a crowd of men were holding two 'scab' miners at Dutch Henry's saloon, treating them at the bar, and telling them that the union had decided to call off the strike. The real intention, however, was to murder these two unfortunates at midnight and throw their bodies into the creek.

Thereupon I slipped into the saloon with the intention of warning the two men of their danger, but before I could get near them an attack was made on me by a rabid anarchist, known as 'Johnny-Get-Your-Gun,' and about twenty of his followers. I stood them off with drawn pistol until I got back to my own house, when their leader shouted:

'Never mind, you traitor, we'll get you before morning!'

On reaching my room I picked up my rifle, stowed the hundred cartridges away in my pockets and then left by the window using a ladder which I had placed there for the purpose. Going to the high board fence in rear of the back yard, I peeped through a crack and detected the shadowy figures of two men with rifles, who had evidently been posted there to cut off my retreat. They were some distance away, however, so I made up my mind to risk a bolt.

Pulling aside a board I had purposely left loose, I wriggled through and lay flat on my stomach between two fallen trees. Between this point and the creek, about a hundred yards away, there was a stretch of heavily-timbered swamp land with much undergrowth. Yard by yard I crawled across it, and presently found myself on the bank of the swiftly flowing creek some fifty yards above a bridge, on which stood three more armed men.

Lowering myself noiselessly into the water, I worked my way across under the low, overhanging branches of spruce trees, and once on the other side rose to my feet and ran to the Gem Mine, where I found Superintendent John Monihan and a squad of armed guards. He was expecting the riot to start at any time, and had a hundred and twenty non-union miners sleeping with their weapons beside them.

I reported to Monihan the plot to murder his two men in the saloon, and while we were still discussing it the town constable arrived and informed us that the two poor fellows had already been attacked and beaten almost to death. The smaller man had lost his nerve, after being severely injured, and had promised to leave the country, but the other, a giant in size, had fought his assailants desperately until he became unconscious. He had then been dragged down to the bridge near the company's office, and left.

Monihan and some of the guards promptly went down to the bridge, found the wounded man, and carried him into the mill. He was only just alive, having been most cruelly beaten, and Monihan begged some of the men to go down to Wallace and bring back Dr. Simms. Only one man, however, would volunteer, and as he dared not go alone I said that I would accompany him.

We duly reached the doctor, who returned with my companion while I went on to report to Mr. Finch, the secretary
of the Owners' Association. He advised me not to go back to
Gem, as it would mean my death, but I told him that my
work there was not yet done.

I took the train back to Gem, and in the coach, as ill luck
would have it, encountered Pettibone and a delegation of
union officials from Wardner. Pettibone stepped up to me and
angrily demanded to know why I was carrying a rifle.

'Because I was attacked last night,' I told him, adding that
I had sent in my resignation as a member of the union.

'That's all very well,' he said, 'but you can't go into Gem
with that rifle.'

'Can't I?' I answered. 'You just watch me and see!'

No more was said, and when the train reached Gem, I
stepped out and walked up to Mrs. Shipley's store without
molestation, though the town was seething with excitement.

That night I slipped out to the Gem Mill as before. We all
expected the riot to begin between midnight and daylight, but
when dawn came, and everything remained quiet, I determined to return to Mrs. Shipley's to find out just what was
happening, though Mr. Monihan did his best to dissuade
me.

I got through to the store all right, but Mrs. Shipley was
horrified at my rashness in venturing into the town. The outbreak, she told me, was timed to start at any minute, and she
implored me to leave at once, as it was now definitely known
that I was a detective and I had been marked down to be
killed directly the row started.

Going upstairs to one of the front rooms which commanded
a view of the street, I looked carefully out. Not a soul was to
be seen anywhere, but all at once, right under the window, I
heard voices. They came from beneath an awning over the

store door, and peering down through the six-inch space between this awning and the wall I recognized Tom Whalen, an
ex-prizefighter, and another man, a blacksmith. Both carried
rifles.

It was now six o'clock, and just as the hour struck I saw
Jimmy Irvin, one of the clerks in the mine company's store,
lean out of the window and look up and down the street.

Thereupon Whalen raised his rifle.

'Watch me knock that fellow's nose off,' I heard him growl,
and forthwith he fired. Irvin disappeared with considerable
abruptness, and I learned later that the bullet had actually
grazed his face.

As though Whalen's shot had been a prearranged signal, a
perfect fusillade of firing came echoing down the canyon. The
riot was starting!

There was no time to be wasted, so I hurriedly ran to my
own room, shinned through the window, and down my emer-
gency ladder. Peering through the garden fence, I saw a
group of armed strikers crouched against the wall of a saloon
building next door. To attempt to leave through the gap in
the fence meant certain death, so I slipped through a window
of the Nelson Hotel, which adjoined my ground, and entered
the kitchen of that building.

Two French cooks occupied the room, and I passed quickly
through it and swung open the inner door with the intention
of running along the rear of the buildings to the company
office, whence I hoped to fight my way past the three guards
on the bridge to the Gem Mill.

All at once one of the cooks grabbed my arm.

'For Heaven's sake, don't go out there,' he cried, 'or you
will be killed! I saw fifty men with shot-guns and rifles a few
minutes ago!'

I halted at the warning, and just then through the open

door I saw Ivory Bean, one of the Gem Mine guards, approaching the bridge.

'I'll see what happens to him before I make a move,' I told the cook.

Hardly were the words out of my mouth when Bean was called upon to stop. He did so, and threw up his hands, but next instant toppled over dead, with a bullet through his heart.

That was quite enough for me. I thanked the cook for his warning and hastened back to Mrs. Shipley's.

It transpired later that the unfortunate Bean had been engaged on an errand of mercy. The big fellow who had been so badly knocked about two nights previously was in dreadful agony, and Bean had volunteered to go to the drug store and get something to alleviate his pain, arguing that an unarmed man would not be interfered with. As a matter of fact, he was never given a chance to explain his mission.

Once back in my house, I got a saw and cut a square hole in the floor in Mrs. Shipley's living-room. Then, putting on an old leather jacket and a black slouch hat as some sort of disguise, and hiding my own cowboy hat and raincoat, I squeezed through the opening into the foundations of the house. Mrs. Shipley gave me a cup of coffee and a sandwich to take into my dark refuge, and then, rearranging the carpet, pulled a large trunk over the hole.

CHAPTER XIV

MRS. SHIPLEY'S COURAGE — I ESCAPE UNDER THE
SIDEWALK — 'THAT TRAITOR ALLISON!'— I TAKE
TO THE HILLS — THE ARRIVAL OF THE TROOPS

AN investigation of my hiding-place showed me that the only
way of escape from it was to crawl along under the board sidewalk, which was raised about two feet above street level. I
was not at all certain, however, where this would eventually
lead me; I might emerge under the very feet of the men who
were hunting me!

I was still debating the matter when I caught sight of a
glimmer of light on the eastern side of the building, and, ap-
plying my eye to a wide crack, found myself looking out on a
narrow alley which divided my house from the saloon next
door. Within five feet of me stood my sworn enemy Dallas —
or O'Leary as he called himself — leaning on a double-
barreled shot-gun!

My first thought was that here was a good chance of paying
off old scores. All's fair in war, and this man was certainly doing his best to put 'paid' to my account. I had actually taken
aim at him through the crack, when, just in time, I realized
the folly of my action. There were other guards about. They
would see Dallas fall, and the smoke and sound of my rifle
would immediately reveal my place of concealment. Reluc-
tantly I lowered the rifle, and as I did so the earth shook and a
loud explosion sounded from the direction of the Frisco Mill.
Dallas immediately ran out into the street, followed by another man carrying a gun.

After the explosion I heard rifle-firing for some minutes.
When it ceased, Mrs. Shipley's voice came to me in agitated

THE WRECKED FRISCO MILL

GEM, IDAHO

A. The author's building, where he sawed a hole in the floor. *B.* Jenny Nelson's hotel, where the author escaped through a window. *C.* Saloon building, where the author crawled from under the sidewalk. *D.* Miners' Union hall. *E.* Where the author entered the culvert. *F.* House where the author emerged from the culvert. *G.* Daxon's saloon. *H.* Company store.

tones. She had pulled away the trunk and was speaking down the hole.

'Oh, Mr. Allison,' she cried, 'run for your life! Mrs. Weiss says the Frisco Mill is blown up, and many 'scabs' killed and wounded. Now they are coming to get you and burn you at the stake as a traitor!'

This was distinctly pleasant hearing, but I told Mrs. Shipley that there seemed to be no way out from under the building, so that it was safer to remain where I was.

'Oh!' she exclaimed, blankly. 'Well, I hope they won't find you.' With that she pulled the trunk back into position over the hole, leaving me alone in the darkness with my thoughts, which were none too cheerful.

Soon I heard loud cheering and yelling coming from the Union Hall. I learnt later that the 'scabs' captured at the blown-up Frisco Mine were being placed there under a guard of strikers. And now, as Mrs. Shipley had said, the rioters turned their attention to me. A mob of close on two thousand men crowded into the street in front of our building. There came a loud pounding on the locked door, and then I heard Dallas's voice shouting to Mrs. Shipley:

'Open this door, or we'll break it down!'

'Break it down, then,' came the plucky response. 'You'll suffer for it.'

A moment later there was a crash, as the heavy double doors were burst in, and in a twinkling the store was full of angry, cursing men.

'Where's that infernal detective Allison?' I heard Dallas demand.

'What do you want him for?' asked Mrs. Shipley.

'To burn him at the stake, as an example to other curs of his kind,' was the savage retort. 'You know where he is, and if you don't tell it will go hard with you.'

'Allison is not here,' replied Mrs. Shipley. 'I haven't seen him since last evening.'

'You are a liar!' came the snarling answer. 'He was seen to come in here early this morning, and the house has been watched ever since. You'd better tell us where he is or it will be the worse for you.'

'I tell you he's not here,' she declared once more.

I felt like patting the plucky little woman on the back, for not one in ten thousand would have defied that infuriated mob. Meanwhile her little boy was crying as though his heart would break, and I was afraid he would reveal my hiding-place. However, the woman's dauntless attitude evidently had its effect on Dallas, for presently I heard him growl:

'Search the place, boys; he's here somewhere.'

The tramping of feet echoed everywhere as the mob rushed into the back yard and all over the house. I concluded it would be only a matter of time before the trunk was moved and the hole discovered, so I determined to take a gambler's chance by crawling under the sidewalk toward the Union Hall, in the hope of finding some way of escape.

Accordingly I wormed my way slowly along, dragging my rifle after me. There was not room to crawl properly on my hands and knees; I had to lie flat on the ground and wriggle. It was a nerve-trying business, for up above me the sidewalk was packed with howling strikers, and some of the cracks in the boards were so wide that I could look up and actually see the men and hear what they were saying. If one of them happened to glance down and spot me, my life would not be worth a second's purchase!

Most of their talk referred to the blowing-up of the Frisco Mill, but I heard one Irishman say: 'I wonder why they are so long in bringing out that traitor Allison? I want to smash his face in!' Altogether they were a nice crowd, and I vowed they should never take me alive.

After wriggling the length of three buildings — a distance that felt like a mile — I came to a saloon, and found an open space through which I was able to crawl right under the building. Here I was overjoyed to see daylight streaming through another opening in the rear.

This saloon was built over a brushwood swamp, and soon there was enough room for me to walk in a stooping position. Crossing to the rear, I cautiously worked my way out into the open.

Thirty feet away from me stood three men. Evidently they had been posted to guard the back of the saloon, but in their anxiety to see the 'traitor' brought out to be burnt alive they were eagerly watching the movements of the mob in the street behind me.

Once more I longingly fingered my rifle, only to realize afresh that to attract the attention of the crowd would be suicide. About a hundred yards in front of me was the high railway embankment, on the other side of which was the Gem Mill, where I knew my friends were waiting to receive me. To scale the embankment, however, meant running the risk of being shot by mistake, for the Gem Mine watchers would very naturally take me for one of the enemy. Some other plan had to be thought of.

A short distance to the left was a boxed culvert through which the fast-flowing waters of the creek passed under the embankment, and I made a quick rush for this, in the hope that I could make my way through to the other side. I knew that my footsteps would be heard by the three guards, but trusted to luck that they would think I was a union man on some errand. I did not dare to look back, and just as I was springing into the creek a bullet whizzed past my ear. This was the only shot fired.

The water came up to my arm-pits, and the force of the current was so great that I could hardly keep my feet, but I managed to get hold of a heavy cross-timber on the wall of the culvert, and so haul myself forward against the flood.

Once out of sight in the darkness of the tunnel, I braced myself between two upright timbers and prepared to fire back, if necessary, at the three men, who had now reached the bank of the creek. Their rifles were held ready for action, but from the way they staggered in their walk I could see that they were the worse for drink. I concluded, therefore, that I had not much to fear, and having no wish to reveal my hiding-place, I left them alone and recommenced my struggle against the current.

When I reached the farther end of the culvert I came to the conclusion that I must risk the bullets of both friends and foes by sprinting across the open space of about two hundred yards that lay between me and the mill.

I was only a few yards from the building when a guard hailed me:

'Drop that gun, or off goes your head!' he shouted.

Halting, I called out that I was a friend.

'Drop your gun,' the voice repeated, 'and walk up here with your hat off so that we can see who you are.'

I did as ordered, and was asked if I were Allison, the detective. I replied in the affirmative.

'Get in, then, before a bullet hits you in the back,' said the sentry, and a few moments later I was shaking hands with the guards.

Inside the mill I found Superintendent Monihan and a crowd of others congratulating Fred Carter, the cowboy, who had been the only man to escape from the Frisco Mill after the explosion. Amidst the hail of shots he had run for a quarter of a mile along the railway track to the Gem Mill, and later I saw the marks of the hundreds of bullets which had been fired at him. One had taken a knuckle off his right hand, and another had wounded him in the heel, but apart from this he was unhurt.

It was a mystery to him, he said, how the union men had blown up the mill. A previous attempt to destroy the place by sending an ore car containing a lot of giant powder down the tramway had miscarried; the fuse had been cut too short, and the powder had exploded some way from the mill.

It was at this point that I suggested to Mr. Monihan that he should lend me a few men to climb up the Gem tramway and tie some heavy poles across the track in order to derail a car should the strikers attempt to send a cargo of explosives down from the upper workings of the mine. He agreed, and while we were carrying out the job we saw many union men moving about in the trees above the mine. I duly reported this, whereupon Monihan put out extra guards.

About 10 A.M. a striker carrying a white flag came out to the Gem Mill. He bore a message to the effect that the union officials would allow Monihan half an hour to surrender, failing which the mill would be blown up. Monihan promptly refused, and the messenger returned to Gem.

Half an hour later, however, Edward Kinney, John A. Finch's private secretary, arrived under a flag of truce with an order from the Mine Owners' Association to Mr. Monihan to surrender, and so prevent the loss of the valuable mill. Monihan asked my advice about this, and I said that in my opinion surrender would be a mistake which might mean the death of himself and his men, but after thinking it over for a while he said he would have to obey the Association and take the consequences.

Thereupon I told him that I would leave him and fight it out alone; I felt sure the strikers would kill me if they once laid hands on me.

At this juncture a young man named Frank Stark, who had come to the district with Joe Warren's first batch of non-union men, asked if he might go with me, as he, too, was afraid of the strikers. I consented, and we both bade Mr. Monihan good-bye. Crawling away up the mountain-side, through the heavy timber, we secreted ourselves in a position from which we could see Monihan and his men surrender.

They all marched out, carrying their arms across the bridge to the railway track near the Gem Mining Company's office. Here they were confronted by more than a thousand union men, all yelling and cheering. Their guns were taken from them, and they were lined up in double rows facing the railway. From where we crouched we could see several strikers walking up and down the ranks peering intently into each man's face. It did not take much acumen to guess they were looking for *me!*

Leaving our hiding-place, Stark and I skirted the side of the mountain toward a low gap to the southward through which ran a footpath leading to the large mining camp of Mullen. On nearing the gap, we discovered three men with rifles blocking the trail, and I suggested to my companion that it would be better to fight these men and force a passage rather than struggle up the steep mountain-side through the brush and fallen timber.

'You're boss,' replied Stark, 'I'll follow your orders.' Thereupon I worked a little stratagem. We covered two of the unconscious men with our rifles, and then, in a loud voice, I said: 'You shoot the one on the right; I'll kill the fellow on the left!'

I had an idea this would startle them, and it most certainly did. All three jumped as if they had actually been shot, and next instant they were tearing away down the canyon for their lives, dropping their rifles, and even turning somersaults over fallen trees in their eagerness to get away. We were compelled to laugh as we watched their frantic progress — never were three men more thoroughly scared!

Leaving the well-beaten trail, we made a detour through the undergrowth toward the town of Wallace, and just before sundown, with Wallace in sight a couple of miles away down the mountain-side, we reached a small ranch house where we begged a meal, giving out that we were returning from a hunting trip. I was ravenous, having tasted nothing since Mrs. Shipley's sandwich and cup of coffee at daylight.

The old couple at the ranch gave us a good warm meal, and refused all payment. They asked us what was the meaning of the heavy explosion and the rifle-fire, but we professed ignorance of the matter.

It was nearly dark when we set out to continue our journey along the wagon road leading from the ranch, which presently crossed the creek and emerged into the main road connecting Wallace, Gem, and Burk. This road almost immediately made a sharp bend to the left between a high bluff on the right and the swift-flowing stream. At the bend stood four armed men, two on one side of the road, and two on the other.

I consulted with Stark as to what was to be done about it, and again we decided to fight, if necessary, rather than abandon the road. I told him to watch the two men on the left; I would look after the others. If any of them made a move to stop us or shoot, we were to drop to our knees and start firing.

We kept to the middle of the road, and passed them without a word. It was evident that they did not know what to make of us, and directly we had passed, my two men ran across to confer with the others. Next instant we were round the bend.

Here I realized at once that we were in a bad fix. The railway station was only a couple of hundred yards away, its electric lights making the roadway as bright as day — and I knew just how sharply our figures would stand out against those lights!

Without a word to Stark, I sprang suddenly into the creek, where the water reached my arm-pits. He followed me, and we waded across and hid in the undergrowth on the opposite bank. We were not a minute too soon, for hardly were we concealed before we saw the four men, their rifles held ready for action, come running around the bend. They stopped in amazement at not seeing us outlined against the light, for they knew that we could not possibly have reached the station in the time.

They talked together for a time; then three of them retraced their steps, evidently to go back to their post, while the fourth ran toward the town, looking in at the station as he went. Meanwhile Stark and I made our way to the rear of the Carter Hotel, which was a rendezvous for mine owners.

Knocking at the kitchen door, I asked the porter if any of the owners were inside, but he replied that all but Mr. A. L. Gross had left early that morning by special train for Spokane, Washington. Mr. Gross and Mr. Monihan had gone upstairs to bed. I asked him to go and tell them that Allison wished to speak to them at the back stairs.

Presently they arrived in their nightshirts, and in a great state of excitement, saying that they would be murdered if caught talking to me. I was still being searched for, they added, and they urged me to get out of the town at once if I wanted to save my life. There was evidently no safety in Wallace, so Stark and I struck the trail once more, heading south up Placer Creek.

We snatched a few hours of sleep, and about noon next day came across a miner's cabin. In front of it sat a man whom I recognized as a member of the Gem Union and a warm friend of mine while I had been recording secretary. At the time the strike was declared, he told me in confidence that he was not in favor of the union's action, and that he was going up to his mining claim on Placer Creek so as to keep out of trouble.

I felt that this old German could be trusted, so we approached him, and he gave us a hearty welcome, though he, too, said that he would be murdered if caught harboring a traitor to the union. Moreover, he expected his Irish partner back at any time — he had been absent for several days helping in the riots — so he advised us to hide in a rock cabin near by until he could cook us something to eat. He gave us the key of his cabin, and we duly locked ourselves in.

An hour later he arrived at our door and told us that his partner had arrived, and was now asleep. The old man was to wake him up at 4 P.M., as he wanted to go back to Wallace. At 5 P.M. my friend came back again and announced that the Irishman had returned to Wallace, so we emerged from our hiding-place and ate a fine meal.

Supper over, our host gave us a bag of food, and an old coffee-pot, with two cups, to take with us, and we struck out east toward the top of a high timbered mountain, where we pitched camp and erected a brush 'wickiup,' such as the Indians make, to shelter us from the drizzling rain that was now falling.

Early next morning we tramped to the top of another hill overlooking the town of Wallace, and from here we witnessed the union's great day of reckoning against all 'scabs' and others who had opposed them in their fight with the Mine Owners' Association.

First, John Monihan and his hundred and thirty 'scabs,' guards and miners, including all the Frisco Mine 'scabs' who were not in hospital, were put aboard a train for the Cœur d'Alene Lake, there to be deported to Spokane, Washington, with a warning never to set foot again in the Cœur d'Alene district at the peril of their lives. Before being put on the train they were taken to the Wallace bank and compelled to draw out all the money they had on deposit.

Next, squads of merchants and clerks were marched to the railway track, where they were told to 'hit the road' to the State of Washington, and shots were fired over their heads to improve their speed as they hurried away.

Stark and I spent another night in the 'wickiup,' and next day, when we returned to our look-out, we were delighted to witness the arrival of several train-loads of United States Regulars and State Militia. We learned later that these troops had actually started on the day the riots began, but that the union in Montana had blown up the bridges with dynamite so that the trains had been compelled to make a detour of several hundred miles.

However, they were here at last, and we watched more than a thousand soldiers march up to the Carter Hotel and erect their tents in the adjoining streets. The American flag was hoisted on the roof of the hotel, and Stark and I gave three cheers all on our own for the 'Star-Spangled Banner.' Then, feeling we were safe at last, we bade farewell to our 'wickiup' and started for the Carter Hotel.

On the way down the mountain we passed near the house of 'French Pete,' one of the union leaders, so I determined to do a little more detective work by calling on 'French Pete's' wife and passing myself off as a union man, Stark in the meantime lying down behind a log and covering me with his rifle.

'French Pete's' mother-in-law, Mrs. Hollihan, an Irishwoman, answered my knock, accompanied by Pete's ten-year-old son. I told the old lady that I was a union member from Gem, worn out from the long fight with the 'scabs,' and that

I wondered what was the best thing to be done now that the soldiers had arrived. I also expressed a fear that they would put the union officials in prison.

'Don't you worry about that,' she laughed. 'They'll never find them, for they happen to be hiding in the cellar of my house in town. I shall feed them until they get a chance to leave for Butte City, Montana, where they will have protection.'

Concealing my satisfaction at having got this valuable information so easily, I asked Mrs. Hollihan if she could furnish me with some late Spokane newspapers, as my partner and I would be glad to read the latest items about the strike. She went into the house and brought out the last two issues of the 'Daily Review,' and then she and the little boy accompanied me to Stark, to whom I read the sensational accounts of the blowing up of the Frisco Mill, and the killing of many guards and non-union miners; also the blowing up of the bridges to prevent the soldiers from coming to Wallace.

That morning's paper, too, gave an account of a raid made on John Monihan and his men at the Cœur d'Alene Lake, stating that many of the non-union men had been killed and robbed and their bodies thrown into the lake.

Stark and I pretended to be greatly elated at this 'good news,' and the old woman patted us on the back. We then bade her good-bye, saying that we were going up to Placer Creek to hide. What we actually did was to get out of sight and watch Mrs. Hollihan's movements. It was not long before she came out of the house and started off toward the town at a fast walk. We followed more leisurely, and were presently held up by a military picket and arrested as suspicious characters.

Shortly afterward we were taken before General Carlin, the officer in command, to whom I explained our identity.

'Why,' he said in astonishment, 'you must be that man Allison whom I sent a company out to rescue a short time ago!'

This was news to me, and I asked for an explanation.

'Well,' he replied, 'half an hour ago a man friendly to the mine-owners came over to tell me that a big crowd of armed union men had just gone up to Placer Creek to capture a detective by the name of Allison.'

I found out later what had happened. Mrs. Hollihan had told the union officials about meeting 'two worn-out union men,' and from her description of them my old enemy Dallas had recognized myself, and started out at once with a band of his desperadoes to look for me.

Runners were immediately dispatched to recall the troops and meanwhile I told the General what Mrs. Hollihan had said about the union leaders' hiding-place. A squad of men was sent to search her house, and succeeded in capturing O'Brien, president of the Central Union, and other 'wanted' officials. Through being absent, looking for me, Dallas escaped arrest. Later he made his way to Butte City, Montana, and was never brought to trial for his part in the riots.

That night Stark and I slept in the Carter Hotel, with the United States flag flying over our heads, and a thousand bayonets outside to insure our safety. It was the first peaceful night's rest I had had since resigning from the Gem Union.

The district was put under martial law, and I had several exciting experiences in helping to round up the principal authors of the trouble. Most of them were taken at last, and sentenced to varying terms of imprisonment. Among them was my old friend George A. Pettibone, who had been the prime mover in the blowing-up of the Frisco Mill, and who, it transpired, had been injured by the explosion.

After the failure to destroy the mill by means of the runaway car of dynamite, he had hit upon another ingenious scheme. From the mill engine-room a large iron 'penstock' extended a quarter of a mile up the mountain-side, connecting with a big board flume through which water was led to run the mill machinery. Pettibone and his men carried boxes of giant powder along this flume and threw them down the mouth of the open 'penstock' so that they lodged in the machinery. A lighted fuse was then sent after them.

All the other men climbed out of the flume, but Pettibone remained with his ear glued to the 'penstock,' waiting to hear the welcome sound of the explosion. When the crash came its force was so great that the ingenious conspirator was hurled into the tree-tops and badly injured.

With the arrival of the troops the trouble in the district gradually subsided, but not before several 'scabs' and other opponents of the union had been set upon and killed. One of these victims was Dr. Simms, who had been made United States Marshal, and who was shot through the head by an unknown assassin. Lurid threats continued to be made against me, but none of them were put into execution and in due course I was able to betake myself to more peaceful surroundings, my mission having been satisfactorily accomplished.

My work in the Cœur d'Alene had cost me three thousand dollars cash when my furnished-room building in Gem was burnt to the ground. It pained me to know that the hole sawed in the floor went up in smoke. It would have been a satisfaction could it have been bottled up and handed down to my grandchildren as a relic of the time their grandsire had crawled into a hole in time of danger!

CHAPTER XV

SAYLES AND I GO TO ALASKA — WHISKEY PEDDLING
FOR A PURPOSE — A VENTURE IN GOLD SMELTING —
A GOOD SHOT

About February, 1895, Superintendent McParland called me into his office and told me to get ready for a trip to Alaska. The Treadwell mill on Douglas Island had been robbed during the winter of ten thousand dollars' worth of gold. Operatives from the Portland office of the agency had failed to find the thieves, and although the loss of time made the task more difficult than it should have been, it was determined to make another attempt to solve the mystery. I was to start at once and W. O. Sayles was to follow me to Alaska a few weeks later.

In the early part of March I boarded the Topeka, at Tacoma, for Juneau, Alaska. The trip on smooth waters among whales and 'totem-poles' opened my eyes to a new world of which I had never dreamed. On arriving in Juneau, a swift little city built mostly on stilts, I at once wrote to Superintendent Duncan on Douglas Island, across the bay, of my arrival. At night in a secluded place I met Mr. Duncan and his assistant, Mr. Corbus.

It was agreed that I should apply for work in the big Treadwell gold mill, the largest in the world, in a regular way, and Mr. Corbus would make a place for me. No one but Mr. Duncan and Mr. Corbus were to know of my identity or my business. I secured a job as machine oiler. This work took me to all parts of the mill where I could make the acquaintance of all the employees. Part of the time I was on the day shift, then I changed to the night shift. In oiling the machinery, I had to climb around in ticklish places where a misstep or a false move would land me in the 'kingdom come.'

By the time Sayles arrived, three weeks after my arrival, I concluded that we had a clue and that Charlie Hubbard and Hiram Schell, two mill hands, who had quit work and bought a small schooner and sailed westward a month after the robbery, were the thieves. No one knew what had become of these men, as they didn't tell any one where they were going with their little schooner.

Sayles and I discussed matters in Juneau. We decided to buy a large canoe, one that would hold two cowboys (Sayles had been a cowboy in Montana) and twenty-five gallons of whiskey and go on the trail of Hubbard and Schell. We had both trailed horses, cattle, and men, but never a schooner on water.

It was agreed that Sayles keep his weather eye open for a good Indian canoe, while I returned to the mill to break my arm and recover from the injury. In order to keep down suspicion, it was necessary for me to have an excuse for quitting my job, therefore I concluded to break my arm that night, which I pretended to do by falling down the basement stairs.

Just before I drew my wages and quit the mill job, Sayles had found Hubbard and Schell and their schooner lying on the water-front among the other boats in Juneau. The news cured my sore shoulder quickly. On my arrival in Juneau we bought one of the large Indian canoes which Sayles had 'spotted.' It was forty feet long and painted with all the colors of the rainbow. Her bow and stern were built high above the water to ward off the heavy seas.

After our new ship was rigged up with a sail which could be taken down, mast and all, we loaded up with the necessaries of life, including twenty-five gallons of good Canadian rye whiskey. The main object in taking the whiskey along was to pass ourselves off as whiskey peddlers among the Indians, and as bait for Schell and Hubbard in case we found them. Before starting, we bought a fine chart of the Alaskan coast.

From Indians, who could talk and understand a little English, we heard of our little schooner and the two strange white men sailing westward. Thus we knew we were on the right trail.

From now on, we had some narrow escapes from being swamped. Once in a storm we got our canoe tangled up in about a hundred acres of seaweed, and couldn't get out for a long time. But at last, we made a landing on a small island and camped for the night.

After following the mainland and searching many channels and inlets, we crossed over a wide water to the east coast of Bishcoff Island, thence south nearly to Sitka, the capital, thence east across the big water to the west coast of Admiralty Island. This island is over a hundred miles wide, and I think from one hundred and fifty to two hundred miles long. After traveling about six hundred miles, counting the waste miles when we were lost and went backwards, we found the little schooner up in Chieke Bay, about twenty miles south of Killisnoo, a place where steamers plying between Juneau and Sitka stop. She was anchored in front of the Indian village of Chieke.

We found Schell and Hubbard taking life easy. Here they had a friend by the name of Hicks, a reconstructed Missourian, from his looks. He was married to 'Hias' Jennie, the richest Indian woman in the village, her wealth being in the form of blankets. She had tons of them.

Hicks had saved up some money and had recently gone into the stock business. He sent his money to a stock-dealer in Seattle, on one of the steamers, and wrote him to send a start of hogs, chickens, and cattle. They were finally unloaded at

Killisnoo, and Schell and Hubbard brought them from there to Chieke in their schooner.

The stock consisted of a razor-back barrow hog, one dozen Leghorn hens, no rooster, and a black muley cow which had a papoose shortly after her arrival. Many of these Indians had never seen or heard of cattle before, and they regarded old muley and her black papoose as evil spirits. Even 'Hias' Jennie wouldn't go near them or drink the milk, so muley and her calf were turned out on the tall grass to rustle for themselves. But while we were there, they were kept pretty busy fighting flies and mosquitoes.

We didn't tarry long in Chieke Village, but went on up to the head of Chieke Bay, three miles distant, to look for the 'Lost Rocker' gold mine, which tradition says is near a water-fall which falls over a cliff about two thousand feet high. In Killisnoo we had heard of such a waterfall being at the head of Chieke Bay, so this was our excuse for going there. We found the waterfall to be grand and near it we pitched our tent. Then we began prospecting for the gold that never was there. Here is where the bait we brought along proved a winner, for Charlie Hubbard liked the bait and put in most of his time in our camp.

Days ran into weeks, and while Sayles and I were out hunting for the 'Lost Rocker' mine, we would come back to camp and find Hubbard and a warm supper. Hubbard knew where the whiskey was cached out in the timber, therefore he helped himself during our absence. He had a small canoe of his own, and he could go and come to and from Chieke at his pleasure.

Sayles and I were always testing rock for gold. We were both posted on assaying, and we talked a good deal on that subject.

Finally, Hubbard asked us the best treatment for chlorination gold. We told him, and now we were satisfied that we were on the right trail, for the ten thousand dollars' worth of gold stolen from the Treadwell mill was chlorination gold taken from the bottom of a tank.

One evening Hubbard came from a visit to Schell in Chieke, where no doubt they had both talked matters over, and confessed that they had stolen ten thousand dollars' worth of gold from the Treadwell, and he offered us four hundred dollars to melt it into pure gold for them. Of course we had to swear secrecy. We explained that it would be necessary to expend some cash for material to build a furnace to treat the gold.

That same night after the sun went down about ten o'clock, Hubbard took me and a quart bottle of rye-juice to where they had the gold cached. It was across Chieke Bay from the Indian village, three miles, and about four miles from our camp. On arriving at the place, Hubbard dug up a frying-pan, the inside of which was coated with at least two hundred dollars' worth of gold. This was as far as he and Schell had got with their treatment. They succeeded in melting the stuff, but on trying to pour it into a mould to make a brick, it would cool and stick to the frying-pan. He also showed me their bellows, made of a cracker-box and a raincoat. They had used bark for the fire. He designated the place where the rest of the gold was cached, but wouldn't tell me the exact spot, nor did I press him to know.

For several days following, we three discussed the subject of melting the stolen gold. I had previously told Hubbard of scrapes which I had been in down in Texas and New Mexico, and how officers of the law had chased me out of that country. Therefore, he seemed to place confidence in me.

It was agreed that I go alone to Juneau and secure material to build a furnace, and the chemicals and crucibles for melting the gold. Leaving Sayles in camp with Hubbard, I started in a canoe with an Indian, whom I had hired to take me to Killisnoo, a distance of twenty miles. At Superintendent Duncan's residence on Douglas Island, I met Mr. Corbus and Duncan and told them of our plans.

After securing some clay to make a furnace, and material to melt the gold, I returned on the Topeka to Killisnoo. Before leaving, I arranged for Deputy United States Marshal Collins to be on board a United States man-of-war which was spending the summer at Killisnoo, on a certain day two weeks later, so that he could help us make the arrests, for fear the Indians might assist the prisoners.

When I returned to camp I found Sayles cooking supper and Hubbard sitting by the fire. I could see that something was wrong, but pretended not to notice it.

The camp-fire was outside and Sayles stepped into the tent to get something and while in there he wrote on a scrap of paper, 'It's all off. They are suspicious of us and say they won't dig up the gold.' This was slipped into my hand at the first opportunity. Later I read it in the tent, but I continued to look cheerful against my will. It took me several days and a lot of careful talking to restore their confidence.

When the furnace was completed, we figured it would require several days to dry, so as to be fit for use, and during this time I concluded to visit Killisnoo and buy a few luxuries.

On arrival there I consulted with Marshal Collins on board the man-of-war. I set a day when we would aim to have the first batch of gold melted. On that day it was agreed that Collins should be at the extreme head of Hood's Bay and camp on the south side in the open, so that we could find him. I then returned to camp and found the furnace and charcoal ready for business.

One night after dark, Hubbard brought in what he thought was about a fourth of the gold. It looked just like black mud and was very heavy. Next day we made experiments and

melted some of the stuff into fine gold nuggets. The day following, the furnace was kept going, and some nice nuggets
were turned out. Hubbard worked hard, as he was anxious
to get this batch finished so that he could get the nuggets
cached in a safe place. But Sayles and I had agreed that we
shouldn't quite finish the batch, so we worked with that end
in view, although we had not planned a mode of action. That
was left to my two-by-four brain, to act whenever I got a
'hunch' that the time was ripe. The main point was not to
let Hubbard re-cache this gold.

Towards sundown I had a fine supper cooking — clam
chowder and pies. I went out to see how the boys were getting
along. Hubbard was sweating like a 'Nigger' at election, in
his haste to finish the batch before supper time. While I was
out there we weighed the nuggets and made an estimate of the
value of the gold, including that just put into the crucibles to
melt. This would make nineteen hundred dollars' worth. Here
I went back to see that my clam chowder wasn't burning. I
knew how long it would take to melt the stuff now in the furnace, so I regulated the cooking accordingly.

Hubbard and I slept together on one side of the tent, while
Sayles slept on the other. Hubbard kept his rifle under the
head of our bed, buried out of sight in the grass which we
slept on. I secured this rifle and was looking for a safe place to
hide it. Near the camp there was a deep hole of water not less
than ten feet deep. All of a sudden I got a 'hunch' that this
would be a good place to hide it, so out the rifle went in the
pool, which was quite wide, and no doubt it is there yet, as we
never looked for it. Then I cached my Winchester rifle, so I
could get it without Hubbard seeing me.

Now supper was ready, and I began to call the boys. Ten
minutes passed and they didn't come. I called with an oath
attached, to let them know I was getting angry. After another

minute's wait I ran out to where they were at work. They had just emptied the crucibles and Hubbard was insisting that they fill them up with the last 'mud' on hand, as he would rather finish than go to supper. As he had agreed to stay and keep the furnace hot, Sayles had to give in, as he had no excuse. So I found them preparing to put the last 'mud' in the crucibles. I began swearing and said my nice supper was getting cold. I finally grabbed the crucibles and 'mud' and cached it behind a log near by. I then picked up the can containing the nuggets and started out in the brush to cache them. Hubbard followed me and helped dig a hole in the moss by the side of a log, where the can was deposited. This was quite a distance from the furnace, so that Sayles couldn't see us.

My supper didn't agree with me, for I began to have cramps in my stomach an hour afterwards; this, of course, being a blind. I went to bed the same time Hubbard and Sayles did, but I couldn't sleep. After one or two false starts, I got away. With my Winchester on my shoulder I slipped through the brush to where the gold was cached. Securing the nuggets and the balance of the 'mud,' I struck out for the northeast through the timber. Half a mile from camp I re-cached the gold, then continued up an open glade covered with skunk-cabbage, on which the hundreds of bears feed. From the head of this glade over to Hood's Bay was an unexplored territory to me.

By this time it was quite dark. I could see the bears running into the timber at the head of the glade, just where I had to go. This made me feel a little ticklish, as I had heard it said that Alaska bears were dangerous when they had young ones, or if surprised by a person coming on to them suddenly.

From the head of the glade I found it hard navigating, owing to the fallen timber and 'devil-clubs' — a tough briar bush with thorns like an eagle claw, which is poison to the flesh. I had to follow the bear trails. Often I had to crawl on my hands and knees for a hundred feet or more, under fallen timber. During all this time I would whistle or sing to scare the bears out of my path. Judging from the sound of the brush cracking ahead and up the sides of the mountains, there were a great many of them.

On top of the mountain range I came to a lake. There were no bear trails around it, and to go through the brush was too slow and tiresome, so I waded around the edge of the timber in the lake, up to my waist in water. Reaching the opposite side of the lake I found myself going down a creek, and by keeping in the middle of it half-knee deep in water, I could make pretty good time. In going down this creek I couldn't resist the temptation of firing my pistol twice, once to kill a large dog salmon, and the other, at a large bald eagle. I cut the eagle's claws off as relics. I had fired offhand at the monster bird sitting in the top of a large pine tree, a distance of about two hundred yards. This was the last crack shot I ever made with that gun, which is now owned by my dear friend, Earl L. Baum, M.D., of Milwaukee.

It was after daylight when I woke up Marshal Collins in his tent. While he was dressing I made some coffee. Before starting, he gave orders to the two Indians to take his camp outfit back to Killisnoo.

We returned the way I had come.

On reaching the top of a high hill overlooking our camp, we saw Sayles and Hubbard getting breakfast. We slipped down through the brush and reached the tent on the opposite side from the camp-fire. Stepping around the tent, we advanced toward Hubbard. Collins pointed his pistol at him and demanded that he throw up his hands, as he was a prisoner.

I was standing with the butt of my rifle resting on the

ground. Hubbard paid no attention to Collins's demand, but, straightening himself up to his full height, with both thumbs under his suspenders, he walked up to me and looking me square in the face said: 'Davis, how in h—l can you ever face the public again after the way you have treated me?' I told him that my conscience wouldn't bother me on that score.

This ended our work. The company got back its ten thousand dollars' worth of black 'mud,' as it had all been found and dug up where Schell and Hubbard had cached it. The gold-plated frying-pan was also taken along, as it was worth a few hundred dollars, there being that much gold sticking to it.

When the United States Court convened late in the fall, Hubbard and Schell were sent to the penitentiary. Hubbard received a sentence of only one year in the Sitka Pen. Schell received a longer sentence, so I heard.

During his stay in the Sitka Pen, Hubbard used to correspond with Sayles and me regularly. The last letter received was after his sentence had expired, and while he was preparing to start for the Dawson City gold diggings to make his fortune. We only hope that he has become rich, for the world is full of worse men than Charlie Hubbard.

After receiving the blessings of Mr. Duncan and Mr. Corbus for getting back their black 'mud,' Sayles and I boarded the steamer Queen for Sitka, so as to take in the capital of Alaska before returning to civilization.

On the return trip from Sitka, we visited the great Muir Glacier, one of the wonders of the frozen North.

At the Muir Glacier I did a little stunt which should forever brand me as a fool. The tourists on the Queen had climbed the hill and mounted the glacier. Most of the people had rented sticks with spikes in the end to keep from slipping on the ice, but I didn't, as I regarded them a foolish fad to make one look like a 'globe-trotter.'

We finally came to a natural ice bridge across a chasm hundreds of feet deep and about thirty feet wide. The bridge was only two or three feet wide with a slippery surface. A nice-looking young woman bantered some of the men to show their courage by crossing this bridge. No one responded. Then she gathered up her skirts with the independent air of a Boston schoolmarm, and went across. On the opposite side she laughed, and dared one of us men to come across. Instead of complying with the dare, most of them got farther back as though the mere thought of crossing the chasm gave them the shivers. I told Sayles that if some one didn't go I should, as women are not built for holding as much courage as men, and for that reason I couldn't stand to see the whole male population of the world disgraced by one little woman.

Finally I plucked up courage and started, but before getting halfway over I wished to be back on the starting side. If my hair didn't stand up on end, it surely felt like it. I dare not shut my eyes, and with them open I could see too far below, where there seemed to be no bottom.

On reaching the lady's side, she gave me the 'glad hand,' which helped some, but it didn't relieve the strain on my mind as to how I should get back, for I was on an icy island with chasms all around. I followed the lady back, but it required every ounce of courage in me to make the start. Hereafter when a foolish girl wants to test the courage of men, she won't get me for a tool, no matter if she is a good-looker!

I enjoyed the trip from Alaska immensely, for it gave me my first chance to study nobility at close range. We had on board a Duke from Italy and a Prince from Germany. The Prince's name was Bismarck, he being a nephew of the 'Heap Big Chief' Bismarck, ruler of the German Empire. The Italian Duke was a nice sociable gentleman with sense enough not to be a Duke, if it wasn't for the money there was in it.

But the other rooster, his Royal Princeship — he didn't have a thimbleful of brains. He wouldn't speak to any one on the boat but the Captain, and he wouldn't stoop so low as to eat with the common herd. He got up on his high horse once because I called him 'partner.' He asked the Captain what that 'bloody American' meant by calling him 'partner.' He had taken the wrong route to see an Indian village, when I called and said: 'Partner, you are on the wrong road.' His Royal 'Ighness was on a trip around the world.

On arriving in Denver, Superintendent McParland gave Sayles and me the 'glad hand' for our work in Alaska, and the operation was closed after an absence of six months.

CHAPTER XVI

THE SENTIMENTAL HOBO — DODGING THE SIBERIAN
BLOODHOUND — INTO JAIL AND OUT — WARNED
OF DANGER BY A DANCE-HALL GIRL — THE
GOVERNOR'S BODYGUARD

NEXT I was sent to Minas Prietas and Guaymas in the State
of Sonora, Mexico, to run down twenty thousand dollars in
gold. It was recovered and my work ended. In the seaport
city of Guaymas, a forty-five-calibre pistol bullet scorched the
skin on my forehead, which convinced me that a 'miss is as
good as a mile.'

On returning to the United States, I worked on a big mining
case for United States Senator William A. Clark, in Jerome,
Prescott, and Tucson, Arizona. My work was a success after
I had consumed a lot of kill-me-quick whiskey with old
'Hasiampa' sinners.

In the fall of 1897, I was sent to British Columbia to run
down a young man. I had nothing to work on but his photograph and the fact that he had skipped out for British Columbia after having robbed his employers in Milwaukee of
several thousand dollars. I found my man at the head of a big
mining company in Greenwood City, on the head of Kettle
River, in the new Boundary Creek mining district. He was
going under an assumed name, and to save his reputation and
his chances of becoming a millionaire, he dug up the amount
of the stolen money through his father who was a banker in
Illinois.

One of my next operations was for some money brokers of
the East who had loaned a cattleman, whom I will call Bill

Bronson, a large sum of money to buy a herd of cattle. At three o'clock Christmas morning, a Denver & Fort Worth train dumped me off at Amarillo, Texas, the town built at Amarillo Lake on the Staked Plains, where, in the early winter of 1877, I had seen about a million buffaloes.

Knowing that my old cowboy pal, Jack Ryan, owned a saloon in this town, I steered for his place. I found Ryan behind the bar and about a dozen men stretched out on chairs and asleep on the floor. After shaking hands with Jack, he asked me if I could pick out any of my friends among the sleepers. Glancing over the bunch, I recognized Burkley Howe asleep on a chair. Slapping him on the shoulder, I said: 'Hello, Burkley, old boy!' Before opening his eyes he yelled: 'Well, I'll be d——d, if that ain't Charlie Siringo!' He had recognized my voice.

Jumping to his feet, Howe began hugging me and declaring to the others, who had awakened, that I used to be the best wild-horse rider in the whole United States. In order to choke him off, I called the crowd up to the bar to take a Christmas drink on me.

When Burkley Howe came to the L X ranch in 1878 to learn the cattle business, he was a fine-looking young man of wealthy parents in Massachusetts. Mr. Beals had brought him from the East and turned him over to me to be taught the cattle business. At that time I had charge of four herds of L X steers grazing on the Staked Plains. Now, after the lapse of about twenty years, here is that same Burkley Howe, a total wreck and aged beyond his years. He died soon after, which shows the power of John Barleycorn over robust manhood.

Jack Ryan told me that my old cowboy friend, John Hollicott, now the manager of the large L X ranch, with its fifty thousand cattle and thousands of horses, was at a saloon across the street. I found him dancing a jig and having a rattling good time, as he expressed it. I joined him in the celebration.

After daylight, Hollicott had his coachman bring up the carriage and span of mules for our twenty-mile drive north to the L X ranch. He had insisted that I eat Christmas dinner with him on the ranch. We arrived at the ranch about ten o'clock. I was introduced to Garnett Lee and his family, two of them being pretty young women. Several of the L X cowboys were there to eat Christmas dinner. Two of them, Charlie Sprague and Johnny Bell, had worked under me when I was a boss on this range.

About two P.M. the fat turkey gobbler and 'fixings' were set on the same old table from which outlaw Billy the Kid and I ate meals together twenty years before. It was a dinner fit for a king and queen, and we all did justice to it. When we got through, Mr. Turkey Gobbler looked as if he had been to a bone-picking match.

The afternoon was spent harking back, and the evening in dancing.

After breakfast next morning, I asked Hollicott to take me back to Amarillo, as I had to buy a horse and saddle for my ride into the Indian Territory. He insisted on my lying over until the next day, when a horse and saddle would be presented to me for my trip.

The following morning, we went to the headquarters ranch in the carriage. Tied to the hitching-rack stood a five-year-old bronco, sixteen hands high and every inch a model piece of horseflesh. On his back was Johnny Bell's saddle. This horse had lately been broken, he having run on the range all his life. I had known his sire and his grandsire on his dam's side, and they were of the best blood. The sire was Glen Alpine, a four-mile running horse.

On mounting Glen Alpine, Jr., after bidding everybody, including the two pretty Lee girls, good-bye, Hollicott told me never to sell this horse, but to shoot him when I had no further use for his horseship. I promised that he should never be sold.

Some of the boys rode with me a few miles and told how Hollicott and the Lee family were disappointed at my horse not bucking, as they had expected a free show with me as the star actor. They said Glen Alpine, Jr., was a vicious bucker, and they couldn't account for his not bucking that morning. But he made up for it next morning and on dozens of occasions afterwards.

A couple of months' work in the Indian Territory and parts of Texas solved the mystery of how Bill Bronson had beaten the money brokers out of their money. He and another man had each bought a herd of long-horn steers near Uvalde, Texas, west of San Antonio. The ranch brands on the steers were the same. The other man, whom I will call Daniels, paid cash for his, while Bronson had the Kansas City money brokers pay for his.

To tell them apart, as both herds were to be fattened on adjoining ranges in the Wichita Mountains of the Indian Territory, the tips of both horns on Daniels, steers were sawed off, and the tip of only one horn on the Bronson steers. This was to answer in lieu of road-brands. During the summer the cowboys were kept busy cutting the tips from the horns of the Bronson steers. Thus they became the property of Daniels. In the fall when fat, they were all shipped east by Daniels, who divided the money received for them with Bronson. When the money brokers found they had no steers on which to foreclose their mortgage, they employed me to unravel the puzzle, with the above result.

In winding up the operation, I trailed one of the Bronson cowboys, whom I will call Cunny, to San Pedro, New Mexico. From him I secured a confession of how his employer had beaten the Kansas City money brokers. This corroborated information I had secured from others, among them being cowboys who had helped cut the steer horns in Southwest Texas, to which point I had gone on trains.

When on the trail of Cunny, I crossed the Pecos River at the Lewis ranch, between Roswell and Fort Sumner, New Mexico. I got an early start, as I had a ninety-mile ride to make across a desert to the Capitan Mountains, without water. There were no roads or trails to follow, but I could see the Capitan Mountains off in the distance to the southwest. About dusk, after the sun had set, I dismounted to tighten my saddle for the thirty-mile night ride to water. First I tightened the front cinch, but when I pulled up on the hind one, Glen went to bucking. I held on for dear life to the bridle reins. He took me round and round with him. Finally, I had to turn loose, and he ran back the way we had come at a clip which did credit to his sire. He was soon lost to view. There I stood in the twilight cussing myself for not drinking the last cup of water in the canteen, which hung on my saddle, when I had the opportunity.

I could still see the tracks of Glen, and I started out in a dog-trot — all same an Indian following a wounded deer to get his supper. After going a mile I could no longer see the tracks. Then I stopped to consider whether to turn around and walk the thirty miles to the Capitan Mountains, the outlines of which showed on the horizon. It would have meant a sixty-mile walk to the first water on the Pecos River.

Seeing a dark object which looked like a bunch of bushes off to the eastward, a faint hope sprang up in my breast that it might be Glen. It proved to be the horse, but when I drew near, he snorted and ran out of sight again. I trotted in the direction he had gone. Soon the dark object was in sight. I walked around it, knowing it was Glen. I kept whistling and singing until I was on the east side. He began to snort, then I sat down and whistled. My tongue was so badly swollen, I could hardly whistle.

When finally I got hold of the bridle reins I was happy. The rifle and canteen were still hanging to the saddle. The water was gone — out of sight, just as soon as I could get the canteen to my parched lips. At daylight, Glen and I were drinking water out of a reservoir on the wagon road between Roswell and White Oaks.

An all-day ride brought me to White Oaks. Here I lay over next day to rest and to shake hands with old friends. This former rich gold camp had been my stamping ground in '80 and '81, when I was chasing Billy the Kid with my Panhandle warriors.

Glen Alpine, Jr., lived a retired, easy life on my Sunny Slope ranch at Santa Fé, New Mexico. He died at the age of fifteen, though he never quit the habit of bucking, even in his old age.

Now I was employed by the Anglo-Continental Mining Company of London, England, to get at the bottom of the salting of the Jersey Lily Mine near Prescott, Arizona. Their German expert had reported the values to be eight dollars in gold to the ton of rock. On the strength of this, the company had bought the mine at a high price. But when they became the owners, the best gold value that could be squeezed from the rock was one dollar to the ton of ore.

After landing in Prescott, Arizona, I selected a man named Alex as a good subject for me to work on. In partnership, we bonded a claim on Groom Creek and sunk a shaft, in hopes of finding pay rock. About six months later Alex and I went on a pleasure trip to Southern California. In Los Angeles, after we had seen all the sights, Alex was arrested by a United States Commissioner, and had to face Lawyer Bryant, who represented the Anglo-Continental Mining Company. The result was Alex made a full, sworn confession of how he and the owner of Jersey Lily Mine had fooled the old German expert by salting his samples of ore.

My next big operation was for the same Anglo-Continental Mining Company, whose German expert had been fooled again when they bought the Butterfly gold mine from a saloon man of Silverton, Colorado. After the company had built a twenty-thousand-dollar mill to treat the ore, they found they had no mine.

By making trips out in the mountains with the saloon man, I secured a confession of how the Butterfly mine had been salted. This resulted in the Anglo-Continental Mining Company washing their hands of the whole American continent — so Mr. James McParland told me.

Now for a hobo operation over the whole Oregon Short Line Railroad in the States of Utah, Oregon, and Montana, for the Union Pacific Railroad Company, who wished to learn the way their branch system was being worked by their employees.

While on this operation I experienced how a hobo feels when he falls in love. A bunch of us bums had beaten our way to Salt Lake City, to take in the great Mormon Jubilee, the fiftieth anniversary of the settling of Utah. We made our headquarters under a water tank in the railroad yards. When the big street parade started, I was standing on the outer edge of the sidewalk, in the hot sun. Directly in front of me stood a small woman holding her silk umbrella over her head. I finally became impatient, and, tapping her on the shoulder, asked if she wouldn't let me hold her umbrella high above her head, so that I could see the parade.

When this pretty young woman turned her face towards me to size me up is when little Cupid shot my system full of his darts.

While holding the umbrella, which shielded both of us from the hot sun, the girl became talkative and explained all the interesting sights. One of them was a sailing vessel on wheels. It represented the Brookline, which brought Mormon emigrants from England. She pointed out her aunt, Mrs. Watson, sitting on the deck. I concluded that my fair companion might be named Watson. I was going to ask her name so that I could dress up and call on her. Just then one of my 'Weary Willie' chums tapped me on the back, saying: 'Say, cully, drop dat rag [meaning the umbrella] and come wid me. I'll steer youse to a joint where dey sell two whoppin' big schooners of beer for a nickel.'

Turning around and seeing my unwashed and ragged chum, the lady reached for her 'rag' and at the same time gave me a look with her pretty dark eyes that froze poor little Cupid to a standstill.

The Denver law firm of Thomas, Bryant, and Lee had a client in California who had bought a gold mine in Mexico, from a Californian whom I will call George Hamlin. When it was found that the mine had been salted the case was put into the hands of the Pinkerton agency in San Francisco, which had recently been established.

Operatives had been sent into Siskiyou County to locate Hamlin through his father and mother and other relatives. This they had failed to do. It was then that I was sent to San Francisco to learn the facts in the case. The Superintendent informed me that it was useless to work on the relatives of Hamlin, as that had been tried by some of his best detectives. He advised me to run down a prospector in the Fort Steel country of British Columbia, who had the same name as the man wanted.

In Nelson, British Columbia, I boarded a steamer for the head of the Kootenai Lake, where a new railroad had started to build to Fort Steel. On a construction train I rode to the end of the line. There I hired an open cutter and a team of horses to drive over the deep snow to Fort Steel, a distance of twenty-eight miles.

I started east one morning when a blizzard was blowing from the north and the thermometer registered forty degrees below zero. It was early in December; the wind kept whistling a tune through my whiskers which sounded like: 'Say, old boy, why didn't you save your summer's wages and buy an overcoat?' I had on only a light leather frock coat. This pure and innocent newborn blizzard from the frozen North would never have asked the question had it known of the many inducements for spending a summer's wages in Salt Lake City. It may have frolicked behind the curtains in an Eskimo Indian village, but that isn't sporting by gaslight in the Mormon capital.

After running down the prospector, Hamlin, and, finding he was not the man wanted, I decided to start right by working on the relatives of the mine salter in order to learn his whereabouts. Toward Christmas a train dumped me off in the sleepy village of Gazelle, in Siskiyou County, California, near the foot of Mount Shasta. For a couple of days I roasted my shins at the open fireplace in the rotunda of the Edson brothers' ranch house, which was used as a hotel.

First I drove out to the home of Hamlin's old father and mother and formed their acquaintance. Finally, I put spurs to my two-by-four brain and started out to work on the sister of Hamlin's wife.

A short ride on a train brought me to the town of Montague. Two miles from that town lived Hamlin's sister-in-law. Her husband, whom I will call Hughes, owned a valuable ranch stocked with fine blooded cattle. I decided to walk out to the Hughes ranch after dark, for if I rode out there would be no excuse for staying all night.

The night was dark, and it was eight-thirty when I stood at the front gate of the large white house. The only light in the building was coming through curtained windows in the rear. Just as I turned the corner of the house and was within a few feet of a rear door, a Siberian bloodhound loomed up like a mustang in a fog. She was as large as a good-sized colt. She had sprung out of a dog house in the farther corner of the back yard. I did a double stunt with lightning rapidity — sprang for the door, turning the knob with my left hand and pulling old Colt's 45 with the right. The door was slammed in the dog's face just in the nick of time to prevent a tragedy. She had thrown her weight against the door, and it was all I could do to close it. She was growling and raving.

As soon as the catch snapped in the door, my pistol was back in its place in my hip pocket, out of sight, and I faced the big fat man and his small young wife. Both were on their feet and thunderstruck. I begged their pardon for intruding so suddenly. The lady replied that it was lucky I did, as the 'doggy' would have eaten me up alive, as she had pups and was more vicious than usual.

After introducing myself as Charles Le Roy, and telling how I had made a little fortune mining up in British Columbia, I told how I had heard in Montague that their ranch was for sale. My brother and I wanted to settle down in California and raise fine stock.

Hughes replied that he would sell, but his price would be way up into the thousands of dollars. I told him that a few thousands of dollars, more or less, would not affect a sale if the place suited me. I was invited to stay all night and look the ranch over next day.

By 10 P.M. the fat man was dozing in a rocker after reading

a newspaper, while the little lady and I were going over the family album which I had picked up from the center table, in this rear lounging room adjoining the kitchen.

When we came to the photographs of herself and her married sister, along with a pretty single sister, taken in a group a couple of years previous, I got from Mrs. Hughes facts that I wanted. After finding out that George Hamlin and his wife, and her single sister, lived on the Alberni Canal, west of Victoria, British Columbia, my work was done for the night.

It was past eleven o'clock when the fat man showed me to my room upstairs. I was soon stretched out between white sheets dreaming of my coming trip to Vancouver Island, British Columbia.

This proved the finish of Hamlin's career. I found him operating a small mine, with several miners employed, twenty miles south of the Alberni Indian Village, on the west coast of Vancouver Island. The family lived near the mine, which was a rough mountain canyon four miles from the Alberni Canal. I became their guest, as a supposed wealthy mining man from New Mexico hunting good investments.

When valuable property owned by Hamlin in California could be attached and tied up in the courts, the arrest was to be made by our San Francisco branch agency, they sending an operative to Victoria, the capital of British Columbia, to keep track of the man until the arrest could be made. I learned later that he was sent to the penitentiary for ten years and died soon after his prison term had expired.

I then returned to Denver, Colorado, to be sent in haste to the Cripple Creek mining district, to relieve operative Billy Sommers who had been working two months trying to get a clue as to what had become of the two thousand dollars' worth of rich gold ore stolen from the R. P. Russell lease on Bull Hill. A noted safe-blower and ore thief, George Shaul, was suspected. But Sommers couldn't even get a chance to speak to Shaul, as he was too foxy to make new acquaintances.

Five days after I had landed in the Cripple Creek district, I had a full confession from George Shaul as to how he and Kid Wilson had stolen Mr. R. P. Russell's gold ore. In order to get this confession, I had to get drunk with George Shaul and Wilson. We shot up the town of Victor at three o'clock one morning. Shaul and Wilson made their getaway, while my room was raided by the mayor, millionaire Jimmie Doyle, and his squad of policemen. I was thrown into jail. The proprietor of the Redlight Dance Hall went on my bond for three hundred dollars. Then we explained matters to the police judge who tried my case and I was liberated.

We were now ready to arrest Shaul and Wilson, but 'Win' Boynton, sheriff of El Paso County, got permission from my superintendent to let me work up a murder case for him while I was in solid with Shaul and his tough gang. Unknown parties had recently held up a saloon in Goldfield, murdering one man and wounding another.

Two more weeks of carousing and drinking in the dance-halls of Victor and Cripple Creek solved the Goldfield murder mystery. A chum of George Shaul's, by the name of 'Baldy' Bob Pelton, had committed the crime.

Just before I was ready to spring the trap and make the arrests, a blackmailing detective, who knew me as a Pinkerton man, 'tipped me off' to the gang, who laid a trap to murder me and throw my body into an old abandoned shaft. A few hours before this stunt was to be pulled off, after midnight, a tough dance-hall girl, Nelly Taylor, in Cripple Creek, saved my bacon by warning me, as she couldn't believe me degraded enough to be a detective.

The arrests were made, and with me as the star witness in the district court in Colorado Springs, Pelton received a life sentence for the Goldfield murder. George Shaul and Wilson were sentenced to the penitentiary for a term of six years for stealing the Russell gold ore.

This was one of the quickest operations I ever performed, with the exception of the day's work I did as a bronco buster near Longmont, Colorado.

After several brief operations in Arizona, I reached Denver just in time to see the State legislature seat James H. Peabody in the Governor's chair for a second term in spite of the protests that the Democratic candidate, Alva Adams, had been elected. I was made bodyguard for the Governor to see that the Western Federation of dynamiters didn't blow him off the face of the earth. Still, it was only an accident that saved us both from being blown up by a dynamite bomb, manufactured by George A. Pettibone and Harry Orchard.

One morning, Governor Peabody and I started from his residence on Capitol Hill to walk to the Capitol building, as was our habit. The bomb had been planted in a pile of old snow at the foot of a telephone pole, on the corner of a street where we always turned west, close up to this telephone pole. As we made the turn, Harry Orchard took hold of the small wire attached to the bomb to pull on it. Just then a heavily loaded coal wagon emerged from the alley and buried the wire in the soft earth, thus saving our lives. This came out in Orchard's confession at his trial in Boisé, Idaho, later.

CHAPTER XVII

TWENTY-FIVE THOUSAND MILES ON THE TRAIL OF THE KID CURRY 'BUNCH'

DURING the early summer of 1899, I was detailed with my friend W. O. Sayles, who had just returned from South Africa, to go on the trail of train robbers for the Union Pacific Railroad Company. One of their passenger trains had been held up at Wilcox, Wyoming, and a large amount of unsigned money stolen, and in a fight which followed, Sheriff Hazen was killed by the robbers. From the best information obtainable, the Hole-in-the-Wall gang had committed the robbery.

In Denver, Sayles and I bought a 30-40 smokeless-powder Winchester rifle each, also blankets and camp outfit. Superintendent John S. Kaiser instructed us to go to Salt Lake City, Utah, and there buy horses and saddles and ride into Brown's Park, Colorado, just over the line of Utah. In Wyoming some of the robbers had been seen driving a bunch of horses south, headed for Brown's Park. These were the particular men we were going after, but any one who looked suspicious of ever having robbed a train, was to be 'spotted.'

A five-hundred-mile ride over the continental range of mountains on the Denver and Rio Grande Railway brought us to the Mormon capital. The first thing we did was to hunt up our friend 'Doc' Shores, special agent of the Rio Grande Western Railway, and tell him of our proposed man hunt, for he was in a position to help us. Sayles and I then bought a good saddle horse apiece, and a pack animal, also saddles, grub, etc., and a good supply of rifle and pistol cartridges.

Just as we were ready to start, Shores received a letter

from one of his men in Hanksville, Utah, stating that two men supposed to be the Union Pacific train robbers had just passed there going south; that they were driving thirteen head of good horses. Shores let us read the letter and we felt confident these were the men we were after, as they had the same number of horses as seen in Wyoming.

We arranged with Shores to furnish us a stock-car on the narrow-gauge Denver & Rio Grande Railway so that we could ship our horses and outfit to Marysvale, Utah, and from there we could make a fast ride and reach Dandy Crossing on the Colorado River about the same time as the robbers. Shores's man had stated that they were headed for the Dandy Crossing ferry. We telegraphed in cipher the contents of the letter and our intentions to Superintendent Kaiser, and asked for his advice. Soon we got an answer to follow our first instructions, which meant to 'hit the trail' for Brown's Park.

We selected our route through Emigration Canyon to Park City, a large mining camp, thence to Heber and east over the range of mountains to the head of Strawberry Creek on the Duchesne Indian Reservation and down that stream to the Duchesne River. On Strawberry Creek we had good fishing, although Sayles didn't enjoy the sport on account of the mosquitoes.

On arriving at Fort Duchesne, a United States military post on the Indian Reservation, after a five days' hard ride, we found a telegram from Superintendent Kaiser in Denver, stating that the two men and thirteen loose horses seen in Hanksville were undoubtedly the train robbers that we were after, and for us to give up the Brown's Park trip and turn south on trail of these men.

It was evident that some one had made a blunder by not letting us ship our stock to Marysvale and thereby reach Dandy Crossing the same time as the robbers, if not before.

We might have been saved a tiresome five-hundred-mile horseback ride. We were not mad, but the cuss-words hurled over toward Denver left a sulphuric taste in our mouths for a week.

From Fort Duchesne we headed south for Price, Utah, on the Rio Grande Western Railway. On the way to Price I learned from a rancher that my Wyoming friend Tom Hall, who had so kindly prevented a rope being placed about my neck, and who made the crutches for me to walk with, now lived in Price and ran a saloon there, although he was now going by his right name, Tom Nichols, the old charge in Texas having been canceled.

A ride of three days brought us to Price early one afternoon. My first desire was to get a good look at Tom Hall, to see if he had changed from of old. I didn't dare enter his saloon for fear of being recognized by him, in which case my work might be spoiled by our identity being made public. Furthermore, I didn't know but that our meeting might end in a fight, for the chances were a bitter feeling against me existed on his part, and in that case he wouldn't hesitate to use his gun.

When directly opposite the Nichols saloon, Tom walked out in his shirt-sleeves and seated himself in a chair facing me. He was the same Tom, tall and good-looking, but a little older and fleshier.

The next morning Sayles and I pulled out for the south in a driving rainstorm, which had been falling since midnight. About five miles out we came to a raging creek which couldn't be crossed without danger to ourselves and our horses. Therefore we started back to Price only to find ourselves cut off from that place by another swift creek which had risen over its banks in the past half-hour. There was nothing for us to do but wait in the rain for this creek to go down. This it did toward night.

On arriving back in Price, we put up at the same hotel where we had stopped the night before, and while in our room upstairs, a knock came at the door, which was opened and the visitor invited to enter. He introduced himself as the editor of the local paper, and explained to us that we were virtually under arrest as Union Pacific train robbers; that he had been sent up by the sheriff of the county to advise us to surrender peacefully. Of course we laughed and told him that we were prospectors on the way to the Henry Mountains south of Hanksville. The editor then told us that the sheriff and a posse with Winchester rifles had the hotel surrounded, and to verify his assertion we were told to look out of the window. This we did, and saw men with rifles.

We gave a history of how we had outfitted in Salt Lake for a prospecting trip and that we had pick and shovel, gold pan and other prospecting tools in our pack. He said there was no doubt in his mind but that we were all right, and he would so report to the sheriff. Thus the matter ended, and the 'dogs of war' were called off.

The next morning when we were ready to make another start, a photographer took our pictures.

For the next three or four days we had a wet ride, swimming creeks and traveling in sticky mud up to our horses' knees at times. We went through several Mormon towns to Emery, thence over a desert to Dirty Devil Creek, and up that stream to Hanksville, where the two supposed train robbers had been seen.

In Hanksville we made the acquaintance of Charlie Gibbons, who ran the only hotel and store in the place. In a general talk with him and his brother and other men, we found out that two suspicious characters with thirteen head of horses had crossed the Colorado River at Dandy Crossing about ten days previous, and that nearly a week later, a third man with

MR. KIPLING'S SALOON IN PECOS, TEXAS, IN 1880 OR 1881

The proprietor with white apron is taking orders for drinks. The man next to him, sitting at a gambling-table, is Jim Miller, who had recently killed the sheriff of the county and then killed all the witnesses

five head of horses crossed. Charlie Gibbons's brother helped this last man swim his horses across the river, and from the description given us he was evidently the notorious Kid Curry.

After Sayles and I crossed the river, we trailed this man up White's Canyon. We found where he took his horses up a rocky bluff several hundred feet high, which looked to be an impossible feat. By this time it was late in the evening so that one of us had to return to Dandy Crossing after some grain for our horses. It was agreed that Sayles should go back and that I should follow the trail till dark. It was all I could do to get my horse up the steep bluff.

On top of the mesa the country was level. I followed the trail to a wide rocky arroyo where all traces of the horses' tracks were lost. They had evidently gone down this rocky canyon. I searched the canyon for two miles down and then gave up the chase to get back to camp before it became too dark to see my way down that steep bluff.

A year later I found out, through Mr. John Duckett, of Bluff City, Utah, that I was within a half-mile of this lone outlaw's camp when I turned back. Duckett was working a mining prospect across White's Canyon and could see every move made. Duckett said the fellow camped there two weeks. They were only a couple of miles apart, but couldn't visit each other without traveling ten to twenty miles, owing to bluffs and canyons. So, the chances are I came very near running into my game. In that case there would have been 'something doing.' And it is possible that this outlaw saw me trailing him. In that event he would have had the best of the fight.

All is well that ends well.

Owing to the fact of my losing the trail of the lone outlaw on the rock-bottom bed of the canyon, Sayles and I concluded to follow the tracks of the two men and their thirteen head of loose horses. The tracks still showed plainly in the valley of White's Canyon, as there was no travel to speak of in that country.

To recite our ups and downs in finding water and keeping the dim trail and of having our pack horse killed by a rattlesnake bite, would require too much space. Suffice it to say that we reached Bluff City, a little Mormon settlement on the San Juan River, in good health, the distance being about one hundred and twenty miles with not a habitation on the route.

In Bluff City we learned that the two Union Pacific robbers had been there two weeks ahead of us; also two of our operatives. Alvin Garman and Alvin Darkbird had arrived a couple of days ahead of us and had taken up the trail of the robbers who were headed east.

By this time we knew that they were the Union Pacific train robbers, as they had passed some of the unsigned bills stolen in the Wilcox, Wyoming, train hold-up.

Darkbird and Garman had been sent by Superintendent Kaiser to Flagstaff, Arizona, there to buy outfits and cut across the country to Bluff City, Utah, to assist Sayles and me, or to intercept the robbers in case they headed south for Arizona.

Sayles and I figured that we were born leaders of men; hence we didn't like the idea of bringing up the rear, three days behind the other two operatives. Therefore, in Mancos, Colorado, on the Denver & Rio Grande Railway we put our jaded horses in a pasture and stored our camp outfit, taking our saddles along with us, and boarded a train for Durango. Here we overtook Garman and his chum. From Durango, Sayles and I led the chase by riding upon trains, in buggies, and on hired saddle horses. We left the other two boys far in the rear, and they finally lost the trail entirely and returned to Denver.

In Lumberton, New Mexico, my friend J. M. Archuleta, who was one of my chums in the Archuleta, Colorado, uprising, had seen the two robbers and the thirteen head of horses, two of them being very noticeable, one being a pretty cream color and the other a large dappled iron gray. After leaving Lumberton we lost the trail, but we heard of two men and a bunch of horses headed south toward Bland, New Mexico. It was agreed that I should follow this clue, while Sayles searched the country around Pagosa Springs, Colorado.

By riding on a Denver & Rio Grande train about five hundred miles, I landed in Santa Fé, New Mexico. There I went out to my ranch and saddled up Glen Alpine, Jr. He was fat and bucked like a wolf.

A forty-mile ride brought me to Bland in the Cochiti mining district, where lived my friend Cunny. He had seen the two men with the bunch of horses, and they proved not to be the robbers.

On returning to Santa Fé, I received a telegram from Sayles, saying that he had found the right trail, going through Pagosa Springs, and over Mosca Pass into the Wet Mountain Valley. Shortly after rejoining Sayles south of Canyon City, Colorado, we lost the trail again. He then went to Cripple Creek on a false scent, while I went east and picked up the trail by tramping afoot ten miles from a little railroad station where there was no horse to be hired. In Cucharas Junction the trail crossed the railroad and headed for Rattlesnake Buttes, toward the Arkansas River.

Of course I kept the Denver officials of our office posted by wire. Sayles was called in and sent to Montana to work on a clue as to where some of the stolen money which had been sent to the city of Washington had come from. I continued to follow the trail down the Arkansas River.

Finally I landed in Dodge City, Kansas, and found that my men and horses had passed through there on their way down the Arkansas River; but I concluded to lay over a half-day and note the changes in this, the toughest of all early-day Western cattle towns.

In looking over the prosperous town, I found many old landmarks in the way of buildings, etc., but only one live one, the live one being old 'Dog' Kelly, the early-day mayor of Dodge City. He was nicknamed 'Dog' Kelly because in the early days he always had a pack of greyhounds following at his heels; and the strange part of this story is that the dogs were still with him, though not the same dogs, of course.

I continued on the trail of my two train robbers, on horse-back, in buggies, and on trains. They passed through the out-skirts of Wichita, where I spent one night visiting old friends and acquaintances.

From there I followed the trail south to Caldwell, Kansas. In this former hurrah cattle town, where I once made my home for about two years, I met many old-time friends. Among them were only two ex-cowboys, Jay Willis and Dick Malone, and a solitary ex-cattle king, Sol. Tuttle.

My friend Dick had drifted to bleeding Kansas with a herd of long-horns from southern Texas. And his inclination then was to help paint towns red. But now he does his painting with a brush instead of with 'red licker' and a six-shooter.

From Caldwell the robbers followed the Indian Territory and Kansas line to Arkansas City, Kansas. Here I continued on the trail to Winfield, thence through the Indian Territory to Fort Smith, Arkansas.

Before reaching Fort Smith I was joined by operative Dark-bird who had been sent from Denver to assist me. We trailed the men and horses through Pine Bluff and to Hot Springs, Arkansas. Here we lost the trail. We split up and searched the surrounding country. Soon I received a telegram from Darkbird in Tennessee telling me to meet him in Nashville, the capital city of that State, as our men had got rid of their horses and boarded a train for there. I hurried to Nashville by way of Saint Louis, Missouri, where I spent one night with my sister and her family. In Nashville I met operative Darkbird and found he had followed a wrong trail. The men he had followed were evidently desperadoes, but not the ones we wanted.

Here Darkbird became sick with malaria and returned to Denver.

A couple of years later, in looking over correspondence on this operation, I found one of Mr. W. A. Pinkerton's letters to General Superintentent McParland. It was dated Chicago, December 22, 1899, and stated: 'I note that operative Siringo has picked up the trail of these men at Benton, Arkansas, and that operative Darkbird has returned home, being very sick with malaria. I am sorry to hear of operative Darkbird's illness. The swamp country through which he passed has evidently knocked him out. I fear it may do the same with Siringo, but he is as tough as a pine knot and I never knew of a man of his size who can endure as much hardship as he does.'

It gave me much satisfaction to know that I was considered tough, in more ways than one.

Arriving back in Hot Springs, Arkansas, I hired a saddle horse and searched the mountains for a trace of my men. This brought me among a queer class of people, some of them moonshiners. One old moonshiner assisted in putting me on the right trail of the robbers. Their trail led through Little Rock, the capital of the State, thence down the Arkansas

River through the swamps to a wild, unsettled country twenty-five miles south of Stuttgart. Here the loose horses were turned over to a long-haired old man by the name of La Cutts, who lived not far from the mouth of the Arkansas River.

The robbers mounted the pretty cream-colored and the dappled iron-gray horses and headed north to White River, thence down that stream to Clarendon, then due east to Helena on the Mississippi River. Crossing the Father of Waters, they passed through Glendale and Lula, Mississippi, thence east one hundred miles through the 'Black Belt,' where in some places negroes are thicker than flies on a syrup keg in August. They then rode one hundred miles south, thence back west to the Mississippi River at a boat landing above the town of Rosedale. Here they hired a man to ferry them across the Mississippi to the mouth of the Arkansas River, after their horses and saddles had been turned over to a strange negro who disappeared in the swamps.

At the mouth of the Arkansas River one robber, whose name I had reason to believe was Owens, went up the Arkansas River in a skiff, while his companion boarded a little tramp steamer and went down the Mississippi. They had agreed to meet in two weeks, but I couldn't find out where. This put me up a stump with no chance to proceed.

I went to the city of Vicksburg, Mississippi, and posted officers to be on the lookout for my men; also did likewise in the large towns of Indianola, Greenville, and Cleveland.

Finally I received orders to give up the chase and return to Denver, as my services were needed in Montana on the same operation. On quitting the chase I was about three weeks behind the two train robbers.

In Denver I was informed by Assistant Superintendent Frank Murray, who had charge of the Union Pacific Railway train hold-up operation, that W. O. Sayles had run into a brother, Loney Curry, and a cousin, Bob Curry, of the noted outlaw Kid Curry, in Harlin, Montana; that Loney and Bob owned a saloon there and had sent some of the unsigned bills stolen in the Wilcox, Wyoming, robbery, off to be cashed. In this way they were located, but they sold their saloon and skipped out before Sayles had a chance to arrest them.

Sayles had found out that the right names of Kid and Loney Curry were Harvey and Loney Logan and that they were born and raised in Dodson, Missouri, near Kansas City, and that for years they had been making their headquarters in the Little Rockies, a small range of mountains fifty miles east of Harlin, the railroad station where Bob and Loney had owned the saloon. Therefore, I was instructed to meet Sayles in Helena, the capital of Montana, and then buy a horse and saddle at some point and ride into the Little Rockies and get in with the friends of the Logan brothers.

In Helena, Montana, I visited with W. O. Sayles and detective N. P. Walters a couple of days. It was thought best for me to outfit in Great Falls and ride about two hundred and fifty miles across the 'Bad Lands' to Landusky, the small cattle town in the Little Rocky Mountains.

Bidding Sayles good-bye, I boarded a train for Great Falls, Montana, where I bought a bucking bronco mare and started east for Lewiston, Montana, about three days' ride. In Lewiston a severe blizzard was raging, it being the latter part of February. I waited two days for it to moderate, but it seemed to grow worse. Therefore, a start was made one morning when the thermometer registered twenty degrees below zero, and with the wind blowing a gale. The people at the hotel advised me not to start, and I wished before night that I had heeded their advice.

My route lay over a flat country north to Rocky Point on

the Missouri River, a distance of about eighty miles, and only one ranch on the route. It was the ranch that I aimed to reach before night. After traveling against this cold wind about fifteen miles, I could stand it no longer. My mare could hardly be kept headed toward the blizzard. I had a woolen hood over my face and head, and even then my nose and ears were about frozen. I could see the mountains off to the east where I had been told the mining camp of Gilt Edge was situated, so for there I headed, not caring to return to Lewiston. About night I struck the wagon road between Gilt Edge and Lewiston, and then I was happy.

A long climb over this mountain range brought me into the live camp of Gilt Edge about four hours after dark. I felt like a half-frozen fool for ever having undertaken such a journey. But after I had got on the outside of a large porterhouse steak and trimmings, I began to thaw out and feel better.

Next morning I concluded to take a different route to the Rocky Point crossing of the Missouri River. Therefore I obtained a sketch of the route to the Red Barn ranch on the south border of the Bad Lands. A hard, cold ride brought me to the ranch, where I found a crowd of cowboys congregated waiting for the weather to moderate. From here it was thirty miles across the Bad Lands to Rocky Point, and I was advised to lay over a few days and wait for a Chinook wind to melt the snow so that the dim road could be followed. I did so, and while waiting, I gained some information about the Kid Curry gang. Loney Curry had stopped here before and after the Wilcox train robbery on the Union Pacific Railway.

I started one morning after a Chinook had been blowing all night, so that the snow was almost gone, but the sticky mud on the Bad Lands was something fearful. It would stick to the mare's feet till the poor animal could hardly gallop. I had seen many kinds of sticky mud in my life, but nothing to equal this.

Just as night was approaching, I found a piece of glass from a telegraph pole. This satisfied me that I was on the right road, hence I was happy. I had been told that in the early days the Government had a telegraph line on the road to Rocky Point, but that the line had been moved away years before. I still keep that piece of green glass, as it had brought good cheer to my drooping spirits.

I arrived in Rocky Point on the south bank of the Big Muddy River three hours after dark. Here I found old man Tyler and his son running the ferry and keeping a small Indian trading store. My mare had traveled only thirty miles, but she had carried about seventy-five pounds of mud across the Bad Lands, hence she was almost played out on arriving at Rocky Point. I had often heard of the Bad Lands and wanted to visit them, but now that desire has vanished.

Before reaching the Little Rockies, I learned that Harvey Logan, alias Kid Curry, had a half-interest in a horse ranch with a man I will call Jim Thompson; that they owned about five hundred head of good horses which ranged in the Little Rockies.

As luck would have it, on reaching Landusky, the small village in the Little Rockies, I made the acquaintance, through an accident, of the man I have called Thompson. In riding by the saloon in front of which were a crowd of rough-looking men, my mare shied and I spurred her in the flanks. She began bucking and my Colt's 45 flew out of the scabbard, striking a rock in the street. When the mare quit bucking, Thompson gave me the pistol, which he had picked up. This meant a treat for the crowd, and I became acquainted with the partner of Kid Curry, the slickest and most bloodthirsty outlaw of the age.

To recite all my ups and downs and the valuable information about outlaws and tough characters secured for my agency would take up too much space. Suffice it to say that I played myself off for an Old Mexico outlaw and became 'Solid Muldoon' with the worst people of the community. I had adopted the name of Charles L. Carter.

Harvey Logan had killed old Pike Landusky, the man for whom this town was named, several years previous, which first started him on the road as a genuine desperado. Thompson informed me that he advised Harvey to kill Landusky, and for that reason he would always be his friend through thick and thin.

Pike Landusky's widow, Julia, still resided on their ranch two miles out of town. The family consisted of two boys and three girls. One of these girls, Elfie, twenty years of age and good-looking, had a three-year-old son by Loney Logan. They had never been married by law, which seemed no disgrace here.

In trying to capture Loney Logan at Dodson, Missouri, where he was in hiding with his aunt, Mrs. Lee, mother of Bob Lee, alias Bob Curry, officials of the Pinkerton Agency had shot him through the head and killed him.

I had made myself solid with Elfie Curry, as she was called; hence read all of her letters and was told all of her secrets. She had stacks of letters from her husband, as she called Loney, and also from Mrs. Lee and her daughter, and during Bob Lee's trial in Cheyenne, Wyoming, she received letters from the lawyers whom Mrs. Lee had sent from Kansas City, Missouri, to defend her son. As I had access to Elfie's trunks I could read these letters at any time.

The Kansas City lawyer came to Landusky after evidence to prove an alibi for Bob Lee, and while he was working with Elfie and Thompson, I was introduced to him, and learned all of his secrets.

During the round-ups and horse-branding trips I showed

my skill in throwing a rope. This made me solid with Thompson, who lived with his common-law wife on a ranch a few miles south of Landusky. They had a bright little three-year-old boy named Harvey in honor of the outlaw, Harvey Logan. This little fellow felt at home with a small pistol buckled around his waist — then he would go wild. A high picket fence had to be built around the house to keep him from running away.

One evening during the past winter when the thermometer was hovering about zero, little Harvey struck out for 'tall timber' with his pet dog, a large yellow cur. They tramped the hills all night. Next morning the whole population of Landusky, in the male line, about twenty-five men, were out searching for the child's corpse, as it was thought impossible for a boy of his tender age to endure the bitter cold night. But the little fellow proved to be tough like his daddy. He was found in the afternoon many miles from home, huddled up by the side of his pet dog, fast asleep. The warmth from the dog's body had no doubt saved his life.

Shortly after my arrival in the Little Rockies, I went to Harlin on the Great Northern Railroad, with Puck Powell, the ex-cowboy postmaster of Landusky. We were the only passengers in the open stagecoach drawn by four horses. On reaching the swollen Milk River, which was full of broken ice, we persuaded the driver to swim the team across. When out in midstream the large chunks of ice struck the stagecoach, carrying horses and all downstream. The spring seats were all that showed above water, and Puck, the driver, and I were upon these. We were having a free ride with the poor horses trying to swim upstream. Something had to be done to save the horses from drowning, so with all my clothes on I jumped into the icy cold water. On reaching the bank in a bend of the creek, the driver threw me the lines. The lead horses were pulled ashore and the vehicle swung around against the steep clay bank, so that Puck and the driver could step off without getting wet. Undressing in the cold wind to wring the water out of my clothes gave me a taste of old-time cowboy life. We didn't reach the stage station until dark.

During the month of June, I came within an ace of losing my breath, which would have put me out of business for all time. I was at Jim Thompson's ranch and he got me to drive a bronco team to Rocky Point on the Missouri River twenty-five miles. This team of four-year-old browns had been hitched up in harness only a couple of times. The broncos were hitched to an old buckboard and a bottle of water put under the seat, as the weather was hot and there was no water on the road.

Before starting at 7.30 A.M. Thompson cautioned me to be careful, as this team had run away and smashed up a vehicle the past fall, since which time they had been running wild on the range.

The twenty-five-mile drive to Rocky Point was over a broken, rocky country, with a very dim wagon road to follow, and there was not a habitation on the road.

Thompson opened the gate and I started with the browns tugging at their bits. For the first few miles the horses made several efforts to run, though I managed to get them checked up, but when about five miles out, business started. As we flew over the rocky road as fast as the horses could run, I remember seeing something black, which must have been one of the tug-straps, hitting the broncos on the hind legs. I also remember seeing a deep gully ahead, and to avoid it, I threw my weight onto one line to turn the team around the head of the short gully. I cannot account for my not jumping and letting the outfit go to the devil, for I've been in runaways before, and I generally sprout imaginary wings and fly out of the rig. I am all right on a horse's back, but a rank coward in a vehicle.

When I woke up, the sun was about two hours high, it being about 5 P.M. I was lying flat on my back with the hot June sun shining in my face. I couldn't move or open my eyes, and I wondered what was wrong. Finally, by making a strong effort, I got my right hand up to my eyes — the left arm couldn't be raised. Raising my head I saw the hind wheels and the bed of the buckboard upside down, and only a few yards from me lay my Colt's 45 and the bottle of water which was put in the buckboard on starting. Then it all came fresh to my mind — the runaway. The last that I could recall was turning the team around the head of the gully.

As I was dying for a drink of water after lying in the hot sun for eight or nine hours, every nerve in my body was strained to crawl to the bottle of water.

The water and the crawling had revived me so that I could sit up. On feeling the top of my head I found that my high stubborn bump had overflowed and filled up the hole where the religious bump ought to have been, according to phrenology rules. In fact, the top of my head was badly swollen, which showed that I had landed on the ground wrong end up. My back pained the worst, and it was like pulling a tooth to try to get onto my feet. Therefore I started out to crawl back to the Thompson ranch — about five miles. After crawling a few hundred yards I managed to gain my feet. Several times I was on the point of giving up and lying down to rest, but the fear that I shouldn't be able to get on my feet again kept me pushing ahead.

When within a mile of the ranch, after the sun had set, I saw a man afoot running toward me. I was reeling from one side to the other like a drunken bum, and this had brought Thompson to my rescue. He saved me from a fall by grabbing me in his strong arms just as I was falling. I had given up and couldn't have walked another step. I was carried to the house and put to bed. Thompson kept a good supply of horse liniment in the house and he used this on me with a lavish hand as though it was water. There was no doctor nearer than the railroad, fifty miles. Two days later the bronco team were found, still dragging the front wheels of the buckboard.

While recovering, I had a good chance to get information about the 'wild bunch,' from Thompson, but he would never give a hint as to where Kid Curry was, though I found out enough to convince me that they kept up a correspondence through the post-office in the town of Chinook, on the railroad, not far from Harlin, but under what names I couldn't tell. He informed me that his mail addressed to Landusky was watched when it left the railroad station of Harlin.

In talking, Thompson showed a very bitter spirit against the Pinkertons for killing his friend Loney Logan, and for sending Bob Lee, alias Bob Curry, to the penitentiary.

Our agency had lately captured and convicted Bob Lee for his connection in the Wilcox, Wyoming, Union Pacific train hold-up. He was caught in Cripple Creek, Colorado, and convicted and sentenced to the penitentiary for ten years, in Cheyenne, Wyoming.

Thompson assured me that Loney's brother Kid Curry would soon get even with the Union Pacific Railroad Company and the Pinkertons by robbing another Union Pacific train; that the Kid was then in the south making preparation for a deal of that kind.

It was three weeks before I had fully recovered from the runaway, and even to this day I can feel the effects of the fall in my head and arm.

I had found out many secrets of past crimes in the West. We knew that Flat Nose George Curry (who was not related to Kid and Loney Curry) was one of the robbers of the Wilcox, Wyoming, train hold-up, and Marshal Joe LaFors of Cheyenne had written the officials of the Union Pacific Railroad that he had learned through a reliable source that Flat Nose George Curry was with a tough character named Henry Smith, somewhere in the northwestern part of the State of Chihuahua in Old Mexico. Therefore I received orders by mail to meet LaFors in Denver and go with him to Old Mexico in search of Flat Nose George.

We had decided that Kid Curry, Thompson's partner, would steer clear of the Little Rockies, where every one knew him, but in this we were mistaken, for not long after I left he slipped back and killed Ranchman Winters, who had killed his brother Johnny. Winters was a prosperous stock-raiser and he told me that he expected to be waylaid and killed by Curry.

In the latter part of August I slipped out of the country on my red roan horse for which I had traded the bucking mare. No one knew I was going but my supposed sweetheart, Elfie Curry. I told her that my partner was to be executed for a crime we had both committed in Old Mexico, and that I feared he would confess and give me away; that if he did, she would never see me again, as I intended to cut my suspenders and go straight up, where my friends would never hear of me. Otherwise I should return. She was given a certain address in New Mexico from whence letters would be forwarded to me.

Nearly a year afterwards a letter from her reached me through that address. In her letter she wrote that poor little Loney, her four-year-old boy, was heartbroken over my long absence, and kept asking, 'Mamma, when is Mr. Carter coming home?' The little fellow was pretty and bright, and we had become greatly attached to each other. Of course the letter was not answered, and I heard no more of them.

In Harlin my horse and saddle were sold and I boarded a train for Denver.

On reaching home, Joe LaFors met me and we went to El Paso, Texas, together. In El Paso, LaFors located until I could run down Henry Smith and his chum who was supposed to be Flat Nose George Curry.

It had been agreed by Mr. Horace Burt, the president of the Union Pacific Railway Company, that LaFors should stay in El Paso until I ran the men down. Then I was to notify LaFors and he would come to me to identify Flat Nose George, whom he had seen.

In El Paso I boarded a train for Casas Grandes, Mexico, at the foot of the Sierra Madre Mountains. There I secured a horse and saddle and the strenuous part of my work began. About a hundred miles northwest of Casas Grandes, in Janos, a large Mexican town, I got on the trail of my men. But in the wind-up two weeks later, I concluded that Henry Smith's chum was not Flat Nose George Curry.

From the Mormon Colony of Dias I wired to LaFors, in El Paso, Texas, that we were on the wrong trail — hence he could return home to Cheyenne, Wyoming.

Soon after this Flat Nose George Curry was shot and killed in Utah, while trying to resist his capture. This confirmed my decision that Smith's chum was not the man wanted.

On this trip into Old Mexico I recognized several former cowboy chums, but I didn't make myself known. Among them was one who was outlawed from Texas. He was going under an assumed name and was living with a native woman. They had a house full of little half-breeds of all sizes, from the cradle up into the teens. So, why disturb him when he was faithfully assisting Mother Nature to improve the human race.

From Dias I rode on a stagecoach to a station on the Sierra Madre Railway, and returned to Denver.

CHAPTER XVIII

THE 'WILD BUNCH' AGAIN — A HORSEBACK RIDE OF
A THOUSAND MILES — 'BUTCH' CASIDAY — CURRY'S
ARREST AND ESCAPE — THE END OF A
FOUR-YEARS' HUNT

WHEN I reached Denver, I found out the particulars of a late train hold-up on the Union Pacific Railroad at Tipton, Wyoming. Assistant Superintendent Goddil had been on the ground investigating this late robbery and had decided that Kid Curry, Bill Cruzan, and a man who might be Longbough did the job.

Jim Thompson had told me that Kid Curry was planning to rob the Union Pacific Railway again to get revenge for the Pinkertons' killing his brother Loney; hence I concluded that Thompson knew what he was talking about.

Our agency had just received a tip through an ex-convict in Grand Junction, Colorado, that he had talked with Kid Curry and a tall companion at their camp on a mesa twenty miles south of Grand Junction, and that they told him they were going south where the 'climate would fit their clothes,' and that they had just broken camp and started south on horseback. Therefore, I was hustled right out to get on the trail of these two men.

I was instructed to pick up their trail if possible, and stay with it wherever it might lead, and should the trail not be found, then I was to drift southwest through Utah and Arizona and into New Mexico to Alma, in western Socorro County, where some of the stolen unsigned United States bills from the Wilcox, Wyoming, robbery had been passed.

A three-hundred-mile ride over the Continental Divide on

the Denver & Rio Grande Railway, brought me to the little city of Grand Junction where my friend Shores and his lovely wife — she who had fed me so well while I was a prisoner in the Gunnison jail, years before — have a beautiful home.

While purchasing horses and getting an outfit ready for the trail, I made my headquarters at the Shores residence, but on the sly, so no one would see me coming and going, as every man, woman, and child in that town knows Shores as an officer. During my stay I made the acquaintance of Charlie Wallis, the sheriff of Mesa County. He was an ex-cowboy from Texas and New Mexico, and an old friend of Tom Hall's; hence we had some pleasant chats of old-time cowboy days.

I started south with a blue-roan saddle horse and a red-roan pack horse, and they were both good ones for such a trip, more especially the saddle animal which could make a meal on greasewood or any kind of rubbish when it came to a show-down during deep snows when the feed played out.

Before reaching the Paradox Valley, the home of the notorious Young boys who are known far and wide as 'bad' men, I made the acquaintance of a Mr. Elliott and his brother-in-law W. B. Moss, and found out for sure that my men had passed their ranch only a week ahead of me. I showed Mr. Elliott the photograph of Kid Curry and he was positive that the small dark man was the same. Before making a confidant of young Elliott, I satisfied myself that he was all right and could be trusted.

From Elliott's ranch the two train hold-ups were trailed into the Paradox Valley and right up to Ed Young's ranch, and from Ed Young's father-in-law, who had no idea that I was a detective, I found out that the two robbers had gone south with Lafe Young, who was an outlaw and dodging the officers. He had last seen them in the La Salle Mountains, where they had a bunch of range horses rounded up with a view of stealing a fresh mount.

I remained in the Paradox Valley about a week and became quite chummy with Bill Young and met his mother and pretty black-eyed young sister. There was a store in the valley, and from the proprietor, Thomas Swain, I gained much valuable information. He was an honest old Englishman and I made a confidant of him.

I had got on the wrong trail by following two men into the La Salle Mountains, and through Thomas Swain I found out that one of them was my friend Cunny, of New Mexico. They were on a prospecting trip to Utah and Nevada. Seeing Cunny's handwriting where he had written to have his mail forwarded convinced me that I was on the wrong trail, but I soon got on the right trail and headed south through a wild, unsettled country, for the Blue Mountains of southern Utah.

In the Blue Mountains I got in with a tough gang, one of whom was the manager of the Carlisle Cattle Ranch. From him I found out that my men, Kid Curry and his tall chum, the latter a stranger in that country, had left a hidden haystack the morning previous to my arrival, Lafe Young being with them. The two train robbers he said were broke, as they had failed to get any money from their last train hold-up at Tipton, Wyoming, hence he gave them a supply of grub. They told him that they were going where the 'climate would fit their clothes.' He figured that meant Arizona or New Mexico, as their clothes were light for cold weather.

Every fall the manager put up a stack of hay for his outlaw friends so that they wouldn't have to feed their horses at his ranch. This haystack was hidden in a heavy grove of piñon and cedar timber a couple of miles from the ranch. My men camped one night at this hidden haystack and then pulled out for Indian Creek.

I drifted over to Indian Creek, a place noted for tough characters, and got in solid with an outlaw named 'Peg Leg.' His chum Kid Jackson was afraid of me for fear I might be a detective.

Peg-Leg had been to the camp of my two men, and Lafe Young had told him that they were Union Pacific train robbers making their getaway, but he didn't learn their names. His description of the small dark man tallied with that of Kid Curry to a dot.

One day Peg-Leg and I rode twenty miles into Monticello, the Mormon county seat of San Juan County, Utah. On the way we rested for an hour on top of a high mountain ridge from which we could view the whole country around for a hundred miles or more. It was a clear, sunshiny day. Looking to the westward beyond the Indian Creek settlement, the great Colorado River could be seen with its jagged cliffs and canyons, which made a beautiful sight. And beyond the Colorado River Peg-Leg pointed out the 'Robbers' Roost' which 'Butch' Casiday and the 'Wild Bunch' used as headquarters for several years until Joe Bush and a posse of Salt Lake City officers made a raid on the Roost and killed some of the gang.

Beyond the Robbers' Roost were the Henry Mountains, mere bluish blotches on the lovely blue sky. The distance to them from where we lay, as the bird flies, was about seventy-five miles, but in order to reach them one would have to travel about two hundred miles, as the country between is almost impassable and devoid of inhabitants.

Peg-Leg told of secret trails to the Colorado River, and of the 'Wild Bunch' having a boat hidden in the rushes at a certain point so they could cross the river and reach the Henry Mountains quickly. He said that Kid Jackson had used this boat a week previous.

Southwest from where we were there is not a human habitation for about three hundred miles down in Arizona, and it is a very rough country with a scarcity of water, therefore it can be realized what a haven of rest it must be for the 'Wild Bunch' and their kind.

Peg-Leg and I aimed to reach Monticello after dark, so that he wouldn't be seen until he found out if the coast was clear; in other words, if there were any outside officers in the county looking for criminals. After we had put up our horses and had a lunch in a cabin on the outskirts of town, Peg-Leg borrowed my pistol so that he would have two, leaving his Winchester rifle with me, and struck out in the dark to find the sheriff of the county. He had told me that the sheriff stood in with the outlaws and kept them posted as to when there was danger in the air, but I didn't know whether to believe it or not. To satisfy myself, I followed Peg-Leg in the dark, keeping my rifle hidden under my coat.

Peg-Leg found the sheriff at a dance and they met under some trees in a dark place and had a long pow-wow. This seemed strange, considering that the sheriff had warrants in his pocket for Peg-Leg and at least half a dozen for Peg-Leg's chum, Kid Jackson.

On returning to the cabin Peg-Leg reported to me that the coast was clear and that no outside officers or detectives were in the county. We then put in a few hours with Peg-Leg's sweetheart and her mother.

Peg-Leg told how the past winter two officers left the railroad with a team and buggy to search for Kid Jackson in the Indian Creek country, there being big rewards out for his arrest; that these officers wrote to the sheriff asking that he meet them. The sheriff then sent for Jackson and told him to 'hit the high places' until these officers left. But instead of hiding out, Jackson and Peg-Leg went to the officers' camp one night, running off their horses and shooting into their tent, the result being the two sleuth-hounds had to 'hoof it' back to Moab, where they secured transportation to the railroad.

After leaving the Blue Mountains I drifted south to Bluff City on the San Juan River, thence west one hundred and twenty miles over that uninhabited, rocky, desert country, over which Sayles and I had passed, to Dandy Crossing on the Colorado River.

On reaching the foot of Elk Mountain a deep snow covered up all trails and the clouds and falling snow prevented my seeing familiar landmarks to guide my way. The result was that I was lost for a couple of days and nights; and one dark night I saw the camp-fire of Jim Scorrup down in a deep canyon. I was then twenty miles off my road to the southward. Jim Scorrup of Bluff City was camped all alone under a ledge of rock, and had a whopping big fire burning. The sight of this fire raised a cowboy yell in my throat that startled Scorrup and his shepherd dog. I was wet, tired, and hungry.

Scorrup was out hunting lost stock. Next day the sun came out and Scorrup put me on the right trail to Dandy Crossing. He went with me as far as White's Canyon and we camped together that night. We bade each other good-bye next morning and I haven't seen him since, but there will always remain a warm spot in my heart for Jim Scorrup, as he knows how to put new life into a lost sinner.

On reaching Dandy Crossing about night, during a severe rainstorm, Colonel Hite, formerly a wealthy politician of Springfield, Illinois, helped to swim my two horses across the Colorado River. In doing so the Colonel got his two hundred and fifty pounds of flesh wet to the skin. We had trouble making the horses 'take the water,' and Hite let me do all the swearing, as he said he had been brought up a Christian and preferred to do his swearing by proxy.

From Dandy Crossing I rode north through the Henry Mountains to Hanksville. As Sayles and I had been in Hanksville, I felt at home here with Charlie Gibbons and his family, with whom I put up. I made a confidant of Mr. Gibbons and told him my business. He gave me some new pointers about Butch Casiday and the Wild Bunch. He had first become acquainted with Casiday after he helped to rob the Montpelier, Idaho, bank of a large pile of gold. This gold was turned over to Gibbons for safe-keeping, he not knowing of the robbery. Later it was taken to the Robbers' Roost, fifty miles east of Hanksville, where the Wild Bunch used twenty-dollar gold pieces for poker chips.

I had received orders from Assistant Superintendent Frank Murray, through the mail, to drift over to the Sevier Valley, where Butch Casiday was born and raised, and find out all I could about that outlaw, for future use; and from there drift south through Arizona and New Mexico to Alma, in the latter territory, Alma being the southern rendezvous for the Wild Bunch, while the Hole-in-the-Wall, in Wyoming, was their northern hangout. This of course meant a horseback ride of over a thousand miles through the most God-forsaken desert country in the United States.

On leaving Hanksville one morning a traveling photographer took a snapshot of me and my horses. This photograph is reproduced as the frontispiece and shows what a cowboy detective looks like when on the warpath, with bedding, grub, and kitchen fixings tied to his saddle-pony's tail.

A day's ride due west up the Dirty Devil River brought me to the Mormon settlement of Cainsville. Here I put up for the night. On leaving the Dirty Devil next morning to cross an unsettled rough desert called San Rafael Swell, I bade good-bye to civilization for a few days.

After the first night out, I lost the dim trail and concluded to head due west over a high snowy range of mountains for the town of Emery, at the head of Castle Valley. Sayles and I had stopped there; hence I knew by the lay of the mountains where the little Mormon town was located on the opposite side of the mountains. This proved to be a bad mistake, for after camping out in the snow two nights I had to turn back, as the snow became too deep for travel, and I was not yet at the top of the range.

That night I had no feed for the horses, and through kindness of heart I hobbled them out; that is, tied their front feet together so they could hobble around among the rocks on a side hill and pick up a little dry grass. This was mistake No. 2, for next morning I had to shoulder my wrath and follow their tracks fifteen miles to the head of Starvation Creek, where there was a small spring. This was back in the direction of Dirty Devil River. In traveling these fifteen miles afoot I felt like swearing, but I realized the uselessness of uttering cuss-words where they would have been wasted on the desert air. I contented myself by making a vow that hereafter one of the horses would be tied up to a tree, feed or no feed, as I would rather count their ribs than their tracks.

The next morning I found the dim trail over which Sayles and I had traveled. This was followed until dark, where camp was pitched without either wood or horse feed. And to make matters worse it was raining hard.

The following morning I pushed ahead to reach a ranch where Sayles and I had stopped nearly two years previous. At that time a Mormon lady and her pretty young daughter lived there alone, as their lord and master was absent trying to make a living, the soil on their homestead being too poor to grow sufficient food. But imagine my surprise on finding the place vacated and not a blade of grass for my tired and hungry horses in sight. It was about night and raining hard, which made the road slippery and hard on the horses.

About midnight we came to a ranch on the side of the road which was considered as being only four miles from Emery. Dismounting, I went to the house and knocked on the door, and a dog inside made a terrible racket, as though he wanted to eat me up. Repeated knocks and loud calls failed to bring any one to the door. I thought seriously of breaking down the door, and if it had to be done, killing the dog and cooking a supper, providing there was anything to eat in the house. But on second thought I concluded it dangerous, as there might be some one inside with a gun. Thus was my well-developed cautious bump getting in its work.

Finally I started in the cold rain, and the poor horses didn't want to go. A half-hour's ride brought me to a small raging creek which my horses wouldn't go into, despite the severe spurring received by my mount. Then we turned back with the intention of breaking down the ranchman's door, but to my great delight, on coming in sight, a light was shining in the window and before knocking I heard voices inside. On knocking I was admitted, and the frightened woman, who was alone with her small children, explained that she didn't open the door the first time because she was afraid, and that after I had been gone quite awhile, she built a fire to make coffee to quiet her nerves.

By the time the horses were put in the stable and fed, the kind lady had a hot meal on the table and I ate dinner, supper, and a three o'clock breakfast all at one time. Then I lay down by the open fireplace to sleep.

But why waste time to chronicle the hardships of a fool cow-puncher who had started out as a detective to see the world and to study the phrenology bumps on the heads of other people, instead of living the simple life on a small patch of the earth's surface? So I will hurry on to Alma, New Mexico, the outlaws' Paradise, near the border of Old Mexico.

A ride of several days over mountain trails landed me in Circleville, the home of Butch Casiday before he turned out to be the shrewdest and most daring outlaw of the present age, though not of the blood-spilling kind such as Kid Curry and Black Jack.

A week was spent in the straggling village of Circleville, and I found out all about Butch's early life and much about his late doings. His true name was Parker, his nickname being 'Sallie' Parker when a boy. This nickname of itself was enough to drive a sensitive boy to the bad.

I had hard work to keep from falling in love with Miss Parker, the pretty young sister of Butch Casiday. She was the deputy postmistress in Circleville.

Hard, cold rides brought me to the town of Panguitch, thence due south to the Mormon town of Kanab, on the line of Arizona. Here I laid in a good supply of grub, as this was the last settlement for hundreds of miles.

A three days' ride over the Buckskin Mountains and down the great Colorado River, brought me to Lee's Ferry on that stream. Not a habitation or a settler was seen between Kanab and Lee's Ferry, Arizona, and I found water scarce and 'far between.' But it was surely a treat to see this lone ranch down in the narrow valley of the Colorado. It was indeed an oasis in the desert. Here green alfalfa was a foot high and the flowers and the combs on the chickens were in full bloom.

Another three days over an uninhabited desert country brought me to the Indian trading store at Willow Creek. From here I turned due east across the Navajo Indian Reservation and through the Moqui Indian country, my object being to find out if any of the Wild Bunch had been seen lately. Therefore, for the next two weeks I was among Indians all the time, and I learned some interesting lessons, especially among the Mo-quis, who live on the very top of round mountains in the desert. At one of the big Moqui villages I took my horses up the steep trail and rode into the chief's front yard. My horses were fed and the Indians made an idol of me. They dug up old rusty dried venison which had been buried for a coon's age, so as to give me a feast fit for the gods. I remained all night and was invited to take me a squaw and become one of them, but I told the chief that I wasn't ready to settle down, as I wanted to settle up first.

Finally I crossed the Atlantic and Pacific Railroad at Gallup, New Mexico, thence went south through the Zuñi Indian country to a salt lake a few miles east of the Arizona line. Here I found a settlement of Mexicans putting up salt for the markets in far off towns. And here I saw a great curiosity in the form of a bottomless lake on the top of a round mountain. To reach it one has to climb to the top of the mountain on the outside and down a trail on the inside. I went swimming in it, as the water is warm in winter. It is said that the Government tried to find the bottom of this salty body of hidden water, but failed after putting down a line three thousand feet. The lake from whence the salt is gathered lies at the foot of this round mountain.

From here I went to the line of Arizona, where a few days previous two of Pete Slaughter's boys murdered William Beeler, the brave officer who had trailed Kid Curry and his gang to Baggs, Wyoming, the spring previous. The two seventeen-year-old boys murdered Beeler in revenge for the killing of Monte Slaughter not long before.

From here I drifted south to the American Valley ranch, where my friend W. C. Moore, the outlaw cowboy whom I saw in Juneau, Alaska, killed two men, which set him adrift with a big reward on his head.

From American Valley I rode south to Luna Valley and made the acquaintance of many tough characters. Here I made a confidant of a ranchman by the name of James G. Smith, and found out that he had known me in Texas years before. He gave me valuable information about the Wild Bunch, and his good wife filled me up on civilized food.

Finally I reached the sleepy little town of Alma, New Mexico, and my thousand-mile horseback journey was ended. The town of Alma supported one store and one saloon, both being well patronized by the wild and woolly population thinly scattered over the surrounding country.

I started in to make myself solid with the tough element of the district, so as to find out more about the Wild Bunch and as to who passed a lot of that unsigned money stolen in the Wilcox, Wyoming, train hold-up. This stolen money had been passed in Alma a few months after the train hold-up, and when the matter leaked out, Assistant Superintendent Frank Murray of our Denver office, was sent there to investigate. There being no deputy sheriffs in this western part of Socorro County, it being about one hundred and twenty miles from the county seat of Socorro on the Rio Grande River, Mr. Murray had no local officers to assist him. I was told that the sheriff couldn't get a man to accept the deputyship in the western part of this county, as it was too tough and dangerous, being overrun with outlaws and desperadoes.

Mr. Murray had to take some one into his confidence, so he used bad judgment by selecting the two leading business men and citizens of Alma. One of these was the storekeeper and the other the saloon proprietor, Jim Lowe. Of course Murray went into detail of how he was on a hot trail of the Union Pacific train robbers who had passed some of the stolen money in Alma. This was enough. That night Mr. Murray was driven out of town and would have been killed had it not been for the saloon man Jim Lowe.

After getting in with the tough gang, I learned the truth of how Jim Lowe saved Murray's life, and how next morning Lowe sold his saloon and 'hit the trail' with outlaw Red Weaver, for 'tall timber'; that Jim Lowe was none other than the notorious Butch Casiday of the Kid Curry gang.

Among the men whose friendship I made was Jesse Black, one of Jim Lowe's warmest friends, who had figured in the raid on Frank Murray. He was considered a hard case, but no one seemed to know who he was or where he came from.

Part of my time was spent out in the mountains in the Mogollon mining camp and at the mining town of Graham, where there was a gold mill; also at the cattle town of Frisco, near the Arizona line.

In Frisco I got in with a bronco-buster and 'bad' man, who told me the spot in the mountains, about forty miles southwest, where Jim Lowe had established a Robbers' Roost or rendezvous, and at that very time was there with eight outlaw companions, but who these companions were he didn't know, as they were from the north. He was only acquainted with Jim Lowe. He pointed out the particular mountain in the distance where they were camped, and getting ready for some kind of a raid. This bronco-buster had been to their camp lately.

On learning of this, I at once wrote to Assistant Superintendent Murray telling him of Jim Lowe's rendezvous and of my plans to visit their camp and try to get in with the gang.

Soon I received a reply by mail saying that I was mistaken about Jim Lowe being Butch Casiday, as he (Frank Murray) had met Lowe and found him to be a nice gentleman. In the letter he instructed me to sell my horses and return to Denver, as he wanted me to join a tough gang in western Colorado and southern Wyoming, who stood in with the Wild Bunch.

So this ended my work in Alma during the late spring. Putting a stop to my visiting Jim Lowe and his gang may have been a Godsend, as they might have killed me; but still, it might have terminated in the killing or capture of the whole bunch.

After selling my horses in the Mogollon mining camp, I boarded the stagecoach for Silver City, the county seat of Grant County, New Mexico, a distance of about eighty miles to the southward, this being the nearest railroad.

Blake Graham, a warm friend of Jim Lowe, was a passenger on the stage with me. We had a good supply of liquor along and he told me the whole secret of Jim Lowe being Butch Casiday. He told of how, when Assistant Superintendent Murray was run out of Alma, Jim Lowe sold his saloon and skipped; that he (Blake Graham) rode several miles with Lowe and Red Weaver when they were leaving, and of how Lowe said he didn't have the heart to see Frank Murray killed, and for that reason he helped get him out of town in the night.

The driver of the stagecoach was Bill Kelly, who claimed to be the original 'L. S. Kid' of the Panhandle, Texas. I had known the L. S. Kid as a wild, smooth-faced boy, hence Kelly and I became quite chummy. Young Graham and I and the two traveling men aboard kept Kelly loaded with liquor so that he would make good time, and amuse us with his Western songs. He claimed to have originated one of these songs while a cowboy in the Panhandle, Texas, and he sang it half a dozen times. It had a lovely tune and seemed to strike me just right. It ran thus:

> My lover is a cowboy,
>   He's kind, he's brave and true;
> He rides the Spanish pony
>   And throws the lasso, too;
> And when he comes to see me
>   And our vows we have redeemed,
> He puts his arms around me
>   And then begins to sing:

CHORUS

Oh, I am a jolly cowboy,
  From Texas now I hail,
Give me my saddle and pony
  And I'm ready for the trail.
I love the rolling prairie
  Where we are free from care and strife,
And behind a herd of long-horns,
  I will journey all my life.

We rise up in the morning
  At the early dawn of day,
We vault into the saddle
  And quickly ride away.
We rope, brand and ear-mark,
  I tell you what, we're smart,
We get the herd all ready
  For Kansas, then, we start.
Chorus.

When lowering clouds do gather
  And livid lightnings flash,
And crashing thunder rattles
  And heavy rain-drops splash.
What keeps the herd from roaming
  And stampeding far and wide?
'Tis the cowboy's long, low whistle
  And singing by their side.
Chorus.

And when in Kansas City
  The boss he pays us up,
We loaf around a few days,
  We have a parting cup.
We bid farewell to city,
  From noisy marts we come
Right back to dear old Texas
  The cowboys' native home.

Before reaching Silver City about night, the liquor began to work. Then Graham and I pulled our pistols and emptied them through the canvas-covered top of the stagecoach. This set fire to the canvas top and the wind carried the fire to my roll of bedding in the rear; then we all became fire-fighters. We drove into Silver City without a buggy-top and the liquor all gone.

As my daughter Viola lived in Silver City with her aunt and uncle, Mr. and Mrs. Will F. Read, I lay over the next day to visit them. Viola had grown to be a pretty young lady and was just finishing her education in the Territorial Normal College in Silver City.

I then boarded a train for Denver, stopping off in Santa Fé one day to visit my pets. On arriving in Denver, Assistant Superintendent Murray sent me at once to Grand Junction in the western part of Colorado, there to purchase a horse and locate a man I will call Jim Foss, who had been run out of Dixon, Wyoming, by the vigilantes, as he was known to be in with the Wild Bunch. It was reported that he had taken his family and settled somewhere near Grand Junction.

I finally located Foss through my friend Sheriff Charlie Wallis. He had bought a small patch of land in an out-of-the-way place on Grand River near Palisade, twenty miles above Grand Junction, and lived there with his young wife and two pretty little girls.

After much planning and scheming I got in solid with Foss, although he had received a letter of warning from a friend in Dixon, Wyoming, to the effect that the Union Pacific Railroad Company had a detective on his trail. I brought him this letter from Palisade, as he had given me orders to get his mail. On reading it, he swore the most wicked oaths against all detectives and swore to cut out the heart of any detective who undertook to win his friendship. He let me read the letter.

Foss and I became fast friends after he had seen the newspaper accounts of my shooting scrape in southern New Mexico, and of my being an outlaw who was badly wanted by the officers of Grant County, New Mexico. I had these accounts put into the papers and marked copies sent to me.

I was going by the name of Lee Roy Davis. The Palisade paper once referred to me as 'mysterious white-horse Davis,' my saddle horse being white.

During the month of August, Foss and I pulled out for 'tall timber.' We put in a couple of weeks at the head of White River above Meeker. We lived on venison and fish and camped out alone. From here we drifted to Hayden, Colorado, where Foss had friends; thence to Dixon, Wyoming, to show Bob Meldrum, the 'man-killer' town marshal, and the vigilantes that Jim Foss was not afraid to come back. I had promised to help fight his battles, and we came within an ace of having a shooting scrape with Bob Meldrum on reaching Dixon.

On the Snake River, above Dixon, at the foot of Black Mountain, is where Foss lived on his ranch when run out of the country by the Cattle Association, as it was known that he was a cattle rustler and used his ranch for a rendezvous for tough characters.

It was at this Black Mountain ranch that Foss had furnished horses and grub to Kid Curry and his gang when they started out to rob the Union Pacific train at Tipton, Wyoming, about a hundred miles north, the fall previous, and after the robbery Foss kept them hid on Black Mountain until the officers quit searching for them. I was shown the exact spot where they camped high up on the timbered mountain. From Foss I learned that Kid Curry, Bill Cruzan, and the tall Texan, whose right name was Kilpatrick, held up the train at Tipton, Wyoming.

Foss also gave me the secrets of the Wilcox, Wyoming, train hold-up, and many other noted cases. He told how he assisted in a bank robbery in Nebraska, and of his many cattle-stealing and fighting scrapes in the Black Hills of Dakota.

Foss and I were planning to pull out of Dixon and go to Rawlins to meet friends of his, when Ellis, a merchant of Dixon, called Jim to the rear of his store and advised him not to go to the Union Pacific Railroad, as detectives were on his trail and would arrest him. At this Jim concluded to hit the road back to Grand Junction, Colorado. He sold me his pack horse and outfit and gave me a letter of introduction to a friend who stood in with the Wild Bunch, and who had two saloons in Rawlins, Wyoming.

On leaving the Grand River, my name had been changed to Harry Blevins, so that the New Mexico officers couldn't get track of me. Foss selected my new name, and in this name he gave me the letter of introduction, which was short and to the point. It merely stated: 'This will introduce to you my friend Harry Blevins. He is righter than hell.'

After seeing Foss off and headed south for Colorado, I pulled out for the north. I arrived in the hurrah little city of Rawlins, where half the men are railroad employees and the other half, with the exception of the gamblers and saloon men, smell sheepy. Even the cattlemen get to smelling like sheep from the constant chasing of sheep off their ranges. Rawlins is the center of a great sheep country.

Foss's friend welcomed me with open arms on the strength of Jim's letter, and it wasn't long until he told me of the Wild Bunch and their doings. He had made his first stake through Butch Casiday and his gang, after they robbed the Montpelier, Idaho, bank of about thirty thousand dollars in gold. At that time this man, whom I will call Jack, owned a small saloon in Baggs, on Snake River, near Dixon. The gang was headed for the Robbers' Roost in southern Utah and stopped over a few days to rest in Baggs, and while there they threw enough twenty-dollar gold pieces over Jack's bar to give him a stake, so that he could open a good saloon in Rawlins. Jack told how Butch would shoot an old widow's chickens just to hear her swear. Then he would have the old lady smiling by giving her a twenty-dollar gold piece for every chicken killed.

During the winter in and around Rawlins, I led a hurrah drinking life, and made friends among the tough element. Among those met was Bert C., virtually one of the Wild Bunch, but who was slick enough to keep out of the law's clutches. His home was in Grand Junction, Colorado. He and I became chummy, but he kept his secrets to himself. He was noted for being close-mouthed, and no doubt that is why Kid Curry and the Wild Bunch put such confidence in him. But I played my cards so as to open Bert's mouth. In the spring he and I went to Grand Junction, Colorado, where we hobnobbed with his tough cowboy friends. Among them was our friend Jim Foss. During the summer Bert and I rode from Grand Junction to Rawlins, a distance of about three hundred miles, on horseback.

While in Grand Junction, I received a fake letter from my supposed attorney, ex-Governor L. Bradford Prince, requesting that I come to Santa Fé, New Mexico, and sign some papers in order that certain property could be sold. This letter was on Attorney Prince's letter-head and looked genuine.

Foss asked me to visit his friend Bob McGinnis in the Santa Fé penitentiary, and if I got a chance to give him a Wild Bunch cipher code, so that they could communicate with each other through the mail. The code was each fourth word, in a friendly letter on general news; that is, each fourth word to be written down which would convey the secret. And I was instructed to tell Bob McGinnis to hold a stiff upper lip, as his friends would have him out before many years.

Jim and Bert had told me confidentially who Bob McGinnis was, that he was a Utah chum of Butch Casiday's, whose right name was Elza Lay. This was a secret which hadn't yet leaked out.

Jim gave me certain words to say to Bob McGinnis which would convince him that I was all right. He and Jim had been in the cattle-stealing business together several years previous.

In Santa Fé, New Mexico, I took ex-Governor Prince, Attorney-General E. L. Bartlett, and Warden H. O. Bursom, of the penitentiary, into my confidence, so that I got a chance to visit McGinnis and gave him Foss's secrets.

I found McGinnis to be a pleasant fellow, but a hard-looking 'mug.' He acted as though he felt that a job was being put up on him when the guard was called away for a few minutes. It was then that I imparted the secrets to him.

About the time of my visit with Bob McGinnis in the Santa Fé penitentiary, Butch Casiday, Bill Carver, and Harry Longbough robbed the Winnemucca, Nevada, bank and secured thirty thousand dollars in gold. It was plain to me now that some of this money would be used to free McGinnis from prison.

It was early summer when Bert and I started, in company with his young brother, across country for Rawlins, Wyoming. We each had a saddle horse and I had a pack animal to carry the grub and bedding.

On reaching the Green Cattle Company's headquarters ranch on the edge of Wyoming, we learned of the Denver and Rio Grande train hold-up east of Grand Junction, and from now on we were suspected of having had a hand in the hold-up.

Bert gave me to understand that Bill Cruzan was in this last hold-up. It seems that Bert knew it was billed to come off.

In Dixon, Bert got a tip from some one, whom I suspected to be merchant Ellis — knowing that he had given Jim a friendly tip — that the Pinkerton agency had a cowboy detective by the name of Charlie Siringo working in with the Wild Bunch. This worried Bert, and he became sullen for a while, as though suspicious of me. He questioned me as to whether I had ever heard of Charlie Siringo. Of course I hadn't.

Previous to our arrival in Dixon Bert had given me many secrets of the Wild Bunch. He told of how they kept a system of blind post-offices all the way from the Hole-in-the-Wall in northern Wyoming to Alma in southern New Mexico, these post-offices being in rocky crevices or on top of round mounds on the desert. In passing these post-offices, members of the Wild Bunch would look for mail or deposit notes of importance. Also late news of interest would be clipped from newspapers and deposited in the post-office by passing members.

Finally the tall Texan (Kilpatrick), who was with Kid Curry when I trailed him into the Blue Mountains, and who assisted in the Tipton, Wyoming, Union Pacific train hold-up, was arrested in Saint Louis, Missouri, along with Curry's sweetheart. Curry and one of his chums made their getaway and Curry came direct to Rawlins to dig up some of the stolen Great Northern money which he had cached on Twenty-Mile ranch. He wanted this money to hire lawyers to defend his sweetheart, Laura Bullion, who had been passing some of the stolen bills in Saint Louis.

Curry remained in the vicinity of Rawlins only two days. He then boarded a train for the east. I didn't know of his being in Rawlins until two days after he had gone. Then one of Curry's friends named Sid told how Kid Curry had seen me in a saloon one night when he was watching the crowd through the rear door. He singled me out as a suspect, saying that I looked too bright and wide-awake for a common rounder; but Sid assured him that I was all right. I considered it quite a compliment to be called bright by such a wide-awake judge.

But poor Kid Curry ran up against a live issue on this trip east. In Knoxville, Tennessee, he was arrested after shooting two officers. He finally had a trial in the United States Court, for passing money stolen in the Great Northern train hold-up. He was convicted on several different counts.

Curry made his getaway, however, from the high sheriff before reaching the penitentiary walls. The sheriff was arrested for liberating him, but I never heard how this honorable official got out of the scrape.

Kilpatrick received a sentence of fifteen years in the penitentiary, and Curry's sweetheart got a long sentence behind prison walls.

I put in a lively fall in Rawlins and the town adjoining, including Grand Encampment, the big mining camp, and, against my will, I drank poison liquor enough to kill a mule.

In Rawlins I was considered an ex-outlaw, though no one but my friends knew where I came from. Sheriff McDaniels wrote a full description of me to the officials in Denver, and in the letter he said I was the toughest-looking fellow he had ever seen, and he knew that I must be an outlaw.

Having finished my work in Wyoming, I was hurried to Arizona to find out the whereabouts of a certain 'bad' man, who was supposed to be in with the Wild Bunch, so that our agency could keep track of his movements. I had nothing to work on but the fact that he was getting mail at Flagstaff, Arizona.

From the postmaster in Flagstaff, I found out that this 'bad' man had left for parts unknown and had left instructions that his mail be forwarded to Gunnison, Colorado.

I had also been instructed to locate a brother-in-law of the late outlaw, Bill Carver, alias Franks. A trip to Phœnix, Arizona, thence to Douglas on the Mexican border, put me on trail of my man. I had found my old cowboy chum, Jim East, in Douglas, and he assisted me.

Up in the mountains near Rodeo I found Bill Carver's brother-in-law, and got all the information wanted. Then I made a little jump of over a thousand miles to Gunnison, Colorado. Here I located a sister of my 'bad' man. She had a pretty eighteen-year-old daughter whom I had to fall in love with, in order to find out the whereabouts of her 'bad' uncle. For about two weeks I did some swift courting and learned new lessons in human nature.

After getting the information wanted, I went straight up, so far as the poor girl was concerned. Then the train carried me home.

On reaching Denver, I closed the Union Pacific train robbery case after having traveled more than twenty-five thousand miles by rail, vehicles, afoot, and on horseback, and after being on the operation constantly for about four years.

CHAPTER XIX

A TEXAS OUTLAW IN KENTUCKY — THE INDEPENDENCE
EXPLOSION — 'EAT-'EM-UP JAKE' — SENATOR WAR-
REN'S RANGE HORSES — WITH COLONEL GREENE TO
CANANEA — BODYGUARD FOR HARRY ORCHARD, CON-
VICT, AND JAMES McPARLAND, DETECTIVE — THE
TRIAL OF PETTIBONE, HAYWOOD, AND MOYER — SAV-
ING SOME LIVES OF GREATER OR LESS IMPORTANCE —
MISS ETHEL BARRYMORE

THE son of Dr. Wentz, of Philadelphia, Pennsylvania, had
been kidnaped on the line of Virginia, and taken into the
Cumberland Mountains, where it was supposed that he was
being held for a ransom, as the kidnapers had written an unsigned letter offering to liberate young Edward Wentz on
payment of $150,000 cash. The letter stated that if the
money was not paid over in thirty days, the boy would be
murdered and his right hand sent to prove that they had
carried out their threat.

As a supposed Texas outlaw, mounted on a cracker-jack
blue-roan pacing stallion, I visited the toughest illicit stills in
these mountains. It would require too much space to record
my narrow escapes from death. On Christmas Day the noted
feudist, Tilden Wright, threatened to scatter my brains all
over the floor of widow Bee Crafts' house, where dozens of us
were celebrating. Later Wright and his moonshiner pal, Mose
Craft, emptied their pistols down a wooded lane where they
supposed I had just gone. Instead of being in a lane, I was
hidden on a side hill watching them. Both were drunk. I had
jumped a rail fence with my mount, back of the stable, and
made a quick dash to a hiding-place.

Early in the spring, the body of Edward Wentz was shipped

back to Philadelphia for burial by officials of the Pinkerton Agency who came to get it. The body showed a bullet hole in the heart, and the right hand had been cut off at the wrist.

I had got confessions which might have sent many to prison, or the gallows. But it was decided an impossibility to convict any one in that county, as the people were all related by blood or marriage.

Just before leaving the country, I had a narrow escape from death. It had been planned to murder me at a farm two miles below Whitesburg, on the Kentucky River. I had been warned to keep away from this place as the woman who ran it was a sister to one of the noted Hatfield-McCoy feudists. Soon after this he was killed in a bloody battle. The plot to kill me at this farm proved a failure, but it resulted in the wounding of two of the would-be assassins and the killing of the woman's nephew, Jim Day.

I landed back in Denver, Colorado, after my eight months' strenuous life among the moonshiners of Kentucky. During my stay about thirty men had been assassinated — some of them revenue officers. On returning to Denver, I found great excitement over the Miners' Union strike in the Cripple Creek district, and the recent blowing-up with dynamite of the Independence depot, with great loss of life and limb.

My dear friend, Charles J. Smith, of the agency in Chicago, had been sent to ferret out the dynamiters responsible for the Independence explosion. In order to give Smith clues to work on, I went with him to the second-hand furniture store run by George A. Pettibone, the dynamiter whom I had sent to the penitentiary from Idaho in 1892. There, on the sly, several pals of Pettibone's were pointed out. In the wind-up Mr. Smith's evidence showed that Pettibone's chum, Harry Orchard, had touched off the bomb which sent thirteen men to their graves and maimed dozens of others for life. But all trace of Harry Orchard was lost when he boarded a west-bound train in Cheyenne, Wyoming.

Soon after this, I was hurried away to Cheyenne, Wyoming, to work for United States Senator Francis Warren. His Pole Creek ranch house and wool storage rooms had been burned by unknown parties with a loss of $40,000. I held consultations with Senator Warren, Marshal Hadsell, and his deputy, Joe LeFors. The latter had worked on the case and decided that the Pole Creek plant had been set afire by either an ex-convict or two cattlemen living near the line of Nebraska.

I decided to run down the ex-convict first. He was thought to be somewhere on the Laramie plains. In Torrington, Nebraska, I bought a horse and saddle and rode to old Fort Laramie, Wyoming. Thence I traveled west to the foot of Laramie Peak, where I found my man camped all alone in a wild spot. We planned a horse-stealing raid into Nebraska. A month's work convinced me that he had no hand in burning the Pole Creek plant.

I then started overland for Cheyenne to work on the other suspects. At the Jim Kirkbright ranch, I traded my jaded horse for a wild bronco. I also traded a watch for the pick of a litter of half-starved Russian wolf-hound pups. These pups had been weaned and all they got to eat was cornmeal mush at the end of the day.

Early the following morning I mounted the bronco and started east for a forty-mile ride across the unsettled Laramie plains. The Kirkbright boy who had traded me the pup helped us get started by going along a mile or two. He then slipped away from the pup, who trotted along at my mount's heels.

The day was very hot and several times I had to water the pup from my canteen. But finally he played out completely and couldn't be made to travel another step. First I decided to shoot him, then changed my mind and concluded to carry him to water. He was sitting on his haunches panting for breath when I rode up by his side. Reaching over with my right hand, the pup was grabbed by the nape of the neck. When I went to raise up with the bundle of bones and hair, the bucking contest began. The pup was thrown across my saddle in front of me. Here was a bronco-busting contest going to waste on the desert with no one to see it but the Lord, and if His all-seeing eye gathered in any fun from this free show He failed to let it be known by slapping me on the back and saying: 'Well done, thou good and faithful bronco-and-dog buster.' The pup was being 'busted' too, or at least would have been had his stomach contained anything but the lingering memory of his last mush supper. Every time the bronco came down on his front feet with his hind parts up in the air, my whole weight was thrown against the pup, and, of course, the air was full of yelps. I wanted to smile, but didn't have time.

On reaching a lake at the head of Horse Creek, I pitched camp to eat the lunch I had brought along. Seeing a mud hen out in the lake, I shot it so as to give the pup a lunch. I had to pull off my boots and pants and wade out into the lake to get the duck.

While I was ripping the mud hen open, preparatory to skinning the feathers off, the pup, which was sitting on his long tail eyeing the operation, smelled the blood and made a grab for the hen. I tried to take it away from him, but he held on. So, turning my hold loose, I told him to pick his own duck; but, bless you, he ate feathers, bill, feet, and all. It was filling that he was after and not dainties. Here I named the pup 'Eat-'em-up Jake,' and he retained that name to the time of his death eight years later. On reaching the railroad, I expressed him to my Sunny Slope ranch at Santa Fé, New Mexico.

My next few months' work solved the mystery of the Pole Creek fire. I had got a full confession from one of the cattle-men. I had made my home at their ranch and become chummy with the youngest brother. He said they burnt the warehouse full of wool in order to discourage Senator Warren from running sheep on the cattle ranges. He also told how they killed and crippled hundreds of Warren's fine range horses, by stampeding them through barbed-wire enclosures, at the windmills, when the thirsty animals were at the troughs drinking. Then the gates would be closed, and with slickers and blankets waved in the air, the wild horses would be stampeded through the wire fence.

On the strength of my reports, Senator Warren sold his range horses. He said he was going to confront the brothers with my reports and threaten to prosecute them if they didn't quit the country. Later, Deputy United States Marshal Joe LeFors told me that the brothers sold their ranch interests to Senator Warren's friends.

One of the sweet memories of this operation is the meeting with Senator Warren's young daughter, Miss Frances, who afterwards became the wife of General Pershing. But the poor young woman lost her life in a fire which destroyed their California home. Two small children were burnt to death. The oldest boy was saved by being absent with his father.

Now, for a couple of years of excitement. One operation took me to the City of Mexico with Colonel Greene, the famous copper king of Cananea, Mexico. He was traveling in his new private car, the Verde, a palace on wheels. My friend, Scott White, the straight-shooting Texas cowboy of Arizona, was Colonel Greene's bodyguard on this trip. The operation was a success, and proved a pleasure trip for me during the couple of months that I was absent from Denver.

One operation took me into the Horse Heaven country of

eastern Oregon, as a horse trader, under the assumed name of Charlie Lloyd. This country should be called Cowboys' Heaven, as good horses mean heaven to a cowboy. My head-quarters were made in Prineville, the county seat of Crook County, a distance of seventy-five miles from a railroad at Chaniko, on the Columbia River. I bought and sold horses in order to get in solid with cattlemen, who had slaughtered whole herds of sheep belonging to United States Senator Chamberlin, for whom my work was being done. One cattle-man on the Ochico River, from whom I secured a confession, showed me receipts for sixty dollars' worth of Winchester rifle cartridges which he had fired into bands of sheep.

After a winter spent among these thousands upon thou-sands of fine range horses, I departed for Seattle, Washington, to locate Great Northern train robbers. In order to do the work successfully, I had to work on the hurrah girls in the several dance-halls of the city, which meant a few weeks of high life for a once wild and woolly cowboy.

Now for a year's work as the bodyguard of James Mc-Parland, while he was gathering evidence against the Western Federation of Miners, throughout Idaho. This work took me to my old stamping ground in the Cœur D'Alenes, where many of my former friends and enemies were met. On leaving the Cœur D'Alene mining country, we were accompanied by that honest man, Harvey K. Brown, former sheriff of Baker City, Oregon. But the poor fellow soon after met the same fate as former Governor Steunenburg, by being blown up as he opened the gate to enter his home.

Another fine man, blown up with dynamite, but not killed, soon after giving his testimony, was Mr. Bulkeley Wells, manager and part owner of the rich Tomboy mine in Telluride, Colorado. The former manager of this mine, Mr. Arthur Collins, as he sat playing cards with his wife after supper, was shot and killed with a double-barreled shotgun, fired through a window. The villain who killed him was one of the paid dynamiters.

While the trials of Big Bill Haywood, Moyer, and Pettibone were going on in Boise, Idaho, I acted as the bodyguard of Alber E. Horsley, alias Harry Orchard, in addition to being James McParland's bodyguard. I would take Orchard out of the penitentiary and stay with him until court was over, then return him to the prison. It was feared that he would be assassinated for confessing that he had been paid by the Western Federation of Miners to murder ex-Governor Steunenburg and others.

During the times I was with Harry Orchard, Mr. James McParland remained in his private apartment in the Idan-ha Hotel.

One of the most affecting scenes I ever witnessed was when I took Orchard's former pal Denny to the penitentiary to see Harry Orchard, who had no idea whom he was to meet in the reception room. They stood face to face. Denny was all doubled up and on crutches. Orchard was the first to speak. He said:

'My God, Denny, what has happened to you?'

The answer came when Denny said: 'You did it Harry, when you blowed up the Independence depot in Cripple Creek.'

Harry Orchard threw both arms around Denny's neck and wept like a child. When he had recovered from his crying spell, Orchard said: 'You know, Denny, that I never would have blown up the depot if I had known you were in the crowd.'

While the trial of George A. Pettibone, Big Bill Haywood, and Charles Moyer was going on, for the murder of former Governor Steunenburg, Harry Orchard was constantly on the

THE AUTHOR DURING THE CŒUR D'ALENE TRIAL

witness stand, being questioned by Clarence Darrow. But during the weeks of grilling, Darrow failed to change Orchard's testimony one iota. Other evidence corroborated Orchard's testimony.

When the case was finally turned over to the jury, one of the defense lawyers told me that the jury would never bring in a verdict of guilty; that he knew what he was talking about, as one of the jurymen could be depended on.

This lawyer and I had become quite chummy. He was one of the leaders in the bloody Miners' Union strike in 1892, when I was Recording Secretary of the Gem Lodge in the Cœur D'Alenes of northern Idaho. When that strike was over, he had studied law, and was admitted to the bar in Butte City, Montana. After the jury had been locked up all night, he and I were sitting in the Idan-ha Hotel lobby wondering what the verdict would be. He said: 'It will either be an acquittal or a hung jury.'

It being about 10 A.M., the lawyer suggested that we walk over to the court-house and hear the verdict when it was brought in. We strolled arm in arm toward the court-house. On coming within a block of it, we saw twelve men coming toward us. There being no bailiff with them, we knew they had rendered their decision and had been dismissed.

When the twelve men were within a hundred yards of us, they turned west on a cross street. The lawyer squeezed my arm and said: 'Charlie, do you see that tall man in the lead?'

I replied, 'Yes.'

'Enough said.'

We all knew this man to be the former resident of Cheyenne, Wyoming, who was on the jury which convicted stock detective Tom Horn, who was hanged.

Soon after we returned to the Idan-ha Hotel, the 'Daily

Statesman' came out with an extra announcing that the jury had acquitted Haywood, Pettibone, and Moyer.

I told James McParland of what the lawyer had told me about the juryman. He at once detailed a trusted secret operative to work on one of the jurymen and get the truth. The investigation showed that the tall juryman had frightened the jurymen who were for conviction by telling them that if they convicted the defendants, they would meet a dreadful fate. This had the desired effect by giving the jurymen 'cold feet,' and brought about an acquittal.

The prisoners were to be liberated the next morning. About midnight I was sitting in the hotel lobby reading, Mr. McParland having gone to bed. One of my friends called me off to one side and divulged a secret. He said:

'At three o'clock we are going to storm the jail and take Pettibone, Moyer, and Haywood out to the edge of the city and hang them. The jailer is fixed so that we will have no trouble getting into the jail. We are also going to kidnap Clarence Darrow and hang him, too. We will be more than a hundred strong. A special train of prominent men who will take part in the hanging are now on the way from Nampa.'

I didn't have the heart to see Clarence Darrow hanged by an angry mob, just because he is always for the 'under dog.' It is part of his nature, and he can't help it. At the first opportunity I slipped upstairs and awakened James McParland, telling him the secret. He said it would disgrace Idaho in the eyes of the world if these men were hanged, after the jury had acquitted them. He at once put on his clothes and went to the apartment on the same floor occupied by Governor Frank R. Gooding and his wife. The story was told to the Governor and he dressed in a hurry, so as to meet the special train and put a stop to the hanging. He was evidently successful in persuading his many friends in the mob that it would disgrace the State of Idaho forever if these men were hanged, for the three prisoners were liberated from jail next morning, and Clarence Darrow is alive to-day.

The trial of Alber E. Horsley, alias Harry Orchard, now took place. He confessed to the murder of former Governor Steunenburg. For this cowardly crime, Judge Fremont Wood sentenced him to life imprisonment in the State penitentiary, and he is still wearing prison stripes. When Orchard's trial ended, Mr. McParland and I departed for Denver, Colorado, it being in the month of August, 1907.

The lawyers who prosecuted these cases were William E. Borah, now a United States Senator, and James H. Hawley, who was later the Governor of Idaho. This same Jim Hawley had, in 1892, defended George A. Pettibone and the other dynamiters. At that time, Judge Fremont Wood was the prosecuting attorney.

During the summer, in Boise, Idaho, I had a few years added to my life through my meeting with Miss Ethel Barrymore. This beautiful young actress was determined to see Harry Orchard before returning East. But no one except court officials and his guards were allowed to see him, by strict orders from Governor Gooding.

Miss Barrymore had already pleaded with the Governor, so I was told, but his heart was like a chunk of chilled steel. Then some one suggested that I might help her out. Just one smile and a 'good-fellow' handshake, and she had me at her feet, figuratively speaking. I informed her that my hands were tied without the consent of Mr. McParland, but that if she would act her part according to my instructions we could get his consent. She agreed.

Mr. Gifford Pinchot, Chief of the United States Forest Service, was also anxious to see Orchard; therefore he accompanied Miss Barrymore and me to Mr. McParland's private reception room. Mr. S. S. McClure, of the 'McClure's Magazine,' and Mrs. Calvin Cobb, the wife of the principal owner of the 'Idaho Statesman,' also went along. On introducing Miss Barrymore, I started the ball to rolling by telling Mr. McParland that I had assured the lady that he would not deny her request. The play started when the young actress moved her chair close up to the gentleman, so that she could look him in the face. When the one-act drama was over, we all started in a carriage for the penitentiary. Mr. McParland had given me orders to let the lady see Orchard, but under no conditions to let her speak to him. That was sufficient, as all I wanted was an entering wedge.

On reaching the penitentiary, I had Warden Whitney bring Orchard from the steel cell to the warden's private office. Then I turned the natural-born actress loose in the room with this star dynamiter, and she talked with him to her heart's content.

I was repaid for all my trouble by having Miss Barrymore telephone me after midnight to be at her train and say good-bye. This I did, and her happy smile and warm handshake linger with me to this day.

CHAPTER XX

I RESIGN FROM THE AGENCY — A VISIT TO MY OLD
STAMPING GROUND — TWO YEARS AS NEW MEXICO
RANGER — 'SIRINGO'S ROGUE GALLERY' — A 'DEN'
IN HOLLYWOOD

On reaching Denver after the dynamite cases ended in Boise, Idaho, my operation as James McParland's bodyguard was closed. Then I wrote out my resignation from Pinkerton's National Detective Agency. I told Mr. McParland that my twenty-two years' schooling in the agency had taught me all I wished to know about the ways of the world. He tried to persuade me to stay and accept a position as superintendent in one of the western branches, but this I refused, as I had done once before when Mr. Robert A. Pinkerton in New York offered me such a position. I told him there was not kick enough in office work.

It was the latter part of August, 1907, when I landed in Santa Fé, New Mexico, to lead a simple life on my Sunny Slope ranch in the outskirts of the city. Here, I took great delight in helping my foreman, George Tweedy, milk the fine blooded Jersey cows and care for the White Leghorn chickens and Homer pigeons. When the work was done, I could have the Mexican servant, Ben Romero, put my saddle on either Rowdy or Patsy, offspring of Lulu Edson, and start for a gallop over the cactus-covered plains to enjoy seeing Eat-'em-up Jake and his mate, a Russian wolfhound female, pick up jack rabbits and coyotes.

My taste of real heaven on the ranch lasted only a month, as I got an urgent letter from Mr. James McParland, asking me to hurry to Denver and undertake a complicated cattle operation in South Dakota for the Live Stock Association of that State. They were short thousands of grown steers, and no trace of them could be found.

My misery started in October in the Bad Lands of South Dakota. Here I posed as a 'bad man' from Texas, under the name of Charles Tony Lloyd. I bought a horse and saddle and drifted over the cattle ranges, and on to the Pine Ridge and Rosebud Indian Reservations, to work on Indians and cowboys. The long rides through deep snow, when cold blizzards were blowing, gave me a taste of hell.

In the choicest spots along the Cheyenne River and other streams, new settlers had squatted on homesteads. Wood was scarce and some of these 'hoemen' had to haul coal or wood forty or fifty miles. And as they were not able to sink wells, many had to haul water long distances. Many times I put up for the night in one of these sod houses called 'home, sweet home' by these hardy 'hoemen' of the north, when it was impossible to get near the stove or fireplace on account of the shivering children huddled around the fire to keep warm. By rights, Uncle Sam should have furnished them free fuel and water to go with the homesteads.

A few months' work solved the mystery as to what had become of the thousands of missing steers. They had been stolen and butchered for the grading crews on the two railroads, the Milwaukee and the Northwestern racing west across South Dakota the winter previous, to reach Spokane, Washington. Many of the thieves confessed to me as to the easy money they made stealing these cattle and selling them to the contractors on the two new railroads.

I had worked up evidence enough to send several small cowmen and a dozen cowboys to the penitentiary, but it was decided best by our clients to drop the case, as the expense of prosecuting the thieves would cost too much, with only the

THE AUTHOR ON LEFT HOLDING ROWDY, NOLAN KELLER ON
RIGHT HOLDING PATSY, AND EAT-'EM-UP JAKE BELOW

THE AUTHOR WITH HIS RUSSIAN WOLF-HOUND JUMBO IN 1916

satisfaction of getting revenge and no chance of recovering the value of the lost steers.

This decision had been reached through the mail while I was in the White Owl country, over a hundred miles from a railroad. This meant a hard ride through deep snow to the railroad town of Wasta, where my horse and saddle were sold. There a train was boarded for Denver, Colorado, thence to my haven of rest at the end of the old Santa Fé trail, where once grazed the tired oxen and mules after their long journey across the plains.

Once more my term of simple life on the Sunny Slope ranch was short. I accepted an operation from an agency in Chicago. The work came through my friend, Charles J. Smith, who was superintendent of the agency. It was arranged that I be at a side station on the desert west of Ogden, Utah, on a certain day. I was there at the appointed time and met the three clients from Chicago, and their mine manager, John E. Pelton, who had come from National, Nevada, to meet us. Mr. Pelton explained matters, as to how the 'high-graders' were robbing the company, but said he was unable to find out how they did it. He gave me a description of the 'Gumshoe Kid,' who was the leader of the high-graders, and a dangerous gunman. He said that if I could win his friendship I might get onto the secret of where they sold their stolen gold.

A week later, dressed as a tramp cowboy, I boarded a four-horse stagecoach in Winnemucca, Nevada, for the eighty-mile ride across the desert to the northern line of the State. The second night after my arrival in National, under the assumed name of Leon Carrier, I got on a big drunk with Gumshoe Kid. We shot up the town in true cowboy fashion. There were six dance-halls running full blast, and it was the liveliest town I had ever been in.

From now on, Gumshoe Kid and I were pals — as I had

told him of having to leave Texas in a hurry on account of a crime committed in that State. He introduced me to the high-graders who handled the rich ore stolen by the more than a hundred miners working in the richest ore on the National mine. This ore was worth from thirty to ninety dollars a pound, and only trusted employees were allowed to handle it. In visiting miners' cabins with Gumshoe Kid, I was shown the kind of harness the miners wore underneath their clothes to conceal the stolen ore. Each harness had two pockets which pressed against the flanks of the thief, preventing the shift boss from seeing any bulge in the overalls, which would have attracted their attention. Each of these pockets would hold about three pounds of ore, which the miner would sell to the buyers of high grade at half price and often for less.

Before a month passed, I had visited the six different dumps, where the rich ore was melted and run into bars of pure gold. These dumps, as they were called, were in out-of-the-way places in the mountains. I made it a point to take rich ore to all these plants to have it melted into pure gold.

I spent eight months in National and put a stop to high-grading. Change rooms, with armed guards present, were installed, so that each miner coming off shift had to change his clothes before leaving the ground.

Manager Pelton, who owned an interest in this rich mine, would not consent to the sending of men to prison for stealing ore. To illustrate what a great temptation was placed before honest miners, I will cite one case. I had built a cabin to live in on the side of the mountain. Adjoining my lot was the cabin of a young miner. He and I soon became pals. On coming off shift, he would come into my cabin to warm, as I always kept a fire burning in the stove. Often I would go with him into his cabin and see him take off the harness full of rich ore. This he would place in a sack under the floor, first raising a loose plank.

This young man confessed to me that John Pelton had known him as a child, and had great confidence in his honesty, as he had been brought up a Christian. He said that he had worked in rich ore for a month before stealing any of it, but seeing other miners getting rich, he finally fell from grace and became a thief. He said the shift boss under whom he was working was stealing, and he knew that his miners were doing the same. This young man showed me the account he had kept of the stolen ore sold during the few months since he began stealing. It footed up $7000.

After being on this operation eight months, during which time I had led a swift life drinking and dancing at night, often spending as high as fifty dollars between sun and sun, I departed for Santa Fé, New Mexico, with a fat bank account. My chums, Gumshoe Kid, King of the Cacti, and the Katzenjammer Kids, hated to see me leave, as I was considered one of their 'kind of people.' Since the stealing of high-grade had been stopped, the camp had become a dull place, only two dance-halls being in operation.

In the winter of 1913–14, I met my former clients, Buckley, Snydecker and Scotten, in the city of Chicago, where all were members of the Board of Trade. Mr. S. C. Scotten told me that my work in National, Nevada, had saved his company half a million dollars before the rich ore vein 'petered out.' He estimated that more than a million dollars had been stolen by the high-graders.

To break the monotony of leading the simple life at Santa Fé, I worked in 1910 investigating a recent bank robbery in Morencia, Arizona, to ascertain the identity of the lone bandit who held up the Gila Valley Bank. A month's work convinced me that the brave hold-up man was Harvey Logan, alias Kid Curry, of Wild Bunch fame. I had found many people in the mountains who had met the bandit before the robbery, and his description and actions fitted Kid Curry, who had escaped in Knoxville, Tennessee, after receiving a life sentence in a Federal court for robbing a Great Northern railway train in Montana.

In 1912 I ate Christmas dinner in Santa Fé, then put my two pet saddle horses, Rowdy and Patsy, in a box car and started them south, ahead of me. In the same car was my large Russian wolfhound dog, Eat-'em-up Jake, who could whip his weight in wild cats and not half try. My saddle, pack outfit, and bedding were in the same car. On the morning after Christmas, I boarded a passenger train and overtook the horse car at Belin, where the stock were watered and fed, then sent on their journey for Amarillo, Texas, the next feeding place.

I was starting out for the Gulf coast of Texas to visit my boyhood stamping ground, and in the spring to ride up the old Chisholm cattle trail to Abilene, Kansas, its northern terminus, a total distance of about twelve hundred miles. I was anxious to see how much of this old trail had been torn to pieces with ploughs and hoes.

In the little city of Amarillo, built near the Amarillo Lake, where I had, in 1877, seen a million buffaloes in one black mass, I lay over a day and night to visit former cowboy friends. One of these friends owned a butcher shop in which hung a dressed buffalo bull, which he had purchased from Charlie Goodnight, to be sold on New Year's Eve at a dollar a pound. From this buffalo bull, a hump loin was cut and presented to me as a treat.

On leaving Amarillo, the passenger conductor and his brakeman put the hump loin on ice, then telegraphed ahead to the manager of the Harvey House in Sweetwater, the end of the division, to prepare us a fine midnight supper — all but the meat, which we would furnish.

The brakeman of this train, F. A. Dumek, had been a buffalo hunter in the early seventies in Dakota and Nebraska. I asked him how many buffaloes he had seen at one time. He placed the number at ten million head, as far as the eye could reach. Even though Mr. Dumek stretched the truth by nine million head, that would leave a good-sized herd, equal to the one I had seen at Amarillo Lake in 1877.

We arrived at Sweetwater City at midnight. The manager of the Harvey House was waiting for us, so as to fill up on buffalo hump. This was my last taste of buffalo meat!

One of the objects of this trip was to dig up the hidden secret of how the old Chisholm cattle trail got its name. Most cattlemen and cowboys thought it was named after the Pecos cattle king, John Chisum. But I felt sure it was not, as the names are spelt differently, and John Chisum never drove cattle over that famous trail to Kansas.

Here follows the true story of the Chisholm Trail as told to me by Mr. David M. Sutherland of Alamagorda, and confirmed through corresponding with old-timers in Wichita, Kansas:

In the year 1867, the United States Government concluded to move the more than three thousand Wichita and affiliated tribes of Indians to a new reservation in the southern part of the Indian Territory. Their camp was located on the Arkansas River near where Chisholm and Cowskin Creeks empty into that stream. They had been moved there by the Government during the rebellion. Major Henry Shanklin was in charge of them.

Previous to the time of moving these Indians to their new reservation, Major Shanklin made a deal with a rich half-breed squawman, by the name of Jesse Chisholm, to open a trail, and establish supply depots through the Indian Territory to Red River, the dividing line of Texas and the Nation.

With a large train of ox-teams, Jesse Chisholm went to Fort Leavenworth, on the Missouri River, to load up with Government supplies. On his return to the camp on the Arkansas River, a hundred wild ponies were bought for the trip through the Indian Territory. These were used to settle the quicksand in the treacherous streams of Salt Fork, the Cimarron, the North Canadian, and the South Canadian. Ahead of the heavily loaded wagons, this band of ponies were driven back and forth many times, to settle the quicksand. The more than three thousand Indians with their thousands of ponies, along with the many mounted soldiers, traveling in the ruts made by Jesse Chisholm's heavily loaded wagons, made a plain roadway. It was christened the Chisholm Trail, and over its surface passed millions of long-horn cattle in the years following.

After the Indians had vacated their camp, the Government sold the land, and the present city of Wichita, Kansas, was established on the old camp-ground. When the Atchison, Topeka, & Santa Fé Railroad reached the town of Wichita and built shipping pens a few years later, the enterprising citizens began planning to turn the trail herds away from Baxter Springs, in the southeast corner of Kansas, into Wichita.

In the closing years of the sixties, the Union Pacific Railroad had reached Abilene, Kansas, farther north, and that town, backed by the Union Pacific Railroad Company, laid plans to get some of the Texas cattle trade. In the spring of 1870, Mr. David M. Sutherland, who was associated with Major Henry Shanklin, went to Bosque County, Texas, and purchased a herd of long-horn cattle which were driven over the new Chisholm Trail to Wichita, thence to Abilene.

The following spring, 1871, Major Shanklin and Mr. Sutherland were employed by the Union Pacific Railroad Com-

THE AUTHOR ON HIS HORSE PATSY
Roswell, N.M., February 15, 1921

pany to turn the cattle driven away from Baxter Springs onto the Chisholm Trail, through the Indian Territory.

Mr. Sutherland went to Gainesville, Texas, to meet the Baxter Springs trail herds and induce the owners and bosses to turn west to Red River station, where they would strike the Chisholm Trail and have good grass and water all the way through the Indian Territory. During the season Mr. Sutherland and the boosters sent by the town of Wichita succeeded in turning most of the herds to the Chisholm Trail.

Mr. Sutherland says that in April, 1871, he made a cut-off trail with ploughs from Pilot Point to Bolivar, in the State of Texas, for the herds to follow. From Bolivar to Red River station there was already a plain wagon road. It is said that the Wichita boosters paid as high as five hundred dollars to owners and bosses to induce them to change their course from Baxter Springs to the Chisholm Trail at Red River station.

During the next season, 1872, the whole trail drive continued north from Austin, Texas, to Red River station, and the entire route to Abilene, Kansas, became known as the Chisholm Trail. At the Montopolis crossing on the Colorado River, two and a half miles below the capital city of Austin, Texas, the many small trails from all over the Gulf coast merged into the Chisholm Trail, which was now a solid roadway, several hundred yards wide, all the way to Wichita and Abilene, Kansas.

Early in the spring of 1916, my friend Governor William C. McDonald persuaded me to accept a position as Ranger, with a commission as Mounted Police, for the Cattle Sanitary Board of New Mexico. Therefore, on the first day of March I started south, mounted on Rowdy, with the pack on Pat, and Jumbo, an offspring of Eat-'em-up Jake, chasing jack rabbits on ahead. Governor McDonald had selected Carrizozo, the present county seat of Lincoln County, as my headquarters.

Bill Owens, a fighting son-of-a-gun, was selected as my partner. We were to have jurisdiction over seven counties, north of the Old Mexico border, to run down outlaws and stock thieves. But poor Bill Owens lasted only a short time. In a fight with two Mexican cattle thieves, at Abo Pass, he was shot through the lungs and lay at the point of death for a long time. This ended his usefulness as a mounted Ranger. After he had fallen, Bill Owens emptied his pistol into the thief who had shot him. Both of the thieves were killed.

This work as Ranger took me over much of my old stamping ground. During my two years of work there, I made many arrests of cattle and horse thieves, and had many close calls, with death staring me in the face.

While attending one term of court in Carrizozo, I was taught how old 'Father Time' heals wounds. I was introduced to Mr. Augustin Kayser, who owned a cattle ranch near Corona. He remembered my name, and asked: 'In 1872, when you were a boy, did some one steal your rain blanket, one stormy night?'

Of course, I remembered it, as for several years it had left a bitter feeling in my heart against the thief.

He then continued: 'Well, Charlie, I am the thief who kept dry that night under your blanket. Of course, I felt sorry for you, but it was a case of self-protection, as I had lost my slicker.'

We were putting up a herd of long-horn steers for the trail. I, being on the last guard, had gone to bed, leaving my saddled night horse tied to a tree near by. On my saddle was a Mexican rain blanket, used instead of a slicker. These blankets are made narrow and long, with a slit in the center to stick your head into, the fringed ends coming down below the boot tops. On getting wet, they become hard and turn water like rubber.

On this particular night, a severe rainstorm sprang up and every sleeping cowboy had to spring onto his night horse. A stampede followed, and during the rest of the night I suffered greatly from the cold spring rain. The next morning my blanket was found lying on my bed, the rain having ceased.

In southern Texas these fancy-colored blankets were plentiful, but I saw but one of them in the Panhandle country. During a cold blizzard or rainstorm there, if you happened to see a Mexican blanket coming toward you, or going in an opposite direction, you could bet your last dollar that Jim East's head, covered with a gold-and-silver-mounted sombrero, was sticking out of the slit in the center.

In December, 1922, after a severe illness with pleurisy, I decided to get rid of everything I had at Santa Fé and go to San Diego, California, to be with my daughter Viola Reid, and her fourteen-year-old child, Margaret.

Before leaving Santa Fé, I raffled off Sailor Gray for a hundred dollars in cash, and took Patsy out in the woods and put a 45-caliber bullet in his brain. He was hog-fat and I had been offered one hundred and fifty dollars for him. But I wouldn't risk selling him, for fear that he might, in time, fall into cruel hands. As he was eighteen years old, I decided that he would be better off in horse heaven with his daddy, Rowdy.

On the way to San Diego, I lay over a week in Douglas, Arizona, to spend Christmas and New Year's with my old cowboy friend, James H. East, and his good wife. The only hard work Jim does is to get out his pet Colt's 45 pistol and oil it once a month, through force of habit.

I was a sick man when I landed in San Diego. I could

hardly drag one foot after the other, being so weak. But, thanks to the careful nursing of my daughter, Viola Reid, and her fourteen-year-old Margaret, I soon began to improve and gave up the idea of dying. Viola and Margaret are proof that churches do good. Had I not gone to church with Miss May Beals, and there met pretty fifteen-year-old Mamie Lloyd, Viola and Margaret would never have seen the light of day.

After a stay of three months in San Diego, I was strong enough to move to Los Angeles. Soon afterwards, I moved to the heart of Hollywood, so as to be near my dear friend, George T. Cole, who is the youngest son of former United States Senator Cornelius Cole, who passed away at the ripe age of one hundred and two. He was as bright as a silver dollar up to within a month of his death. He had voted for Abe Lincoln as President and hoped to live to vote for Calvin Coolidge as President of the United States, but he died the day before election.

My landlord, Linder Stafford, built a new cabin in the rear of his home for me to live in. By being alone, I can keep my ears primed so as to hear Gabriel toot his horn when he wants me to meet him on the other side of the Great Divide.

Over my cabin door is a sign 'Siringo's Den.' In midwinter I can look out from the windows of my cabin and enjoy Mrs. Stafford's beautiful flowers. On the walls of my 'Den' are hundreds of photographs. Above them is a sign: 'Siringo's Rogue Gallery.' Once, when William S. Hart was visiting me, I saw him reading this sign just above his own photograph. A smile flitted across the face which is familiar in all parts of the world. He was badly mistaken if he thought I was placing him in the rogue class. If there is one person in the whole world who has not a drop of rogue blood in his veins, that man is Bill Hart.

*The postcard photograph of the author on Sailor Gray was sent to
Mr. Gifford Pinchot, then Commissioner of Forestry for Pennsylvania,
and to Mr. Emerson Hough, the author. They sent the following
replies:*

MILFORD, PIKE CO., PA.
June 15, 1922

Mr. Chas. A. Siringo,
Santa Fé, N. Mex.

DEAR MR. SIRINGO:

I can't tell you how homesick for the West your postal-card
made me, or how glad I was to get it. Before I die I want to be
out on a horse again in that great country, but I judge I will
have to hurry up or the things you knew so well and I a little
will all have disappeared.

I knew you would feel as you did about my fight here. Before I get through with it, it ought to produce some real
results.

With all good wishes,

Sincerely yours,

[*Signed*]   GIFFORD PINCHOT

630 FRANKLIN STREET, DENVER, COLORADO
October 5, 1922

Mr. Charles Siringo,
P.O. Box 322,
Santa Fé, New Mexico.

MY DEAR MR. SIRINGO:

Thank you for your nice letter of September 28. . . . Have
you any objection if I should use as a sort of model for a
cowboy picture in the Saturday Evening Post some time, that
part of your postcard photograph showing yourself and horse?
I am trying my best to get the artists of that great periodical
to know what a cowman really looks like. These fancy boys
with chaps and handkerchiefs give me a pain.

.   .   .   .

Yours sincerely,

[*Signed*]   EMERSON HOUGH

THE AUTHOR ON SAILOR GRAY CROSSING THE RIO GRANDE AT
THE COCHITI INDIAN PUEBLO IN 1921

THE AUTHOR WITH BILL HART

Another movie Cowboy Star who has no rogue blood in his veins is Will Rogers.

In February, 1924, I received a letter from Mrs. Betty Rogers in Beverly Hills inviting me to come to their home and meet her husband, Will. I answered this letter stating that I was not feeling well, but would visit them within a month or two.

Soon after this Will Rogers went to Europe and I missed shaking hands with the only cowboy able to throw a loop large enough to encircle the globe.

'The Water Hole' on Caheunga Avenue between Sunset and Hollywood Boulevard, is within walking distance of my Den. I often go there to see the movie cowboys and cowgirls with their silver-mounted spurs and high Stetson hats. They bring back memories of my cowboy days, although such high hats and girls wearing pants were not seen on the early-day cattle ranges.

When the time comes for putting me under the sod, I hope the little verses by Badger Clark, Jr., which follow, will be carved on my headstone. These verses were dug up from the William E. Hawks collection of cowboy songs, as appropriate for the wind-up of a fool cowboy's life history, so that posterity will know the class of dare-devils who paved the way for the man with a hoe.

The hoeman will need no history for the benefit of posterity, as he is here to stay. When once a farmer plants his feet on the soil, neither time nor cyclones can jar him loose.

> 'Twas good to live when all the range
> Without no fence or fuss,
> Belonged in partnership with God,
> The Government and us.
>
> With skyline bounds from east to west,
> With room to go and come,

I liked my fellow man the best
   When he was scattered some.

When my old soul hunts range and rest
   Beyond the last divide,
Just plant me on some strip of west
   That's sunny, lone and wide.

Let cattle rub my headstone round,
   And coyotes wail their kin,
Let hosses come and paw the mound,
   But don't you fence it in.

THE END

www.ingramcontent.com/pod-product-compliance
Lightning Source LLC
Chambersburg PA
CBHW020655270326
41928CB00005B/130